LOCKED IN

The True Causes of Mass Incarceration—
and How to Achieve Real Reform

John F. Pfaff

BASIC
BOOKS
New York

Published in the United States by Basic Books, an imprint of Perseus Books, LLC, a subsidiary of Hachette Book Group, Inc.

Books published by Basic Books are available at special discounts for bulk purchases in the United States by corporations, institutions, and other organizations. For more information, please contact the Special Markets Department at the Perseus Books Group, 2300 Chestnut Street, Suite 200, Philadelphia, PA 19103, or call (800) 810-4145, ext. 5000, or e-mail special.markets@perseusbooks.com.

Designed by Linda Mark

Library of Congress Cataloging-in-Publication Data

Names: Pfaff, John F., author.
Title: Locked in : the true causes of mass incarceration—and how to achieve
   real reform / John Pfaff.
Description: New York : Basic Books, [2017] | Includes bibliographical
   references and index.
Identifiers: LCCN 2016037701| ISBN 9780465096916 (hardcover) |
   ISBN 9780465096923 (ebook)
Subjects: LCSH: Imprisonment--United States. | Criminal justice,
   Administration of—United States. | Corrections—United States.
Classification: LCC HV9471 .P449 2017 | DDC 365/.973—dc23 LC record
available at https://lccn.loc.gov/2016037701

10 9 8 7 6 5 4 3 2

To those impacted by our flawed criminal justice system.
And to those working together toward reform.

CONTENTS

PREFACE

D ONALD TRUMP'S SURPRISE VICTORY OVER HILLARY CLINTON on November 8, 2016, upended most people's expectations of what public policy in this country—including criminal justice reform—would look like over the next four years, if not the next forty. Clinton had met with Black Lives Matters leaders and laid out a proposal for "end-to-end reform" of the criminal justice system; Donald Trump had surrounded himself with "tough-on-crime" advisers including Rudolph Giuliani and spoken favorably of now-discredited aggressive crime control policies like stop-and-frisk.

Yet that fateful Tuesday night was not a defeat for criminal justice reform. Far from it. As voters elected Donald Trump, they also passed a large number of criminal justice referendums—many of them (although, importantly, not all) reform-oriented—and voted out several tough-on-crime prosecutors in red and blue states alike. Consider Oklahoma: while Trump got 65 percent of the vote, the state also passed State Questions 780 and 781, which downgraded many drug possession and property offenses from felonies to misdemeanors, and required that the savings from the resulting reduced prison costs be directed to mental health and drug treatment programs.

Within days, dozens of articles appeared, all making the same point: somehow, surprisingly, criminal justice reform seemed poised to survive even under a Trump administration. Well, yes and no. Reform efforts will continue. Many voters, even those who voted for Trump, still seem to support cutting back prison populations, despite crime rising somewhat in 2015 and despite

Trump's rhetoric. One point I make in this book is that the federal government has little control over criminal justice reform, which is predominantly a state and local endeavor. As long as local voters favor reform, it will move ahead. And Election Day 2016's results suggest that many voters do.

At the same time, reformers still don't understand the root causes of mass incarceration, so many reforms will be ineffective, if not outright failures. Election Night offers a clear case study. Not all the successful ballot questions on criminal justice matters were reform-oriented; some were aimed at making laws harsher. An important split emerged. The reform questions focused on nonviolent drug and property crimes. The tougher-on-crime referendums, however, dealt with violent offenses and included proposals to speed up the death penalty process (passed in red Oklahoma and blue California) and a victim's-rights law called Marsy's Law that is so expansive that even prosecutors opposed it.

These results fit a common pattern in criminal justice reform, which for years has been premised on the idea that we can scale back our prison population primarily by targeting low-level, nonviolent crimes. A major theme of this book is that this is wrong: a majority of people in prison have been convicted of violent crimes, and an even greater number have engaged in violent behavior. Until we accept that meaningful prison reform means changing how we punish violent crimes, true reform will not be possible.

A similar misperception shapes the debate over private prisons. Such institutions receive significant attention and criticism, but their overall impact on prison growth is slight: only about 8 percent of prisoners are in private prisons, and there is no evidence that states that rely on private prisons are any more punitive than those that do not. So although private prison firms saw their stock prices soar in the aftermath of Trump's victory—and even if more prisoners are sent to private prisons in the coming years—reformers' attention should aim at individuals who play a much bigger role in supporting punitive policies and driving incarceration trends, including state and county politicians with prisons in their districts, and at prison guard unions. Yet these public-sector groups continue to face little scrutiny. In short, the state and local commitment to reform may endure. But because that commitment remains focused on the relatively unimportant factors behind prison growth, it continues to ignore the most important causes of this national shame.

John Pfaff
November 2016

AMERICAN EXCEPTIONALISM

THE STATISTICS ARE AS SIMPLE AS THEY ARE SHOCKING: THE United States is home to 5 percent of the world's population but 25 percent of its prisoners. We have more total prisoners than any other country in the world, and we have the world 's highest incarceration rate, one that is four to eight times higher than those in other liberal democracies, including Canada, England, and Germany.[1] Even repressive regimes like Russia and Cuba have fewer people behind bars and lower incarceration rates.

It wasn't always like this. Just forty years ago, in the 1970s, our incarceration rate was one-fifth what it is today. It was comparable to that of most European countries, and it had been relatively stable all the way back to the mid- to late 1800s. It was, in short, nothing out of the ordinary.

In fact, the prison boom started so suddenly that it caught most observers by surprise. In 1979, a leading academic wrote that the incarceration rate would always remain fairly constant, because if it climbed too high, state governments would adjust policies to push it back down.[2] As Figure 1 makes clear, however, the timing of that paper could not have

Figure 1 US Incarceration Rates, 1925–2014

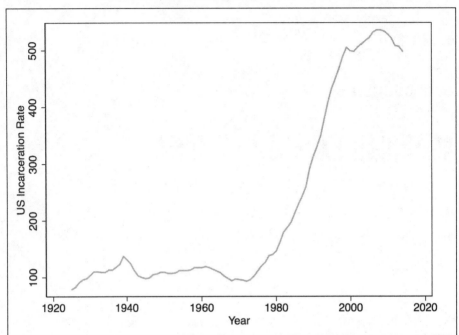

Source: Patrick A. Langan, John V. Fundis, Lawrence A. Greenfield, and Victoria W. Schneider, "Historical Statistics on Prisoners in State and Federal Institutions, Year-End 1925-1986," US Department of Justice, December 1986, accessed October 11, 2016, www.bjs.gov/content/pub /pdf/hesus5084.pdf, and US Department of Justice, Bureau of Justice Statistics, "Data Collection: NPS Program," www.bjs.gov/index.ctm?ty=dcdetail&iid=269.

been worse. The number of people in state or federal prisons rose from just under 200,000 in 1972 to over 1.56 million in 2014; the incarceration rate grew from 93 per 100,000 to 498 per 100,000 (peaking at 536 per 100,000 in 2008). Another 700,000 people are in county jails on any given day, more than two-thirds of whom have not been convicted of any crime and are simply awaiting trial.[3]

Remarkably, these numbers understate how many people are locked in prisons and jails each year. In 2014, approximately 2.2 million people were in state or federal prisons at some point, and perhaps as many as 12 million passed through county jails.[4] Although the data are patchy, it's clear that tens of millions of Americans have spent time in prison or jail since the 1970s. Historians, sociologists, criminologists, and economists disagree over exactly what changed in the 1970s that caused the surge,

Figure 2 Crime Trends, 1960–2014

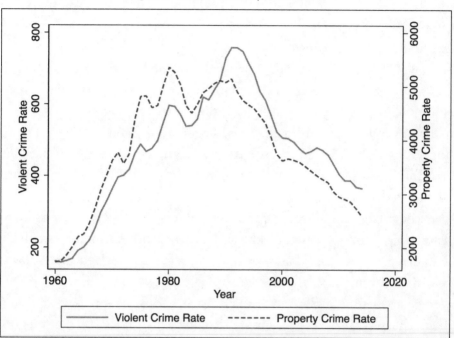

Source: US Department of Justice, FBI, "Uniform Crime Reports," www.bjs.gov/.

but clearly something—or a lot of things—changed, and our prison populations took an unprecedented turn.

One clear cause was rising crime. Starting around 1960, crime rates started to climb steadily. By 1980, violent crime rates had risen by over 250 percent, and property crime rates by over 200 percent; after a brief lull in the early 1980s, violent crime spiked again in 1984, peaking in 1991 at almost 400 percent of its 1960 level (more or less).[5] By the start of the 1990s, violent crime in America had never been worse, and property crime remained as bad as it had been in 1980. (See Figure 2.)

It's not surprising, then, that prison populations also increased sharply during these decades. Surely this was in part just a mechanistic response, since more crime leads to more arrests, and thus to more convictions and more prisoners. But a mechanistic response cannot fully explain what happened with incarceration. The impact of rising crime on prison populations is difficult to measure empirically, and it can only be done with a fair amount of uncertainty, but the best estimate of that impact suggests that rising crime over the 1970s and 1980s can explain, at most, just half the increase in prison populations over those two decades. And that relationship likely weakened during the 1990s, as prison populations continued to rise even as crime declined.

Few, however, pushed back against this relentlessly rising incarceration rate. During the 1980s and 1990s, support for increased incarceration was strong. Crime was rising throughout the 1980s, making tough-on-crime policies popular, and although crime began a slow and steady decline in the 1990s, many viewed incarceration as a primary cause of that decline and thus continued to support it. There were some brief calls for reform at the start of the 2000s, as crime continued to decline and state budgets contracted in the wake of the dot-com crash, but they were fleeting. Economic recovery came quickly, and any nascent reform efforts quickly foundered.[6] With the fiscal crisis of 2008, reformers revived their efforts, and the movement finally started to pick up steam. With prison populations at all-time highs and crime dropping to forty-year lows during a fiscal collapse far deeper and more sustained than the 2000 contraction, the opportunity to push for real reform seemed to be at hand.

In fact, the confluence of low crime and tight budgets has led to a surprisingly bipartisan push for reform during a time when those on the Left and the Right can barely agree on whether it is raining outside. Coalitions have brought together not just left-leaning reformers who have long opposed the social costs and the disparate racial impacts of our prison system, but also a complicated assortment of conservatives, including both budget hawks, who now prioritize cutting corrections budgets over their traditional tough-on-crime perspectives, and conservatives who are more ideologically committed to reform, such as redemption-focused evangelicals.[7]

In 2010, for the first time since 1972, the US prison population edged downward. And then it continued to fall for three of the next four years. By the end of 2014, the last year for which we have national data, it was about 4 percent smaller than it had been in 2010.[8] That's not a large drop, and certainly not one that challenges our position at the top of the international incarceration tables, but—perhaps!—it's a sign of things to come.

For reformers hoping to make deep cuts to our prison populations, these may seem like exciting times. State and federal prison populations are dropping, and every month or so it seems like someone is introducing a new bill in a state legislature or in Congress to change the system even more. The issue is also becoming popular among members of the general public. In a survey of registered US voters by the Pew Research Center in early 2016, 44 percent of all respondents said they believed that "reforming the criminal justice system should be a top priority"; the percentage rose to 73 percent for black respondents and 48 percent for Hispanics.[9] By the start of 2016, the nascent Black Lives Matter movement had forced Democratic presidential candidates to address criminal justice issues more candidly and more often, especially as they pertained to race. Because of all this, many think the reform movement is making great strides.

I am not so optimistic.

At the heart of my pessimism is the fact that the current reform efforts rely on a conventional wisdom about prison (population) growth—what I will call the "Standard Story"—that either substantially oversimplifies or simply gets wrong the factors driving the incarceration epidemic. Reforms built on misconceptions will disappoint at best and fail at worst. My motivation for writing this book is to highlight the mistakes and shortcomings of the Standard Story; to point out the more important, but generally underappreciated, causes of prison growth; and to suggest a set of reforms that are more likely to yield durable change, but that so far seem to be all too absent from reform conversations.

The core failing of the Standard Story is that it consistently puts the spotlight on statistics and events that are shocking but, in the grand scheme of things, not truly important for solving the problems we face. As a result, it gives too little attention to the more mundane-sounding yet far more influential causes of prison growth. For example, a core claim of the Story, made perhaps most forcefully by Michelle Alexander in her book *The New Jim Crow: Mass Incarceration in the Age of Color-Blindness*, is that our decision to lock up innumerable low-level drug offenders through the "war on drugs" is primarily responsible for driving up our prison populations. In reality, only about 16 percent of state prisoners are serving time on drug charges—and very few of them, perhaps only around 5 or 6 percent of that group, are both low level and nonviolent.[10] At the same time, more than half of all people in state prisons have been convicted of a violent crime. A strategy based on decriminalizing drugs will thus disappoint—and disappoint significantly. Yet we see little to no efforts to reform the treatment of people convicted of violent crimes.

The Standard Story also argues that increasingly long prison sentences have driven growth, and thus that cutting back sentences would effectively cut prison populations. President Barack Obama made this claim in a major 2015 speech, and it has been made repeatedly before and after by innumerable academics, journalists, and policymakers. The claim isn't exactly *wrong*: by international standards our sentences *are* long, and if people spent less time in prison, obviously prison populations would decline. In practice, however, most people serve short stints in prison, on the order of one to three years, and there's not a lot of evidence that the amount of time spent in prison has changed that much—not just over the 1990s, 2000s, and 2010s, but quite possibly over almost the entire prison boom.

The far more significant change, as I will explain more fully throughout this book, is the increased rate at which people get sent to prison in the first place. The primary driver of incarceration is increased prosecutorial toughness when it comes to charging people, not longer sentences. Stopping prosecutors from sending people to prison to start with would be far more effective in cutting incarceration rates than reducing the amount of time prisoners spend in prison once they get there—and this fact points to a very different set of reforms than those generally proposed.

The Standard Story also talks extensively about the "prison industrial complex"—a term made famous by journalist Eric Schlosser—and the power of the companies that run private prisons.[11] Tellingly, when 2016 presidential candidate Bernie Sanders decided to show his concern for criminal justice reform, his first step was to submit a law that attempted to ban private prisons altogether. For her part, Hillary Clinton publicly returned the relatively meager campaign donations she had received from private-prison executives once it became public that the donations had been made.

Private spending and private lobbying, however, are not the real financial and political engines behind prison growth. Public revenue and public-sector union lobbying are far more important. As states and counties have become wealthier, they have spent more on corrections (and everything else), and reining in that spending is much harder to do than limiting private firms' access to corrections contracts. Similarly, the real political powers behind prison growth are the public officials who benefit from large prisons: the politicians in districts with prisons, along with the prison guards who staff them and the public-sector unions who represent the guards.

There is one central aspect of the Standard Story, however, with which I agree: the critical role that race has played in driving up prison populations. Race does not come up much at the start of this book, where I focus on defining the factors causing mass incarceration. Showing that recent prison growth has been driven primarily by increased felony filings by prosecutors does not require an extensive analysis of race and punishment.

When turning to solutions, however, race becomes much more important. To figure out what we must do to responsibly reduce the prison population, we must understand why we have seen the results that we have—and that implicates race (along with class and other factors).[12] To address why prosecutors have become more aggressive in filing charges, for example, we must think about the impact of racial segregation. Urban prosecutors are elected at the county level, where political power is concentrated in the wealthier, whiter suburbs, while crimes disproportionately occur in the poorer urban cores with higher populations of people of color. This segregation of costs and benefits is a racial story more than anything else. Identifying prosecutorial aggressiveness as a driver of growth does not necessarily require much consideration of race and punishment—but correcting it does.

Despite my criticisms of the Standard Story, I believe that sizable cuts in the US incarceration rate are possible. But I believe that they will be harder to achieve than many hope, and that they will be far more tentative and vulnerable to reversal than many expect. There will be no moment when legislators sign a bill that will definitively end mass incarceration, allowing reformers to declare victory. The Standard Story explanation suggests that this may be possible. It is not.

To really change prison populations, we need a better model of what caused prison growth and what can reverse it. This book provides that model, reinterpreting the data used to support the Standard Story and calling on data that account has overlooked. In the end, this approach will suggest a set of solutions remarkably different from the ones typically proposed.

WHAT DO WE MEAN BY "MASS INCARCERATION"?

Before we jump into what has or has not caused "mass incarceration," it may help to ask what exactly that term means. Although widely used, it has no precise definition, and it is impossible to say at what point our incarceration rate moved from normal to high to "mass."[13] Furthermore, although pretty much everyone agrees that we need to move away from today's "mass" incarceration to something less, what that number should be is unclear.[14] Most targets—like Cut50's goal of "cut it in half"—seem to be chosen more for their intuitive appeal than for their precise policy implications.[15] The criticisms over "mass incarceration" essentially boil down to claims that we have too many people in prison, although we don't really know how many too many; and that we should reduce that number, although we don't really know what the new goal should be.

Part of the problem is that no one has provided a metric for determining how many people in prison is "too many" (except perhaps prison abolitionists, for whom it is any number much greater than zero). Should we rely on some sort of strict cost-benefit analysis—and if so, what sorts of costs and benefits should we include? Does harm to the inmate count, for example, or harm to the inmate's family? And are there other moral values, such as retributivism or mercy, that argue for more or fewer people in prison, independent of any effect on crime or safety or budgets?

Further complicating efforts to determine where "mass" incarceration starts is the fact that it's not even clear how to define the incarceration rate. Traditionally we look at the number of prisoners per 100,000 people (as in Figure 1). Another way to measure the US incarceration rate is by

Figure 3 Prisoners per 1,000 Violent or Property Crimes, 1960–2014

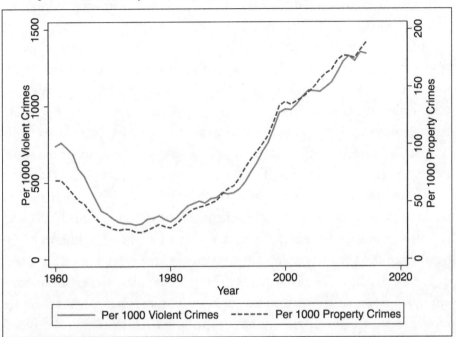

Source: US Department of Justice, FBI, "Uniform Crime Reports," and Bureau of Justice Statistics, "Data Collection: NPS Program," www.bjs.gov/index.cfm?ty.

the number of people imprisoned per 1,000 violent or property crimes, and these statistics tell a very different story. In the first method, incarceration probably becomes "mass" sometime in the late 1980s or early 1990s, by which point it had practically tripled from its mid-1970s levels. The second method, shown in Figure 3, demonstrates that when we scale by crime, not population, incarceration doesn't turn "mass" until sometime in the late 1990s or 2000s, well into the crime drop that began in 1991.

Neither of these methods is right or wrong. They simply represent two different ways of thinking about the incarceration rate, one in general historical terms, the other in terms that account for trends in crime. But they have quite distinct implications about where we now stand and about where we should aim to return. On top of all this, our ability to choose a new "target" incarceration rate is hampered by the fact that we lack a good understanding of the extent to which prison reduces crime. We perhaps know enough to make some broad claims—such as that rising incarceration has little effect on crime today—but we are constrained by not really knowing how much crime each additional prison admission prevents.

In fact, at every turn, efforts to measure the gains and costs of incarceration confront a host of empirical blind spots, an unfortunately all-too-common problem when studying crime and punishment. We lack clear estimates of how many crimes each person sent to prison would have committed if they had not been sent to prison. Nor do we fully understand how that kind of figure might have changed over time. Furthermore, there are all sorts of collateral costs that come from being sent to prison—lost income and family connections, diminished health—that are hard to measure. The possible benefits of incarceration are also hard to calculate, from the benefits to potential victims who escaped harm to the benefits to the general public that come from simply feeling safer.

Yet for all the difficulty with establishing the "ideal" level of incarceration, we can still say with some confidence that prison populations are too large today. Prison growth has certainly started to exhibit diminishing returns. In the 1970s and early 1980s, prison populations were low while crime rates were rapidly growing. Rising incarceration helped stem the rise in crime, even if it couldn't completely reverse the impact of the other factors pushing crime up to begin with. Crime, however, is now low and prison populations are high, suggesting that the return on each additional prisoner is much smaller than it was in the 1970s or 1980s. Although there has been little rigorous work done on this issue, the best results we have (which I will discuss in more depth in Chapter 5) indicate that this is in fact the case. Rising prison populations continue to contribute to falling crime, but their impact has declined greatly, and it is becoming hard, if not impossible, to justify still larger prison populations on crime-fighting grounds.[16]

Moreover, although it is true that prison "worked"—using "worked" to mean only that crime would have been higher had prison populations not gone up, assuming everything else stayed the same—that does not mean that rising incarceration was the best response to rising crime. There were certainly better options available. A growing body of research indicates, for example, that noncustodial rehabilitation programs consistently outperform those run in prisons.[17] Bolstering police forces is another option: the economist Steven Levitt once estimated that from a crime-reducing perspective alone, a dollar spent on police goes at least 20 percent further than a dollar spent on corrections.[18] Yes, problems with policing today clearly suggest that a dollar spent on policing could often be even better spent on non-policing options, but whatever the problems with police, those with prisons are surely worse.

The benefits that incarceration has yielded in terms of reduced crime also have to be balanced against a wide array of often hard-to-estimate "collateral" costs. Some of these costs, such as the income that inmates have lost while they were incarcerated, and the lower pay they face once they have been released, are measurable. Others are harder to estimate, even with good data. How, for example, do we account for the emotional costs of having a family member locked up fifty or one hundred miles away from home? Or the personal and social costs of a prison system that disproportionately impacts minorities, and that in doing so reinforces racial biases and inequalities? Or the increased future health costs (not just the dollar costs, but the emotional and social costs as well) that those who have gone to prison face after release? Of course, there are a lot of benefits to incarceration that might be hard to quantify as well—but many of these could be obtained through non-incarceral measures, so shifting away from prisons wouldn't necessarily jeopardize them.

At the same time, it is possible to oversell the argument that our prisons are too large. Three particularly important problems stand out. First, debates tend to misstate who is in prison. Most prison-reform discussions start with something along the lines of, "We send too many nonviolent and drug offenders to prison." And although it is likely true that we send too many, that doesn't mean that these offenders make up most of the people in prison. In fact, over half of all state inmates are in prison for violent crimes, and the incarceration of people who have been convicted of violent offenses explains almost two-thirds of the growth in prison populations since 1990. Similarly, almost all the people who actually serve long sentences have been convicted of serious violent crimes. To make significant cuts to state prisons, states need to be willing to move past reforms aimed at the minor offender and focus much more on the (far more politically tricky) people convicted of violent offenses.

Second, most arguments in favor of prison reform overstate the impact of prison spending on state budgets. The $50 billion or so that states spend to run their prisons is certainly a lot of money, but that comes to about 3 percent of state spending, a percentage that has been fairly stable for roughly the past fifteen years.[19] This is likely one reason why incarceration was allowed to continue with so little regulation for so long: because, in the end, prison spending did not limit spending elsewhere enough to generate much resistance.

And third, despite the fact that crime has essentially dropped for twenty-five straight years, crime rates are still fairly high. For all the decrease in crime rates since 1991, the official rate of violent crime in 2014 was still roughly twice that of 1960, and the rate of property crime was still one and a half times the 1960 rate.[20] So whatever the target prison population should be, we should be wary about returning to 1972 levels, when prison populations began their slow, relentless rise to the heights they have reached today.

Despite these three caveats, however, the evidence we have strongly suggests that prison populations are simply too large, and that cutting them back is sound policy. It's true that incarceration has focused much more on those convicted of violence than the Standard Story suggests, and that its overall financial cost is less than many think. Yet the costs of the high rate of incarceration are still enormous, not just economically, but socially and culturally as well, especially for the families and individuals touched by it.

Furthermore, recent experiences in many states make it clear that reducing prison populations need not lead to increases in crime. Between 2010 and 2014, state prison populations dropped by 4 percent while crime rates declined by 10 percent—with crime falling in almost every state that scaled back incarceration.[21] After nearly forty years of steadily rising prison populations, we are finally at a moment where we may be able to start to pare our incarceration rate back to levels more consistent with those in other liberal democracies today and in our own past. The political debate over punishment has shifted—and we should be deeply concerned that the reforms that various jurisdictions have implemented in recent years are too anemic, that they are accomplishing far too little and failing to capitalize on the opportunity that has presented itself. The Standard Story is hampering reform, and it is time to move beyond it.

3,144 STORIES OF PRISON GROWTH

A major barrier to reform, however, is the fractured nature of our criminal justice system. In fact, there is no single "criminal justice system," but instead a vast patchwork of systems that vary in almost every conceivable way. Unfortunately, the Standard Story and media accounts often miss this point.

A major reason for this oversight is that they pay too much attention to the federal criminal justice system, and to the various reform bills that have been inching their way through Congress over the past few years. It's easy to talk about the federal system, because it is a single entity with nationwide reach. However, it is also a relatively minor player in criminal justice. About 87 percent of all prisoners are held in state systems. The federal government runs the single largest prison system, but several states have systems that are fairly close to the federal one in size, and if we look at total populations under some sort of correctional observation (not just prison, but also jail, parole, and probation), the federal government quickly falls out of first place.

Furthermore, the federal criminal justice system is a distinct outlier in many ways; indeed, it's likely that the two states that differ the most from each other when it comes to criminal justice policy have more in common with each other than either does with the federal system. Owing to various legal and constitutional restrictions, for example, the federal system focuses much more heavily on drugs than state systems do (half of all federal prisoners are serving time for drug crimes, compared to 16 percent in the states). The federal government also spends much less on punishment than the states spend (0.5 percent of the federal budget, compared to about 7 percent of state budgets), and it faces very different political pressures (rural, white, lower-crime areas are much more overrepresented in the US Congress, and especially the Senate, than in state legislatures).[22]

In other words, both in terms of what is feasible and what is needed, federal reform will look very different from state reform. And federal reform alone will have very little impact on US incarceration rates: if we freed *every single* federal prisoner in prison today, we would still have the highest incarceration rate in the world, and we would still have over 1.3 million people in prison, about what we had in 1999. To really change our prison populations, we need to keep our attention on the states.

When focusing on the states, however, we still can't tell a single story. Punishment is highly localized in the United States, and state and county officials have tremendous discretion over who gets punished and how severely. So while the US incarceration rate in 2014 was 498 per 100,000, state rates ranged from 169 per 100,000 in Maine to 818 per 100,000 in Louisiana. Similarly, the US incarceration rate grew by 288 percent between 1978 and 2009 (its peak year), but the growth in individual states varied greatly: North Dakota and Mississippi, for example, experienced growth rates of 629 percent and 567 percent, respectively, while North Carolina saw a rise of only 85 percent.

If we aren't careful, we can tell a misleadingly national story when talking about what is happening "in the states." Here's a simple example: Between 2010 and 2014, state prison populations dropped by 4 percent, from 1.41 million to 1.3 million.[23] We would be tempted to celebrate that as a national decline. But in reality, twenty-five states saw their prison populations drop and the other twenty-five saw them rise—for a net decline of about 4 percent. So it was not a national decline, but a "half national" one. If we dig even deeper into the data, however, the situation becomes even more complicated. That 4 percent decline in the US prison population represented a reduction by about 56,000 inmates over those five years. But California alone, as part of its unique "Realignment" program, reduced its prison population over those five years by more than 35,000 inmates. So 62 percent of the net national decline, and 45 percent of the gross drop in prisoners, took place just in California.[24]

Are we witnessing a national decline? A broad-but-not-universal decline? Or is the national story basically just a California story? States vary widely in their policies, politics, and outcomes, and we don't want to gloss over those differences. And yet even looking at mass incarceration in a single state can mislead us. Take New York, a state that has experienced one of the longest sustained decarcerations in recent history, with prison populations falling by about 25 percent since 1999. This looks like a state success story, but the entire decline between 2000 and 2011 took place in just twelve of the state's sixty-two counties, with the other fifty counties adding inmates to state prisons during that time.[25] Similar discrepancies likely occur in many states in many contexts: relatively liberal cities act one way, while more conservative and more economically vulnerable nonurban areas act another way. We should be just as curious about differences between New York City and, say, Utica, New York, as we are about differences between Florida and New Jersey.

There are plenty of other examples that show how seemingly national criminal justice problems are really local ones. For instance, more than 90 percent of all three-strike sentences are thought to have been handed down in California; five jurisdictions hold 50 percent of the private prisoners in the country; three states were responsible for half of the executions through 2015 (Texas alone has conducted 37 percent of them, and 42 percent of the executions in Texas were conducted in just three of the state's 254 counties); and five counties have been responsible for a quarter of all juveniles sentenced to life without parole (with Philadelphia alone having sentenced nearly one in ten of these children).[26]

Rather than noting how local criminal justice failures are, however, when discussing our prison systems we too often go in the opposite direction and use extreme examples as if they were representative. It's common in books about the criminal justice system to see statements such as, "Prison guard unions have a lot of power. See, for example, the California Correctional Peace Officers Association [CCPOA]." But the CCPOA is *uniquely* powerful. It isn't an *example*, but a dramatic *outlier* (which is why authors cite it).

In other words, a national story is too blunt of an instrument to convey the complexity of the criminal justice system in the United States. A state story is an improvement, but it still misses a lot of detail. Ideally, we would need to tell 3,144 stories, one for each county in the United States. Even if that were possible, however, the result would be a slog. In the pages that follow I try to identify problems and trends, and I try to point out which of these are more universal and which ones are more localized. By necessity, I often have to paint with a broad brush, but it is important to keep in mind that we are a nation of either 50 or 3,144 distinct criminal justice systems. We must be wary of generalized, one-size-fits-all solutions to the challenges we face.

SMALL DATA

Finally, if we hope to arrive at a new understanding of mass incarceration, it is important to know that the data we have on the criminal justice system in the United States is far from complete. This book is based on fifteen years of close examination of a wide range of data on mass incarceration drawing on a wide range of statistical information gathered by the Federal Bureau of Investigation (FBI), the Bureau of Justice Statistics (BJS), the National Center on State Courts, and other organizations. The more I have dug into the data, however, the more I've come to grasp the magnitude of what we don't know.

Even supposedly basic facts remain beyond our reach. How many people, for instance, have criminal records in the United States? No one knows for sure, although estimates seem to come in around 70 million.[27] How many people have been to prison at least once? We know how many people get admitted to prison each year, but we don't really have any data on how many unique individuals have been to prison (since some of those admissions are recidivists or parole violators admitted in prior years). How many people plead guilty to crimes? There is no clear answer, although we know it is a large fraction of those who have been charged with crimes. How has time served for specific offenses changed? Only rough estimates exist, and only for the past ten or fifteen years. And these are just a few examples among many.[28]

In some cases, we have data, but there are important, often overlooked limitations to its reliability. Take the existing information on arrests. How many people were arrested in the United States in 2014? According to the FBI's official report, *Crime in the United States: 2014*, there were 11,205,833; or perhaps 8,789,559; or maybe 5,267,843—depending on which of the report's tables you are consulting. Not every police department reports crime and arrest data every month, so the FBI has to make tricky assumptions about how to fill in the gaps.[29] Some tables include such extrapolations, and others do not.[30]

There are other problematic assumptions as well. Take how we talk about trends in violent or property crime. The FBI's Uniform Crime Report only tracks incidences of the four "index" violent crimes (murder/manslaughter, forcible sexual assault, aggravated assault, and robbery) and the four "index" property crimes (burglary, larceny-theft, arson, and auto theft). Thus all sorts of other crimes, from simple assaults to drug offenses to date rape, are not included in how the FBI measures criminal offenses in the United States. These are not small omissions: of the 11.2 million arrests made in 2014, 9.2 million of them, or over 81 percent, were for non-index crimes.

Perhaps even more troubling, there are some issues where we simply have no data, where almost nothing at all is gathered. Perhaps most problematically, we have almost no information whatsoever on what prosecutors do or how (or why) they do it. We have almost no data on police-involved shootings.[31] We know practically nothing about the rate at which people sell drugs—and even our sources of information on drug *use*, which are more reliable, suffer from serious biases.

In the pages ahead I will tell you what we know—but I will tell you what we do not know as well. In many ways, perhaps the easiest reform to suggest is clear already: gather better data, so we have a clearer sense of what is happening and why, and thus can design better solutions.[32] But that would only be a very small first step.

THE CHALLENGE AHEAD

Despite the lack of data—and despite the challenges posed by a mistaken Standard Story, by the enigmatic term "mass incarceration," by a federalized system that spreads responsibility across 50 states and more than 3,000 counties—I remain guardedly optimistic about the future of prison reform. The current reforms have yielded only modest gains, but also they have shown that both political parties are willing to tackle the issue of mass incarceration.

What we need to do now is move past the reforms suggested by the Standard Story to take on the far more difficult, but far more important, issues of prosecutorial power, public-sector incentives, and the punishment of violent crimes. There are reforms that can confront these issues, although they are rarely part of the current national discussion. As we will see, options range from plea-bargaining guidelines for prosecutors, to prison closure commissions modeled on the military-base closing commission that Congress established after the Cold War, to incentive-based private prison contracts, and many more possibilities in between.

It's true that there are still many ways for the prison reform movement to falter or fail. Mass incarceration, however, is one of the biggest social problems the United States faces today; our sprawling prison system imposes staggering economic, social, political, and racial costs. The upside from adopting reforms that really work demands that we try hard to push past the misperceptions and political impediments.

PART I

The Standard Story

CHAPTER ONE

THE WAR ON DRUGS

ASK PEOPLE WHAT THEY THINK PLAYED THE BIGGEST ROLE IN driving up incarceration, and my guess is that many, if not most, will immediately say, "the war on drugs." I can't count the number of times I've told someone that I study prison growth, only to have her give me a look that mixed pity (at my denseness) with amusement and reply, "Well, isn't it just the war on drugs?"

It's not surprising that people think this, since leading experts and politicians make this claim all the time. Take Michelle Alexander, in her book *The New Jim Crow*: "The impact of the drug war has been astounding. In less than thirty years, the US penal population exploded from around 300,000 to more than 2 million, with drug convictions accounting for the majority of the increase."[1] President Barack Obama repeated the same point in his highly publicized speech before the NAACP annual meeting in Philadelphia on July 14, 2015, when he kicked off his efforts to reform criminal justice: "But here's the thing: Over the last few decades, we've also locked up more and more nonviolent drug offenders than ever before, for longer than ever before. And that is the real reason our prison population is so high."[2]

I understand why people make this claim: timing. Ronald Reagan declared his "war on drugs" on October 14, 1982, right as prison populations were really starting to rise (although, importantly, nearly a decade after the rise had actually begun).[3] And the 1980s and 1990s did see states crack down on drug offenders, whose share rose from 6.5 percent of the state prison population in 1980 to almost 22 percent in 1990, and the absolute number of people serving time for drug crimes rose from about 20,000 in 1980 to 150,000 in 1990, and up to almost 250,000 by the end of the 2000s (though it dropped to about 200,000 by 2013).[4] Furthermore, even as crime fell steadily over the 1990s and 2000s, arrests for drug offenses rose, from just under 1.1 million in 1990 to over 1.5 million in 2012—although it should be noted that arrests for drug sales and manufacturing, which are the drug offenses that generally result in prison time, fell by about 70,000 over that time, from 348,000 to 278,000.[5]

And so I've relied on a fairly narrow definition of the war on drugs (which, as we'll see, is another term that is hard to pin down). Many argue that a host of non-drug crimes, and thus non-drug arrests, are ultimately tied to the social disruptions caused by drug enforcement: gang wars over drug markets, property crimes to fund drug habits that are more expensive than they would otherwise be due to prohibition, violent crimes arising from addictions that could be managed if we approached addiction as a public health issue instead of a criminal one, and more.

Others have argued that simply putting more police in urban neighborhoods in the name of drug prohibition leads those officers to make more non-drug arrests, increasing both the number of prisoners and the racial disparities in prison populations. Or perhaps the rhetoric of a "war" on drugs has fueled tougher responses to all sorts of crimes, including those not related to drug use or drug trafficking; this indirect effect could matter even if the direct impact of the war is less than believed.

There is much that is troubling here. Prohibition certainly causes some crimes that otherwise wouldn't happen, like a shoot-out over drug territory.[6] And with a few caveats we'll see shortly, many of the 200,000 people in state prisons on drug charges likely would not be there if drugs were legal, or at least if police and prosecutors didn't enforce the drug laws. It's true that those 200,000 people make up only about 16 percent of state prisoners, but that number almost equals the total number of people in US prisons—for any crime—in the 1970s, and the costs to them and to their families are anything but trivial.

Yet when we look at the data more closely, it becomes increasingly difficult to defend the claim that the war on drugs is the main driver of prison growth. This is true for pretty much any definition of the "war on drugs," from one that refers to just the incarceration of those convicted of drug offenses to broader perspectives that include anyone who would not have been in prison if the United States had not prohibited certain drugs or enforced their prohibition. No matter how we define the war on drugs, its impact appears to be important, but unequivocally secondary to other factors.

For the past few years I have been arguing that the "war" against the war on drugs will not cut prison populations nearly as much as its proponents hope.[7] The standard response I get is the "low-hanging fruit" reply: drug reform is the easiest and most politically viable reform to implement. Do that first, then build on that victory to attack the tougher issues, like how we punish violent crimes. On its own terms, it's a fair point. In practice, however, it raises serious concerns. Prison reformers have been pushing hard to change state laws since 2008 or 2009, and seven or eight years later I have yet to see almost any politician take on how we might deal more effectively with violent offenses, perhaps with the high-profile exception of Senator Cory Booker of New Jersey.[8] Political capital and attention are limited, and at some point people's focus will drift away from criminal justice reform to other topics. The window to act is not indefinite.

Even worse, the rhetoric and tactics used to push through reforms for lower-level offenses often explicitly involve imposing even harsher punishments on those convicted of violent crimes. South Carolina, for example, has been widely congratulated for the reforms it passed in 2010, which, among other things, raised the cutoff for felony theft from $1,000 to $2,000 and created various ways for those convicted of drug possession to avoid prison time—but simultaneously raised the sanctions for various violent crimes.[9] Maryland, generally more liberal than South Carolina, passed a reform bill in 2016 that also cut sanctions for nonviolent crimes while increasing punishments for some violent ones in order to avoid looking "soft on crime."[10] Similarly, Georgia's lauded 2011 reforms have cut prison populations, but hidden in that decline is a rise in the absolute number of people serving time for violent crimes—people whose sentences tend to be longer, and whose rising imprisonment may, in the long run, undo the short-run declines.[11]

To be clear, cutting back on drug admissions is almost surely a good thing: a large number of our drug-offense admissions are inefficient, if not immoral, by almost any standard. But it is also true that there are real costs to focusing just on the war on drugs, costs that may not be immediately visible but that may undermine reform efforts down the line. So it is important to understand just what scaling back the war will—and will *not*—accomplish. To start, though, we have to answer a question whose answer is surprisingly elusive: What really *is* the "war on drugs"?

A WAR ON WHO?

When people say, "We should end the war on drugs," what exactly do they mean? Whose arrests and imprisonment fall within the "war," and whose fall outside of it? And when did this war start? These questions seem like they should be fairly easy to answer. They're actually quite baffling.

Start with the easiest case: the people imprisoned for the possession or sale of drugs that are currently illegal. At first blush, none of these people would be in prison but for the war on drugs; if crack or heroin were legal or decriminalized, its possession or sale wouldn't lead to punishment. But already the picture gets complicated. Many of those in prison for selling drugs resorted to that practice because of a lack of other employment options.[12] If drugs became legal, the drug market would surely consolidate, and the number of drug-selling jobs available to those same people would shrink. As long as all the other barriers to legal employment remained in place for many who are now selling drugs (poor schools, racial discrimination), then at least some of those who might have gone to prison for selling drugs would instead end up in prison for some other illegal scheme to make money.[13] From the start, the impact of legalization will likely be less than what it would appear to be from just counting the number of people in prison on drug charges.

How about the people who commit non-drug crimes to fuel a drug habit? Although we do not classify them in the official statistics as "drug offenders"—they would be described as committing property or violent offenses—it seems plausible to tie at least some of these incarcerations to the war on drugs. After all, the war on drugs has raised the price of drugs above what it otherwise would have been; for at least some users, these higher prices force them to resort to crime to afford the drugs.[14] Yet once again, things quickly get complicated. As the prices of drugs fall post-legalization, use will go up, in terms of both quantity per user and the number of users.[15] Some will become serious users who will then find it harder to maintain employment and thus risk turning to crime to support their habit. The net impact may very well be positive, but likely less than many would hope for, and it is difficult to say with much certainty how all this would play out.[16]

Or how about drug-market offenses, such as murders arising from drug gang wars over territory? Unlike theft to support a habit, these crimes seem like they would disappear without prohibition, so perhaps we should count the ensuing incarcerations as "results" of the drug war. Once more, however, there's a complication. In her excellent book *Ghettoside: A True Story of Murder in America*, *Los Angeles Times* journalist Jill Leovy highlights the work of numerous sociologists and anthropologists to suggest that at least some of this causal story—that illegal drug dealing leads to violence—gets things backward. It's not that prohibition causes lethal violence; it's that in an era of prohibition, trafficking in drugs is going to cluster where lethal violence rates are already high. Her basic claim is straightforward: whenever there are a lot of young men with little chance of upward mobility, and the government fails to protect its "monopoly on violence," those young men will form gangs and violence will follow. Anthropologists and historians have shown that this is as true in South Central Los Angeles in the twenty-first century as in tsarist Russia in the nineteenth.

Leovy's three factors certainly hold true in South Central Los Angeles. There are a lot of young men. Upward mobility is often greatly restricted—employers, for example, seem to prefer white applicants *with* criminal records over black ones *without* records.[17] And the state does a poor job of preventing violence in minority neighborhoods. As Leovy shows, the clearance rate for murders in LA as a whole over the period 1994 to 2006 hovered around 50 percent—itself a shockingly low number, given that Leovy estimates that about 30 percent of all homicides are straightforward "self-solvers"—but the clearance rate for murders involving black victims was closer to 38 percent.[18]

Leovy's point is a striking one. Legalizing drugs may have some important collateral benefits—it may improve police-community relations, for example, or free up officers who had to focus on drugs to target more serious crimes—but it does not resolve many of the structural problems that lead to higher rates of violence in the first place.[19] It won't change demographics, it won't really break down the barriers to upward mobility, and it won't necessarily help the state reassert its monopoly on violence.[20] And Leovy's is not the only data to support this view that drugs came to the violence. The black male homicide rate, for example, was almost 20 percent higher in 1970, before the start of the war on drugs, than it was in 1990, at the height of the crack epidemic and crack-related violence; this at least suggests that to some extent the drugs came to the violence.[21]

I don't want to oversell this point: the homicide rate for black males aged eighteen to twenty-four rose by over 170 percent between 1984 and 1993, peaking at almost 200 per 100,000—compared to rates of slightly below 20 per 100,000 for white males aged eighteen to twenty-four at that time.[22] The instability of illegal crack markets, which expanded rapidly in the 1980s, certainly led to violence. But it was against a background of already elevated violence, a background whose root causes will not be addressed by legalization, much less decriminalization, alone.

So the question, "Who is in prison due to the war on drugs, and so wouldn't be if we stopped the war?" is surprisingly hard to answer. To keep things simple, I will define those in prison "due to" the war on drugs as those who are serving time for drug charges. This will both overstate and understate the impact of ending prohibition, but ultimately, it is hard to consider alternate definitions with the data we have.[23]

ORIGINS

It's not just difficult to define who is in prison due to the war on drugs: It's hard to even know when the war started. Most pundits and academics point to one of two dates that are separated by more than a decade: June 17, 1971, or October 14, 1982. Both dates, however, are wrong.

President Richard Nixon gave a major speech highlighting the evils of drugs on June 17, 1971, and although he didn't use the exact term "war on drugs," he certainly talked about drugs as a scourge that had to be eliminated.[24] Yet while Nixon often used aggressive rhetoric, his actual policies tended to favor public health responses over punitive ones.[25] For instance, he oversaw the passage of the Comprehensive Drug Abuse Prevention and Control Act of 1970, which emphasized treatment and rehabilitation and, among other things, abolished federal mandatory minimum sentences for drug crimes (with the vocal support, ironically, of George H. W. Bush, then in Congress, who as vice president and president would oversee the readoption of many of these mandatory minimums).[26] Furthermore, prison populations didn't budge much during Nixon's term, and six years after he left the White House, drug offenders still made up less than 7 percent of all US prisoners. Perhaps some of his rhetoric hardened people's attitudes and contributed to future punitiveness, but that's a much trickier claim to make.[27]

The second time the drug war was supposedly launched was by President Ronald Reagan in a speech on October 14, 1982.[28] Using Reagan's speech as the kickoff, however, has the opposite problem as using Nixon's. By the time Reagan declared a war on drugs, the US incarceration rate had risen by almost 80 percent since 1972; the slow, steady climb was already well underway, and there was no real change in the rate of growth in the years after 1982.[29] If Reagan's rhetoric and policy choices were as critically important as people say, we should be able to see it in prison growth. But we don't.

In the end, though, to focus on either Nixon or Reagan is to approach the issue from the wrong direction. Criminal justice is predominantly local, and even state governments often have little control over county prosecutors and city police. So there won't be a single starting date for

Figure 1.1 Inmates in New York Prisons for Drug Offenses

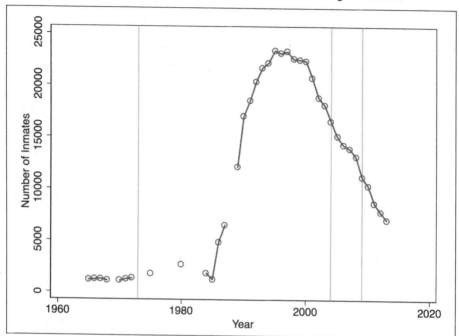

Source: *New York State Statistical Yearbook,* available years.

the war on drugs, because the war started (and, to some extent, stopped or waned) at different times in different places. Two examples from New York State's war on drugs illustrate this point clearly.

First, Figure 1.1 plots the number of inmates in New York prisons on drug convictions. The vertical lines indicate three major legal changes: the adoption in 1973, under New York governor Nelson Rockefeller, of the state's remarkably harsh Rockefeller Drug Laws (RDLs), which for years remained among the toughest in the nation; the relatively minor reforms of the RDLs in 2004; and more substantive reforms to them in 2009. Several interesting stories emerge from this figure. In the first decade after the RDLs were passed, the number of inmates in New York prisons on drug charges barely budged. The laws were tougher, but prosecutors weren't using them. Drug admissions then soared starting in 1984, which is right when crack, and crack-related violence, appeared. Then the number in prison for drug crimes started to drop—in 1997, seven years before the 2004 reforms. And the rate of decline doesn't appear to change following either 2004 or 2009 in response to either reform. In other words, when prosecutors weren't too concerned about drug crimes, they simply ignored the Rockefeller Drug Laws, whether during the rising-crime 1970s or the falling-crime 1990s and 2000s. They appear to take advantage of the laws somewhat in the 1980s—although most of the people sent to prison in New York State for drug crimes still served fairly short sentences—but the decision seems motivated as much by a desire to fight violence as by drugs.

This doesn't mean that the RDLs—or state laws in general—are irrelevant. Although New York obviously couldn't compel prosecutors to be more aggressive in the 1970s or to maintain their aggressiveness in the 2000s, the prosecutors could not have been as aggressive as they were in the 1980s and 1990s without the power granted to them by the state. The timing of the "drug war" in New York State, however, turned far more on local than on state or national factors.

Seen this way, it's worth noting not just how local the changes were, but how *non-legal* they were. The decline in drug incarcerations wasn't driven by the changes in the law, but by some combination of changing local crime rates and changing views of the local police and prosecutors about who to arrest and how harshly to charge them. It was more an attitudinal change, not a legal one. This is an important distinction, one that comes up too infrequently in the reform debate, and one we will return to again. Pessimistically, we cannot legislate ourselves out of large-scale incarceration. Optimistically, we could do so much more right now without any change in the law at all.

The second important point, again using New York as an example, is that not only are the decisions predominantly local, but that even within a state there is great variation across localities. Recall the discussion in Chapter 1 showing how just a few counties drove most of the prisoner decline in New York. It turns out that this observation applies not just to all prisoners, but also to those specifically convicted of drug crimes. A recent study showed that the number of people being admitted to New York State prisons on drug charges rose from 2,000 to 11,500 per year between 1985 and 1992, at which point the number started to decline, falling to about 5,000 in 2008.[30] Yet this decline was driven almost entirely by New York City. Between 1992 and 2008, the number of people the five counties of New York City sent to state prison for drug crimes fell, from around 10,000 to 3,000, while the number sent by the remaining fifty-seven counties rose from 1,500 to 2,000.[31] So when people talk about Richard Nixon's war on drugs or Ronald Reagan's war on drugs—or, admittedly far less frequently, Nelson Rockefeller's war on drugs—they rarely acknowledge that this war is actually waged much more locally. It's more Robert M. Morgenthau's war and Charles J. Hynes's war (the Manhattan DA from 1975 to 2009, and the Brooklyn DA from 1989 to 2013, respectively) than Nixon's or Reagan's or Rockefeller's war.

The war isn't a specific, coordinated set of actions. It isn't the decision to criminalize drugs in the first place—Congress criminalized most major drugs between 1914 and 1937, long before prison populations started to rise. (The Harrison Act of 1914 effectively criminalized heroin, and the Marihuana Tax Act of 1937 did the same for marijuana.) Nor is it any declaration by any one president. It is the decision by state legislators to pass tougher sentencing laws, by county prosecutors to enforce those laws more aggressively, and by city police to arrest drug offenders more frequently. Importantly, these actors need not (and often do not) act in concert with each other. The legislature can pass a law that the prosecutors do not often use (as with the harshest parts of the Rockefeller Drug Laws). The police can arrest defendants whom prosecutors refuse to charge (like the declaration by Brooklyn's DA in 2014 that he would generally not prosecute low-level marijuana charges brought to him by the New York Police Department).[32] Conversely, a prosecutor can continue to go after drug cases harshly even if the police deemphasize drug arrests.[33] In short, there is no single "war on drugs," but rather somewhere between 50 and 3,300 wars on drugs, fought with varying degrees of intensity at different times, in different jurisdictions, and in different ways.

Which isn't to say that national actors are irrelevant. Their impact, however, is indirect, often relatively minor, and frequently far less important than the attention they receive. The federal government can pass laws to try to encourage states to change enforcement priorities, generally through what basically amounts to bribes (grants if states do something) or blackmail (loss of grants if the states do not do something), but states often ignore both of these approaches.[34] It could be that federal rhetoric

Figure 1.2 Percentage of State Prisoners
Serving Time for Drug Offenses, 1980–2013

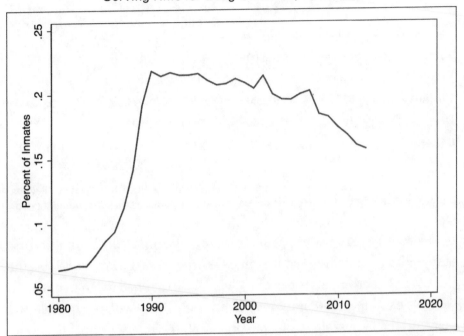

Source: US Department of Justice, Bureau of Justice Statistics, "Correctional Populations in the United States," and "Prison Population Counts." See www.bjs.gov/index.cfm?ty.

shapes what local actors choose to do. But then it is always worth asking if the federal actors getting all the media and academic attention are really driving the process, or if they are responding to more localized conditions that the national media are ignoring—which makes their reaction look more like a cause. Sadly, there is no way to figure out if this is the case, but the possibility cautions us not to give federal and other national leaders too much credit too quickly when it comes to people's attitudes.

20 PERCENT OF THE PRISONERS, 80 PERCENT OF THE ATTENTION

I'll make my core claim bluntly: if we define the people in prison as a result of the war on drugs to be those serving time for a drug conviction, then that war simply hasn't sent enough people to state prisons for it to be a major engine of state prison growth.[35] Given how directly this conclusion flies in the face of the Standard Story, let me show my work.[36]

Table 1.1 Composition of Inmates in State Prisons, 1980 and 2009

	1980	2009	Percent Change	Absolute Change	Percent Contributed
Total	294,000	1,362,000	363%	1,068,000	
Violent	173,300	724,300	318%	551,000	52
Property	89,300	261,200	192%	171,900	16
Drug	19,000	242,200	1175%	223,200	21
Other	12,400	134,500	985%	122,100	11

Source: Data from US Department of Justice, Bureau of Justice Statistics, "Data Collection: National Prisoner Statistics (NPS) Program," www.bjs.gov/index.cfm?ty=dcdetail&iid=269.

Figure 1.2 (on previous page) illustrates my point. Although the share of the prison population serving time for drugs rose during the 1980s, the share was 22 percent at its peak in 1990. By 2013 it had fallen to under 16 percent. Even the 1990 number is surprisingly low—when drug offenders made up the largest share of state prisoners, three in four prisoners were serving time for non-drug offenses. That ratio is now up to about six out of seven. Looking at the numbers a little more closely only reinforces how secondary drug admissions are to prison growth, given how central they are to most popular accounts. Table 1.1 displays the composition of state prison populations from 1980 to 2009. States added over 1 million people to their prisons during that time, with over *half* that growth coming from locking up more people convicted of violence, compared to only about 20 percent due to more drug incarcerations.

Table 1.1, however, is slightly unfair to the Standard Story's emphasis on the war on drugs; there's no reason to assume that the various types of crimes were equally important to prison growth during periods of rising crime (1980–1991) and falling crime (1991–2008). Table 1.2 breaks out these phases: during the 1980s, locking up people for violent crimes and for drug crimes had roughly equal impacts on prison growth but after that, during the 1990s and 2000s, the punishment of people convicted of violence made up nearly two-thirds of the increase in inmates nationwide.

Table 1.2 Composition of Inmates in State Prisons, 1980, 1990, and 2009

	1980	1990	2009	Percent Contributed, 1980–1990	Percent Contributed, 1990–2009
Total	294,000	681,400	1,362,000		
Violent	173,300	316,600	724,300	36	60
Property	89,300	173,700	261,200	22	13
Drug	19,000	148,600	242,200	33	14
Other	12,400	45,500	134,500	9	13

Source: Data from the US Department of Justice, Bureau of Justice Statistics, "Data Collection: National Prisoner Statistics (NPS) Program," www.bjs.gov/index.cfm?ty=dcdetail &iid=269.

These results are actually quite startling. They show that drug incarcerations were more important during the period of rising crime than when crime was in decline. It seems more logical that during a period of rising violent crime, the incarceration of people convicted of violence would drive the process, and that as violent crime fades, police and prosecutors would turn their attention to more discretionary drug offenses. Yet (much to my own surprise) we see the opposite of that taking place here. What exactly does it mean?

Perhaps somewhat counterintuitively, what we see in Table 1.2 actually undermines the claim that drug admissions seemingly mattered as much as violent ones during the 1980s. That drug crime admissions rose more rapidly during a time of rising violence suggests that at least some of these drug admissions, maybe many, were pretextual attacks on violence. In other words, some of those arrested for and convicted of drug offenses were targeted as a way to punish more serious—but harder-to-prove—violent crime. There is other data to support this idea. A large 1997 survey of state prisoners nationwide, for example, found that about 20 percent of all those serving time in state prisons on drug charges admitted to having used a firearm in a previous crime, and about 24 percent had prior convictions for violent crimes.[37]

It is, of course, completely fair to debate the morality or efficacy of using drug charges to tackle underlying violence. These results, however, suggest that some of those incarcerated on drug charges during the more violent 1980s and early 1990s would have been imprisoned even in the absence of a war on drugs (to the extent that the violence itself wasn't *caused* by prohibition, an issue I'll address shortly). The impact that banning or avoiding pretextual admissions would have had on prison populations is thus unclear. On one hand, pretextual arrests allowed prosecutors to target more people. Some of those who went to prison on pretextual drug charges would not otherwise have gone to prison at all, because the "real" violent crime would have been too hard to prove.[38] But in the absence of pretextual drug charges, some of those convicted of drug crimes would have been convicted of more serious violent crimes, and thus likely would have spent more time in prison. These longer terms would have offset at least some of the impact from fewer cases. So it is hard to say if these pretextual cases made prison populations larger or smaller and, if larger, by how much.

There are two important caveats I should raise. First, the fraction of those in prison for drugs who are there pretextually has likely fallen. In the 1990s and 2000s, violent crime fell while admissions for violence rose, suggesting that authorities were attacking violent crimes more directly and relying less on pretextual drug charges. At the same time, the number of people in prison on drug charges still rose slightly. Since drug offenders serve comparatively short sentences, few people admitted to prison for (possibly-pretextual) drug crimes in the 1980s and 1990s were still in prison in the 2000s. Taken together, these two facts imply that a growing fraction of those in prison for drugs today really are there for drug crimes, not pretextually for violent crimes.

Second, while the numbers here suggest that fighting the war on drugs did not play as big a role in driving up prison populations as is commonly thought, the impact of scaling back drug enforcement has yielded noticeable results, at least in the short run. Between 2010 and 2012, state prison populations fell for the first time since the 1970s. During that time, the number of people behind bars for violence decreased by about 17,500, for property crimes by about 2,500—and for drugs by nearly 27,000.[39] Between 2012 and 2013, even as total state prison populations increased by over 10,000 people, the number of people in prison for drugs dipped downward again, by just over 2,000 (and the number in for violent crimes dropped by almost 3,000).

In other words, the single biggest driver of the decline in prison populations since 2010 has been the decrease in the number of people in prison for drug crimes. But focusing on drugs will only work in the short run. That it is working now is certainly something to celebrate. But even setting every drug offender free would cut our prison population by only about 16 percent.[40] There is a hard limit on how far drug-based reform can take us.

THE MYTH OF THE LOW-LEVEL, NONVIOLENT DRUG OFFENDER

Although there may be limits on what a drug-based reform effort can accomplish, 16 percent of the state prison population is still more than 200,000 people—and that's a huge number by any measure. There is, however, another limitation to consider: we may not *want* to release all of those who are in prison for drug crimes. Standard Story narratives often talk about all the low-level, nonviolent drug offenders in state prisons, suggesting that most of the people in prison for drug crimes should not be there. Not surprisingly, the truth is a bit more complicated.

Most of our prisoner statistics provide very little information about why someone is in prison beyond the specific conviction offense. In a world of plea bargaining, however, the conviction offense is an imperfect signal, at best, of what the prisoner actually did. How many other offenses were simply dropped? How many crimes were downgraded at charging (turning trafficking into a possession conviction, for example)? And how many aggravating factors, such as a gun, might have been discarded? There is, however, one way to look beyond the conviction offense to the "real" behavior of people admitted to prison. The Bureau of Justice Statistics periodically conducts a large-scale survey of thousands of inmates in state and federal prisons, asking them hundreds of questions: not just, say, what the official conviction offenses were in their cases, but how many kilos or packets of drugs they really had, whether they actually had guns on them at the time (regardless of what they pled to or were convicted of or were arrested for), what sort of prior crimes they had been arrested or imprisoned for, and so on.

Using the survey from 1997—admittedly slightly stale data—two social scientists tried to determine how many truly low-level drug offenders were in prison, where they defined "unambiguously low level drug offenders" as "nonviolent, first-or second-time drug offenders" who played minor roles and possessed only small amounts of drugs.[41] Only about 6 percent of state drug inmates—not 6 percent of all inmates, but 6 percent of just those inmates convicted of drug crimes, or about 1 percent of all prisoners—and 2 percent of federal drug inmates met that description. At the same time, most of those serving time for drug offenses did not appear to be "kingpins" either, whom the researchers defined as those who described themselves as mid- to high-level drug-ring participants. These people accounted for only about 4 percent of those in state prisons for drug crimes and 6.6 percent of those similarly in federal prisons.

Almost everyone in prison for a drug crime was somewhere in the middle. Some were caught with nontrivial quantities, some had prior histories of violence or gun possession, and some had long lists of prior drug convictions. Most of those in prison for drugs were more than users, and many were not as nonviolent as their conviction offenses suggested. Prison is still an excessive punishment for many of these cases, perhaps even most of them. Yet I imagine that many prison reformers—and certainly much of the general public—still think that some of these midlevel types deserve time in prison.

THE SUBTLER EFFECTS OF THE WAR ON DRUGS

So far, I have used a fairly simple and naïve approach to conceptualizing the war on drugs. What if it matters in less direct, but no less important ways? I recently looked at three such indirect pathways.[42] For two I have some data, for one little more than informed speculation. In all three cases, though, the result appears to be the same: the impact of the war on drugs seems to be fairly slight, contrary to my own initial expectations.

First, it may make more sense to count how many people pass through prisons on drug charges than how many are in prison for such crimes on any one day. It's true that the number in prison on any given day for drug crimes is relatively small. Drug convictions, however, tend to result in fairly short sentences, so it could be that a lot more drug offenders cycle through prisons than the one-day prison counts suggest. Perhaps the war on drugs has a much bigger impact on the total number of people who have entered prison than it does on the number in prison at a specific time. In fact, I think this is what Michelle Alexander generally means in *The New Jim Crow* when she argues that the war on drugs has been the main driver of prison growth. Although she isn't entirely consistent in her book, she often seems to define the "prison population" as anyone currently in prison or anyone who *has been* to prison.[43] If drug offenders churn through prison rapidly, they could make up a much bigger fraction of the "ever been to prison" population than any one-day prison count would show.[44]

To test this idea that people convicted of drug crimes pass through prison at a much greater rate than the one-day prison counts suggest, I looked at data on each person admitted to prison in fifteen states between 2000 and 2012.[45] During this time, these states admitted over 3.5 million people to prison, or about 42 percent of the 8.5 million people admitted nationwide during that time. Once I accounted for people who were admitted multiple times, I found that these 3.5 million admissions comprised just under 2 million unique people. I then divided these people into three categories: those who were never admitted for a drug crime (even if they were admitted multiple times), those who were admitted only for a drug crime (even if they were admitted multiple times), and those admitted multiple times for both drug and non-drug reasons. Table 1.3 breaks down these populations.[46]

The conclusion is clear: the number of people passing through prison for drug crimes over the 2000s is only slightly higher than the number in prison for a drug crime on any one day. In fact, the results become more striking when we look at unique individuals, where the fraction of unique people passing through for drugs was between 20 and 25 percent, right around the 20 percent who were in prison on any given day during the period examined here. In other words, the "churn" rate for drug offenses isn't that much different from that rate for most non-drug crimes:

Table 1.3 People Convicted of Drug Offenses
Admitted to State Prison: 2000–2012

	All Prisoners	No Drugs	Only Drugs	Some Drugs
Total Admissions	3,519,952	2,541,878	644,488	333,586
Percent of Total		72	18	9
Number of Unique People	1,969,703	1,482,860	397,079	89,764
Percent of Unique People		75	20	5

Source: Data from the US Department of Justice, Bureau of Justice Statistics, "Data Collection: National Corrections Reporting Program," www.bjs.gov/index.cfm?ty=dcdetail &iid=268.

although drug terms are shorter than average, they don't appear to be that much shorter than the terms for most other offenses.

The second indirect pathway is parole violations, for drug and non-drug crimes alike. Some 600,000 people are released from prison every year, most of them under the supervision of a parole officer. Many of those who are released end up returning to prison because they violate one of the rules the state imposes on them as a condition for release. The Standard Story generally makes two claims about parole violations: that they are a major engine of prison growth, and that many parolees are sent back to prison because of some sort of "technical" drug-related violation (failing a drug test, missing a drug test, and so on).

Let's start with the macro-claim, that parole violations are important drivers of prison populations. It's easy to see why the link appears plausible. Between 1978 and 2008, the number of parole violators returned to state prison rose by an entire order of magnitude, from about 20,000 to nearly 250,000. The catch, however, is that the prison population, too, soared during this time. Not surprisingly, that meant that the number of people released *onto* parole also climbed, from just under 100,000 in 1978 to just over 500,000 in 2008. An interesting story emerges from these numbers. As prison populations have risen, consistently about 40 to 50 percent of all people in prison have been released each year, and about 70 percent of those released have been released onto parole.[47] Moreover, since 1990 the fraction of those released onto parole who have ended up back in prison because of a parole violation appears to have been steady as well, after rising somewhat over the 1980s. One crude metric of the fraction of parolees returned to prison for a parole violation has hovered at around 40 percent from 1990 onward (after rising from about 25 percent in 1980).

To put all the pieces together: Prison populations are growing. A stable fraction of those in prison are released, a stable fraction of those released are released onto parole, and a fairly stable fraction of those released onto parole violate back. Which means that violations aren't driving growth so much as they are being driven by it. If you're bailing out a boat with a leaky bucket, it seems unfair to blame the bucket's leak for the boat filling up with water. It's true that without the hole in the bucket, there would be less water in the boat, but that hole isn't causing the flooding. Moreover, from the mid-1990s onward, parole violators as a share of all those admitted has remained fairly constant, even as total admissions have risen, further indicating that parole outcomes have not driven prison growth.

The Standard Story's micro-claim is that many of those sent back to prison for parole violations are guilty only of "technical" violations of the restrictions and conditions they face upon release.[48] Some of these are understandable and substantive—don't commit another crime, or (for sex offenders) don't work in a day-care center. But others are more technical and administrative, like needing to show up for drug tests or appointments with parole officers. Violating any one of these restrictions and rules can result in the parolee going back to prison, although some jurisdictions rely on less severe sanctions for smaller missteps. According to the Standard Story, too many people are sent back to prison for violating the more technical restrictions, which needlessly inflates prison populations with low-risk offenders, and which disrupts parolees' chances at successfully putting their pasts behind them. In general, this is a difficult theory to test, because although we can identify how many people return due to parole violations, it is hard to know how they violated parole.

The same large-scale survey that allowed us to examine the real behavior of people in prison for drug offenses, however, helps us here as well. Here, I looked at the most recent version of the survey (2004), which interviewed almost 14,500 inmates nationwide. One part of the survey asked not only if the inmate had been returned to prison because of a parole violation, but if so, why. The results stand in fairly stark contrast to the Standard Story. Over two-thirds of those who had returned to prison because of a parole violation admitted that it was due to a new arrest or a new crime, and over 60 percent of these new offenses were violent or property crimes. The second-biggest category, at under 20 percent, consisted of those who had failed to report to a parole officer, although this could include a wide range of behavior, from fleeing the county to forgetting an appointment to being a few hours late. Less than 10 percent of those interviewed admitted to returning because of a failed drug test, less than 6 percent because they were found to be in possession of drugs (which in many cases is also a crime), and barely 2 percent because they had missed a drug test.[49] Moreover, these numbers overstate the impact of technical violations, since many of those who admitted to technical violations also admitted to being returned for a new arrest or crime. Over a quarter of those sent back for a failed drug test said they were also returned for a new arrest or crime, for example, and nearly 30 percent of those returned for missing a drug test said the same.

It's important to appreciate the implications of these results, which tell another story of pretext. In many cases where a parolee was sent back to prison for a new arrest or offense, the prosecutor likely could have sent him to prison on a new conviction if it was harder to revoke parole.[50] Restricting parole violations might just force prosecutors to pursue new plea bargains instead—it might have more of an effect on *how* people end up back in prison than on *how many* do. I say "might" because the data here are thin to nonexistent. We don't know how many of these new arrests or crimes that triggered violations were for misdemeanors or other offenses that don't carry prison time. We also don't know how many cases prosecutors would simply drop because securing a conviction wouldn't be worth the time; parole violations are faster and easier to process, so they have less of an impact on caseloads.

I don't want to oversell the revisionist claim as something like "parole violations don't matter." If nothing else, violations allow prosecutors to send someone back to prison more easily, and that helps them be more aggressive across the board. Moreover, there are still enough technical and minor parole violators going back to prison to give us pause. Nonetheless, the effect is less than we think in general, further reducing the impact of a "war on drugs" mentality.

The third potential indirect pathway from the war on drugs to prison growth is the impact of repeat offender laws on those with prior records, or at least of internal prosecutor policies toward recidivists. Relatively few people go to prison for drug offenses, but a lot of people get arrested for drugs—between 1980 and 2012, police arrested more than 9.6 million people for the sale, trafficking, or manufacture of drugs, and over 33.6 million for possession of drugs (although these are not all unique people: someone arrested twice counts twice here).[51] A lot of people also get convicted for drug crimes without necessarily going to prison. In 2006, for example, there were approximately 1.13 million felony convictions in state courts, and 33 percent of them, or slightly more than 375,000, were for drug crimes.[52] Yet only about 38 percent of those convicted of drug felonies were sent to prison, and another 28 percent to jail. In other words, more than one-third of those convicted of a drug crime never saw the inside of a prison or jail, and nearly two-thirds never entered a prison. Those convictions, however, still count as prior felonies on people's criminal records.

The number of people passing through prison for drug crimes is thus just a fraction of those who carry the stigma of a drug arrest or conviction around with them. The concern is clear. When someone with one or more of these drug priors later commits a non-drug offense, prosecutors may treat them more aggressively as a result: they may be more willing to file charges, to file more serious charges, to take misdemeanor jail or probation offers off the table, to invoke repeat offender enhancements, or to just demand more prison time in general. In short, a significant impact of drug convictions on prisons could be in how they shape the punishment of non-drug offenses committed by those with prior drug convictions. Looking at the number of people in prison for a drug charge on any one day, or even at the number passing through prison for drug offenses over a year, will miss this effect.

When I examined the rate at which people cycled through prison, I only had data on prior *incarcerations*, not on prior *convictions*. That made it impossible to see how many people had prior drug convictions that did not result in prison time. It is even harder to understand how prosecutor offices take these prior convictions into account. We lack information about how prosecutors organize their offices, and how they determine who they will charge and how they will charge them. It certainly seems reasonable and likely that prior records shape charging decisions, but how much or how often they do is simply unknown. It is hard to stress enough that our lack of data on prosecutors simply blinds us to how our criminal justice system actually functions.[53]

That said, it's still easy to overstate the war on drugs' contribution to prior records. Assume it's true that those 43.2 million drug arrests between 1980 and 2012 created a lot of felony and serious misdemeanor records, and that those records exposed a lot of non-drug defendants to more serious punishments for subsequent non-drug offenses than they otherwise would have gotten. During that same time, there were *444.7 million* total arrests. So those 43.2 million drug arrests—of which 78 percent were for possession—were only 9.7 percent of all arrests made. Whatever sort of prior-record-boosting effect the war on drugs had, the impact of non-drug arrests was surely much bigger.

CRIMES OF PROHIBITION

We still need to ask what would be the broader implications of rolling back the war on drugs, beyond the impact on drug-offense incarcerations I've considered so far. How would the incidences of other crimes, such as robbery or theft or murder, change in response, and how would our prison population accordingly shift? Ending prohibition would prevent some of those crimes—but, as we will see, likely cause others.

Proponents of legalization and decriminalization often point to Portugal. In 2001, Portugal decriminalized the possession of a small amount of any drug (less than that needed for ten days' use). In the years that followed, use by those most at risk (ages fifteen to twenty-four) fell somewhat; the fraction of those in prison for drug-related offenses, such as stealing to buy more drugs, also fell; and even the number of people in prison for drug trafficking fell, despite no change being made in the official trafficking laws.[54] Portugal looks like a stunning success story. Decriminalizing drugs reduced the costs of drug-law enforcement, but it didn't lead to any increase in drug-related harms; if anything, it reduced them.

Of course, the story is never quite as straightforward as it seems. The causal story in Portugal is complicated because the country did a lot of things at once. It not only decriminalized possession, but it expanded treatment options for addicts and improved its social-welfare safety net by introducing a guaranteed income.[55] Treatment and a guaranteed income both likely reduced the demand for drugs, even as decriminalization perhaps increased it. It's therefore quite hard to draw many inferences from Portugal about what decriminalization alone would accomplish.

In fact, it's worth pointing out that Portugal's decriminalization law is actually the same sort of law that the United States had during Prohibition in the 1920s.[56] Drinking alcohol was never illegal during Prohibition; only its manufacture, transport, and sale were. Portugal only decriminalized for drugs what Prohibition never made illegal for alcohol, and what was illegal for alcohol under Prohibition remains illegal in Portugal for drugs. That enforcement appears to have declined in Portugal—even as use, and thus importation, remained fairly constant, and even as the law against trafficking remained unaltered—highlights the importance of cultural or attitudinal adjustments when it comes to changing enforcement. The law can certainly shape these attitudes, but these attitudes are likely far more important than specific legal changes. There is even some evidence that in Portugal the law reflected preexisting attitudes more than it caused later changes.[57] Estimating the impact of Portugal-style reforms, or even more extensive legalization, is thus an important but profoundly difficult challenge. Widespread decriminalization, and especially legalization, is so far outside our realm of experience that empirics fail us.[58]

We can, however, at least point out the various offsetting effects to expect. Take drug-related crimes by addicts, such as stealing to support a habit. On the one hand, drugs would be cheaper to get, if only slightly, with Portugal-style reforms. (Legalization, not decriminalization, produces bigger price drops.) Although in the United States street prices of drugs like cocaine have generally fallen over the years, they would have been lower still, perhaps by about 15 percent or so, but for interdiction efforts.[59] The effect of that price "rise" on demand may be insufficient to justify the billions spent and the millions arrested in the name of the drug war; nevertheless, scaling back enforcement should reduce prices. So if drugs are decriminalized, their prices may fall somewhat; if legalized, they will fall even more. And not just the cash prices, but the legal and social prices, too: the risk of fines and imprisonment, and the social stigma that attaches to using illegal drugs. All of this would imply that users could maintain their habits more cheaply, leading to a decrease in theft and other habit-supporting crimes.[60]

On the other hand, the cheaper price—perhaps especially the elimination of criminal punishments and the decline in stigma—could lead more people to use drugs in the first place. And some of these newcomers, as well as some previous light users, would become serious users who may turn to crime to support their habit as their legal employment opportunities fade. On top of this, with rising drug use we would see rising drug-related DUIs, drug-related DUIs that result in death, drug-fueled fights in bars, and so on. Think of every "alcohol-related" crime that happens, and realize that we would have more of those types of crimes, just fueled now by other chemicals as well.

So some drug-related crimes would drop, but there would be more people using drugs, and more crimes associated with that use.[61] The net effect is impossible to disentangle, but some studies on the relationship between alcohol and crime suggest that we should not necessarily be too optimistic that legalization or decriminalization would lead to as big a drop in use-related crime, and thus use-related imprisonments, as we'd hoped for—unless, perhaps, we see a parallel investment in noncriminal treatment options.

And what about drug-market related violence? As long as decriminalization focuses only on use, not distribution, there's no reason to assume that the drug markets, which would remain illegal, would change all that much.[62] Even if trafficking enforcement decreased, like it did in Portugal, illegal drug markets would still be forced to rely on violence to resolve disputes. Legalization might cut violence more substantially, although work like Leovy's cautions that much of the violence may persist if the underlying barriers to employment and upward mobility remain in place.

A closer look at Prohibition (which ran from 1920 to 1933) also complicates the argument that ending the war on drugs would reduce violence. The conventional wisdom is that Prohibition led to a spike in murders; movies like *The Untouchables* certainly cement that idea in popular culture. The data, however, tell a more ambiguous story. Prohibition coincided with a spike in urbanization, which led to an increase in violent crime independent of Prohibition; murder rates also rose simply because more jurisdictions started reporting murder data during that time. Plus, the increase in alcohol-gang murders (which certainly did happen) was at least partially offset by a decline in more routine drunken killings.[63]

This isn't to say there aren't real costs to prohibition and enforcement. Violence associated with the illegal crack markets of the late 1980s led to a surge in the homicide rate for black males aged eighteen to twenty-four.[64] That the costs involved in prohibition and enforcement are less than expected does not mean they don't exist. Still, in the final count, as long as reformers argue that prohibition itself is a major causal factor of mass incarceration, they will likely be disappointed in the extent to which decriminalization, or even legalization, reduces crime, and thus the extent to which either reduces prison populations.

RACE MATTERS

Beyond its impact on overall prison size, the war on drugs is also frequently blamed for the racial imbalance in US prison populations. That imbalance is stark. In 2015, the United States was 62 percent non-Hispanic white, 13 percent black, and 18 percent Hispanic.[65] Our state prisons, meanwhile, were 35 percent non-Hispanic white, 38 percent black, and 21 percent Hispanic.[66] Standard Story reformers often make two claims: first, that the imbalance in prison populations is driven by imbalances in who we lock up for drug crimes, and second, that the racial disparities in who we incarcerate for drug crimes reflect disparities in enforcement far more than in offending.[67] The first claim is wrong. The second is likely right but suffers from a major empirical blind spot that demands attention.

That the first is wrong shouldn't surprise us at this point. Only about 16 percent of the people in prison are there on drug charges. Such a relatively small number of prisoners cannot alter prison statistics that much, as Table 1.4 shows. The first row of the table shows the racial composition of all state inmates in 2013, the second row the racial composition of those in prison that year just for drug offenses, and the third the racial composition of those in prison for anything but a drug offense. The third row is just the first row minus the second. If we released everyone in prison in 2013 whose top charge was a drug offense, the white percentage would rise by one point (from 35 to 36 percent), the black percentage would fall by one point (from 38 to 37 percent), and the Hispanic percentage wouldn't change. That's it. As is clear from the middle row of Table 1.4, there simply aren't enough drug offenders in prison to have much of an impact.

Of course, using "drug offenses" as the definition of the crimes for which people are in prison on account of the drug war may be too narrow. The broader effects of decriminalization or legalization, however, are hard to predict, which makes it equally hard to know what their effects would be on the racial imbalances in prison populations. Moreover, even if decriminalization or legalization reduces crime, it will not necessarily reduce overall enforcement. Officers who previously served on drug task forces would likely be reassigned, not laid off, which could lead to an increase in the number of arrests for non-drug crimes. Assuming that those officers are assigned to the same neighborhoods in which they were working previously, the net impact on poor minority communities, and thus on prison racial compositions, becomes even less clear (and perhaps less optimistic).

Table 1.4 Racial Distribution of Inmates in State Prison, 2013

	White		Black		Hispanic	
	Number	Percentage	Number	Percentage	Number	Percentage
All Offenders	468,600	35	497,000	38	274,200	21
Drug Offenders	67,800	33	79,900	38	39,900	19
Non-Drug Offenders	400,800	36	417,100	37	234,300	21

Source: Data from E. Ann Carson, "Prisoners in 2014," US Department of Justice, Bureau of Justice Statistics, September 2015, www.bjs.gov/content/pub/pdf/p14.pdf.

The second Standard Story critique about drugs and race focuses on the disparity within the category of drug inmates, not their impact on system-wide disparity. As in so many areas of criminal justice, there is a clear racial imbalance when it comes to those who are in prison for drug crimes. The incarceration rates for drug offenses are 34 per 100,000 for non-Hispanic whites, 74 per 100,000 for Hispanics, and 193 per 100,000 for blacks.[68]

The obvious question is why this imbalance exists. Three reasons have been proposed. The first is just that members of minority groups commit more drug offenses. The second is that even if there is no difference in offense rates across races and ethnicities, blacks and Hispanics are more likely to buy and sell drugs in public, and that outdoor drug markets are easier to police. This is a story of race-class interactions: wealthier (and thus whiter) people have more access to private drug markets. The third reason is explicit or implicit racial bias, either at the micro-level (a black dealer is more likely to be arrested than a nearby white dealer) or at the macro-level (black neighborhoods are more heavily policed than white neighborhoods, even if the white neighborhoods have similar or greater levels of drug crime).

Surprisingly, given how much academic and media attention the war on drugs receives, little rigorous empirical work has been done to test these theories.[69] It's not uncommon to see someone simply assert that the proportions of whites and blacks who use and sell drugs are the same, but with very little data to support the claim, especially when it comes to the sale of drugs.[70] Very little race-based data on drug selling exists, certainly nothing comprehensive. There's some data showing a correlation between use and sale—so data showing similar levels of use would seem to imply similar levels of sales—but it's likely that that connection breaks down for the more serious sellers, where use would get in the way of selling.[71]

The little evidence that we do have points to enforcement choices as important factors in the racial disparities in imprisonment rates. One of the only studies on the topic looked at results from a long-running survey of 9,000 people who were twelve to sixteen years old when the survey started in 1997 (and twenty-four to twenty-eight when the last wave of the survey available to the authors was conducted in 2009).[72] It found that non-Hispanic whites actually sold drugs at somewhat greater rates than blacks or Hispanics, that the white/Hispanic disparity was driven primarily by the class-based public outdoor market problem, and that the white/black disparity appeared to be much more the product of deeper enforcement bias.

So at least some, perhaps much, of the disparity between whites and blacks is due to discrimination, which should come as no surprise. The study's claim that there are no real disparities in offending is somewhat more surprising, however, since the very racial discrimination that leads to biased enforcement should also lead to racial differences in drug offending. Blacks are systematically excluded from the "primary" labor market of full-time employment and diverted to the "secondary" labor market of more erratic, less stable part-time work, thanks to employer biases, underperforming and underfunded schools, family and community institutions that are persistently undermined by the pressures and challenges they face, and the many other costs of structural racism.[73]

If blacks are systematically denied access to the more successful paths to economic stability, they face systematically greater pressure to turn to other alternatives, including selling drugs (as well as other illegal, non-drug actions). The illegal drug market, which generally pays below minimum wage to those on the bottom but offers the urban poor a salient shot at making it big, surely beckons in such situations.[74] So it seems inconsistent to argue, as many do, that blacks face persistent structural barriers to economic and social advancement but do not find themselves forced into illegal "secondary" labor markets, like selling drugs, at greater rates.

To be clear, if it is true that blacks sell drugs at greater rates than whites, that does not inherently justify the higher incarceration rates for drugs. Many of those in the inner city who deal drugs, whether sporadically or regularly, do so as desperate reactions to untenable situations. The culpability of a poorer black kid selling drugs in the inner city is arguably lower than that of the wealthier white kid in the suburbs selling to his friends. And the optimal way to deter or prevent such behavior in the future would be some sort of a constructive, not punitive, response.

We must therefore think more broadly about how to address the racial disparity in drug arrests. Training police to act in a more race-blind manner, for example, will not necessarily yield big returns if there are still real disparities in offending. It is also essential to address the structural barriers that limit access to the primary job market in the first place—to focus on making sure people have first chances before trying to help them get second ones.[75] Yet this is not something that the criminal justice system is equipped to do, which points to very real limits on what reforms that focus on the criminal justice system by itself can accomplish.

THE WAR ON DRUGS IS NOT TRIVIAL: ABOUT 200,000 PEOPLE IN state prisons and another 100,000 in federal institutions are serving time for drug crimes. Some of them are dangerous people who may need to be confined, but most would likely be better handled outside the prison, and many would perhaps be best left alone altogether by the criminal justice system.

Yet the war on drugs is not the primary engine of prison growth. It wasn't in the 1980s, and its role has only declined since the 1990s. Freeing every single person who is in a state prison on a drug charge would only cut state prison populations back to where they were in 1996–1997, well into the "mass incarceration" period. That's not to say we shouldn't think about releasing a lot of those who are in prison for these sorts of crimes, but we need to be realistic about what doing so would accomplish more broadly.

Claiming that the war on drugs is not a primary engine of prison growth does not mean that the core concern of critics like Michelle Alexander—that the criminal justice system is driven by and exacerbates racial inequality—is wrong. It just means that we consistently overstate the role of the war on drugs. The racial disparities in prison populations would barely budge if all the people serving time for drug crimes were immediately released, and it seems likely that scaling back the drug war would not on its own necessarily alter offending or enforcement patterns enough to bring about real change.

Now, to be fair to the Standard Story, whenever people tell me that it's obvious why our prison populations are so large, they never just cite the war on drugs. They always ask, rhetorically, "Well, isn't it just the war on drugs and those long sentences we impose?" We've just seen that it isn't really the war on drugs, certainly not to the extent that many assume. Let's now look at why the longer-sentences argument is also far more complicated, and much less compelling, than people think.

CHAPTER TWO

A BRIEF HISTORY OF TIME (SERVED)

S TUNNINGLY LONG PRISON SENTENCES OFTEN MAKE THE NEWS.
Sometimes they feel justified, like when Bernie Madoff received 150
years for bilking investors out of $65 billion, or when Oklahoma City
police officer Daniel Holzclaw received 263 years for eighteen counts
of various forms of sexual assault and rape he committed while on duty.
Sometimes these sentences are hard to believe, as when a woman named
Sharanda Jones received life without the possibility of parole following
not just her first conviction, but her first *arrest*, on drug charges.[1] And
sometimes they are absurd to the point of implausibility: two men convicted of serious violent crimes in Oklahoma, for example, were sentenced
by a jury to many thousands of years each (11,250 and 21,250, although
the larger sentence was reduced on appeal by 500 years).[2]

One prominent criminologist has argued that since the 1990s, punishment in the United States seems to have focused on "throwing away
the key."[3] Indeed, after the "war on drugs," the most prominent part of
the Standard Story has been its emphasis on the amount of time people
serve in prison. These two factors—drugs offenses and long sentences—
are often linked together, as when President Obama spoke of mass

incarceration resulting from locking up "more and more nonviolent drug offenders than ever before, for longer than ever before."[4]

The impact of time served, however, is not really as important as the Standard Story claims. It's true that by international standards US sentences are long, both nominally and in practice. The amount of time most people spend in prison, however, is surprisingly short, and there's no real evidence that it grew much as prison populations soared. In fact, recent evidence suggests that time spent behind bars may even have decreased over the past few years.

So reformers have accepted a seriously misleading idea: that longer sentences drive prison growth. As a result, they have thrown themselves into the effort to amend and reduce aggressive sentencing laws. The impact of such reforms, however, will be less than expected. At the same time, by dedicating all their energy to reducing the amount of time people spend in prison, the reformers have paid too little attention to far more important factors in the growth of prisons—above all, the actions of prosecutors. There are real costs to emphasizing the wrong agenda.

DOG BITES MAN

It's not at all surprising that people think tougher sentencing laws matter, because sentencing laws certainly have gotten tougher. During the 1980s and 1990s, and even into the 2000s, states nationwide approved an ever-growing array of mandatory minimums; some "abolished" parole or adopted "truth-in-sentencing" laws that required violent offenders to serve at least 85 percent of their term before being eligible for release.[5] Most famously, many states adopted "three-strike" laws, which imposed draconian punishments on offenders for their third (or in some cases even just second) convictions.

There are many reasons why state legislatures in the United States passed tough laws, some of which get more attention than others.[6] In part the phenomenon was a reaction to rising crime—but that reaction alone can't explain the change. After all, other Western countries saw similar increases in crime (except perhaps in lethal violence) during the 1970s and 1980s without responding in the same way. Part of the US response was therefore also something more cultural.[7] The way responsibility and accountability are fractured across city, county, and state bureaucracies also contributed to our punitive decisions. State legislatures often pass harsh laws while trusting local prosecutors to plea-bargain around them; local officials likely encourage state legislators to adopt tough sentencing laws because they hope it will help them avoid having to hire more police. Each free-rides off the other in a punitive "race to thte top."

It is not surprising, then, that when compared to other countries, our sentencing policies are strikingly harsh. The contrast is striking. In some European countries, the longest minimum sentence that a murderer can face is one year; in the United States, the sentence can be life in prison without parole or even execution. Consider the case of Anders Breivik, the Norwegian who killed 77 people and wounded 242 more in 2011. Most of his victims were teenagers who were trapped on an island, where they were at summer camp. His conviction resulted in the maximum sentence for murder in Norway: twenty-one years, with a minimum of ten years behind bars—the sort of punishment that serious robbers and drug dealers in the United States might face.[8] Although he'll likely spend the rest of his life in prison due to preventive detention, he'll be free to petition every five years for release. In the United States, he'd have certainly faced a death sentence or life in prison without a chance of parole, regardless of how much he changed while there.

It's hard to look at the sentencing changes over the past thirty years and not think that time served must have gone up dramatically. Popular anecdotes certainly seem to confirm this conclusion: Under California's three-strike law, for example, a man named Gary Ewing was sentenced to twenty-five years to life for stealing three $399 golf clubs; Leandro Andrade received two consecutive twenty-five-to-life terms under the same law for stealing nine children's videos from two separate K-Marts.[9] There's no way that Ewing or Andrade—whose cases reached the US Supreme Court, which upheld their sentences as neither cruel nor unusual—would have served that much time for their crimes had there been no three-strike law.[10]

Examples like these have become so common that in 2003 the American Bar Association (ABA) established the "Justice Kennedy Commission" to look into US sentencing practices. The commission was founded after US Supreme Court Justice Anthony Kennedy gave an impassioned speech to the ABA about the failings of American criminal justice; so important was the issue to Kennedy that he became the first justice since Earl Warren—who lent his name to the Warren Commission investigating the assassination of President John F. Kennedy—to allow a commission to use his name while he was still on the Court. Not surprisingly, the commission's final report highlighted tough sentencing laws as key drivers of prison growth, particularly mandatory minimums.[11]

Yet stories about individuals can be misleading—or perhaps they are practically guaranteed to be misleading. These stories make the news because they are rare, not because they are commonplace: that's what makes them newsworthy in the first place. Man bites dog, not dog bites man. The reality is quite different. Although it is true that the official sentences as detailed in statutes have gotten longer, time *actually served* appears to have changed substantially less. Just because the legislature passes a law doesn't mean that prosecutors will use it. As the influential law professor William Stuntz explained, "once the defendant's sentence has reached the level that the prosecutor prefers . . . adding more time offers no benefit to the prosecutor. Indeed, prosecutors may actually value 'extra' prison time negatively."[12] Talk to any prosecutor, and he or she will tell you that the goal is to "do justice," not to mindlessly impose the toughest sanction available. Although the prosecutor's definition of "justice" surely differs from that of the public defender sitting at the opposite table, prosecutors are not always going to seek out tougher punishments just because the legislature makes that option available to them (although, of course, they sometimes will).

Consider an example from the federal system. Federal prosecutors are subject to a greater degree of control than their state counterparts, since the president appoints all the US attorneys, and the US attorneys officially report to the US attorney general, whom the president also appoints. The US attorneys and the attorney general, unlike county district attorneys, are all at-will employees whom the president can fire at any time.

Despite this fact, multiple US attorneys general—Richard Thornburgh under President Reagan, Janet Reno under President Clinton, and John Ashcroft under President George W. Bush—have felt compelled to issue memos insisting that federal prosecutors charge the highest readily provable offense. That they have repeatedly faced such commands suggests that despite their higher degree of accountability, federal prosecutors are pursuing their own idea of justice, and their views are systematically less harsh than those which have been codified by Congress and desired by the president.

In fact, Stuntz, who was one of the most astute observers of the American criminal justice system before his death in 2011, argued that legislators pass tough sentencing laws because they *know* prosecutors won't actually impose the maximum punishments. If prosecutors regularly sent defendants away for the maximum times permitted by law, they would drive up state correction costs above what legislators would be willing to pay, and they could generate unwanted political resistance. As long as prosecutors impose something well below the maximum, the legislators get the political credit for passing tough-on-crime legislation while avoiding much of the cost that such legislation could entail.[13] Perhaps it should not be surprising then, that the "throw away the key" claim starts to weaken when we start to look more closely at the data. The times that convicted criminals spend in prison are shorter than one might expect, and they don't appear to have grown that much. The overall contribution of changes in time served to prison growth is less than many think.[14]

TIME (ACTUALLY) SERVED

Let's start with a simple question. If I surveyed people and asked them, "How long do you think a robber or a drug dealer spends in prison?" the answers would most likely exceed what happens in practice, perhaps by a significant amount. In many states, half of all inmates admitted in a given year are released in one to two years, and three-fourths of them are out within about three.[15] And these short times to release hold across a wide range of crimes; they even appear to have declined somewhat over the 2000s.

Table 2.1 25th Percentile, Median, and 75th Percentile
Times to Release (in numbers of days)

Year	25th Percentile		Median		75th Percentile	
	2000	2010	2000	2010	2000	2010
Armed Robbery	377	315	1,951	844	2,305	*
Aggravated Assault	267	237	687	557	1,381	1,097
Burglary	210	179	517	427	1,011	901
Drug Trafficking— Unspecified	176	120	395	313	776	683
Drug Possession— Unspecified	155	120	316	232	657	442
Forgery	124	120	302	263.5	601	555
Petty Larceny	183.5	235.5	423	511	610.5	786
Drug Trafficking— Other	241	193	536	455	1,103	946
Drug—Other	83	114	174.5	281.5	575	519
Weapons	210	239	503	546	908	860

* Given how long armed robbers generally serve, the 75th percentile of those admitted in 2010 had not been released by the end of the dataset (2013).

Source: Data from US Department of Justice, Bureau of Justice Statistics, "Data Collection: National Corrections Reporting Program," www.bjs.gov/index.cfm?ty=dcdetail&iid=268.

Table 2.1 shows how long (in numbers of days) it took for one-quarter, one-half, and three-quarters of all inmates admitted for certain crimes in 2000 and 2010 to be released.[16] The table gives the results for the ten crimes with the greatest number of offenders admitted in 2000. As is quickly clear, the results in Table 2.1 undermine the "sentences are longer" conventional wisdom. There are two important reasons for this.

First, it's worth repeating that two-year sentences for petty larceny never make the paper, because there's nothing noteworthy about them. All we read about are the outliers, the probation-for-manslaughter and ten-years-for-low-level-drugs cases.

Second, terms that ostensibly indicate long sentences can prove to be far more complicated upon closer inspection. Take "life." A report by The Sentencing Project, a prison-reform think tank, calculated that around 160,000 inmates were serving "life" sentences in 2013, and that just under 50,000 of them were serving life without parole (LWOP) sentences. Now LWOP is unambiguous: absent something like a judicial reversal or a pardon or commutation by the governor, someone sentenced to LWOP will almost certainly die in prison. But "life" is another matter altogether. For example, at least in the 1990s and early 2000s, the median time to release for a "life" sentence in Kentucky was ten to fifteen years.[17] Long, yes, and longer than most sentences for the worst offenders in Europe, but not what we immediately think of when we hear "life." Of course, states vary widely, and in many states, many of those sentenced to life are still in prison many years later.

(It's also worth pointing out that fully one-third of those sentenced to life with a possibility of parole were sentenced in California, and nearly two-thirds of those sentenced to LWOP were held by just five states and the federal government.[18] As is so often the case in criminal justice, national statistics make local issues seem more universal in scope.)

So whatever the trends in statutory maximums, time served has remained fairly short. As Table 2.1 suggests, it has also been fairly stable, at least since the 2000s (and likely since even earlier).[19] Figure 2.1, which plots total admissions to and releases from state prisons every year from 1978 to 2014, makes the point even more clearly. If inmates were serving longer and longer sentences in large enough numbers, we should expect to see the number of releases grow more slowly than the number of admissions. That does appear to happen a bit in the early 1990s, but the effect quickly levels out and actually reverses in the 2000s. Other, more sophisticated approaches, including simulations that estimate what prison populations would look like if sentencing

Figure 2.1 Admissions and Releases, 1978–2014

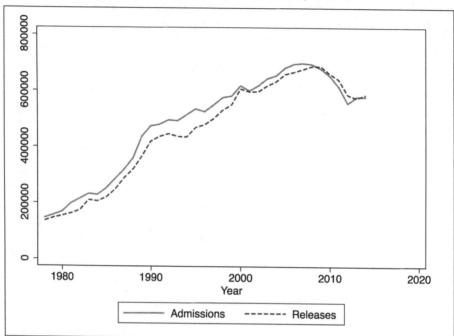

Source: US Department of Justice, Bureau of Justice Statistics, "Data Collection: NPS Program," www.bjs.gov/index.cfm?ty=dcdetail&wd=269.

practices never changed over time, further support the claim that time served hasn't changed much.[20]

Some studies purport to show that increases in time served matter, but even taken on their own terms they do not show that longer sentences have driven prison growth. The Pew Center on the States, for example, reported in 2012 that average time served in state prisons had risen by about 36 percent between 1990 and 2009.[21] Assume this is true, though it is likely somewhat of an overestimate.[22] A 36 percent increase sounds like a lot, but it really isn't. The increases were an extra six months for those convicted of property or drug crimes, and an extra sixteen months for those convicted of violent crimes. If correct, these numbers imply that time served by those convicted of drug or property crimes grew by less than one month each year over the 1990s and 2000s, and that time served for those convicted of violent crimes grew by slightly more than one month each year. Such small increases matter for the inmates themselves, but their impact on more macro-level trends is slight. They cannot explain most of the prison growth over that time.

Some disagreement about the impact of time served may also be more semantic than anything. Some experts, for example, argue that people who would not have gone to prison in the past go to prison today, and therefore, time served has gotten longer. To me, this is a change in the "number of people admitted," not in the amount of "time served." Two scholars who made that claim concluded that "during the past several decades, the likelihoods of serving short, medium, and long prison terms increased greatly for almost all arrested offenders"—which sounds an awful lot like a story of admissions-driven growth, with new admissions taking place at every level of time served.[23]

That said, to call the distinction "semantic" is not to say that it is irrelevant. Viewing the rise in admissions as "more time served" rather than "more likely to be sent to prison" encourages us to think about reforms in terms of cutting time served, not in restricting who gets sent to prison in the first place. Which allows those who determine who gets sent to prison—prosecutors—to avoid attention, and thus regulation.

SMALL-TIME OFFENDERS

Harry Truman famously begged for a one-armed economist, as their "on the one hand, on the other hand" equivocations exhausted him. However, nothing is ever clear-cut, especially in criminal justice. It's important, then, to consider some limitations to my longer-sentences-aren't-important argument. In the end, these limitations do not undermine the core claim, but they do provide some important context.

To start, return to the idea that prison growth is being driven by states increasingly locking up smaller-time offenders who would not have gone to prison at all in the past. It's quite likely—although by no means guaranteed—that rising prison populations in a time of falling crime means that we are sending increasingly minor offenders to prison. If so, shouldn't time served be falling, too? If time served stays flat, as it did in the 2000s, even as the seriousness of the crimes committed by those going to prison falls, then, in a sense, punishment is getting tougher, just in a way that may be hard to see.

A simple example can illuminate the problem. Assume that, at first, a state admits one person to prison every year for fraud; the state focuses solely on serious fraudsters, and they all spend three years in prison. Obviously, the average and median times spent in prison by someone convicted of fraud is three years. Later on, the state becomes more aggressive in punishing fraud. It continues to admit one serious fraudster to prison each year, but now for four years instead of three; but it also now sends two lower-level fraudsters—who previously would have received probation at most—to prison for one year each. The median time served in prison now drops from three years to one year, and the average time drops from three years to two years, even though everyone is serving more time in prison (the serious sentence rose from three years to four, the minor sentence from zero years to one).[24] Everyone is serving more time, but the sentences all look shorter, because of the people convicted of the less serious charge now showing up in prison.

Just how big a threat to my findings is this issue? It depends. If I were saying that time served for "violent" or "property" crimes was steady, this would be a serious concern, since those are broad categories that encompass wide ranges of criminal behaviors. But Table 2.1 uses much narrower categories, such as armed robbery and grand larceny. Obviously, some armed robberies are more serious than others, but in general, the narrower the category the more the conduct in it is roughly similar.

The one exception, unfortunately, is for drugs. As a result of unexplained reporting problems, the data classify drug crimes only as "trafficking" or "possession"; we cannot break these categories down by type of drug or amount. Some of the decline in time served for drug offenders, then, could reflect not only the fact that all types of drug offenders are spending more time in prison, but also that we're locking up more lower-level drug dealers than we did in the past. It's impossible to say, however, how big an issue this is. Outside of drug offenses, though—and perhaps even for those—it seems likely that the stability or decline in time served reflects something real, that people aren't really spending more time in prison, just that more people are spending time in prison.

It also isn't necessarily the case that we are in fact admitting more marginal offenders to prison. Only a small fraction of those we arrest, even for serious crimes, end up incarcerated. In 2012, for example, states admitted about 615,000 people to prison while arresting 12.2 million, including 520,000 arrests just for serious violent crimes—almost as many as were admitted to prison for all crimes—and 1.6 million for serious property crimes. Ideally, prosecutors have always been triaging effectively, sending the most serious offenders in each category to prison. Our complete lack of data on prosecutorial behavior, however, makes this hard to know— perhaps prosecutors often go after the most *provable* cases, which need not be the most serious. If so, incarcerations can rise as crime falls without all (or even without most) of the increase coming from lower-level people going to prison.

THE INSTALLMENT PLAN

Another possible limitation to my argument has to do with parole. It could be that people are serving long sentences, just doing so on the "installment plan," with parole releases and violations making sentences appear shorter than they are.[25]

Say Joe is sentenced to ten years in prison, but he is released on parole after three. A year later, he fails a drug test and is sent back to prison for violating the conditions of parole. He spends another four years in prison and is again released, this time without incident. Bob, on the other hand, is sentenced to six years in prison, and he spends all six years there. He doesn't return after his release. Who served the "longer sentence"? Did Joe go to prison twice, each time serving a shorter sentence than Bob, or did Joe serve a longer, seven-year sentence in two parts? If we've just moved from a world of Bobs to a world of Joes, it's hard to say that we've become less harsh with our sentences.

As we saw earlier, however, the role of parole violations is generally overstated, and we haven't really created a world of Joes. That said, fewer parole violations would rein in prison growth, and our current parole policies often seem to be designed to *cause* violations. So, as with the war on drugs, we should try to fix what is broken with parole, but we should also be modest in our expectations about what it will do to prison populations.

The root of parole's problems is that the Supreme Court has held that parole is a privilege, not a right, and states have generally faced few restrictions on the sorts of conditions they can impose.[26] Perhaps not surprisingly, the number of conditions has grown in recent years. A 1982 study found that most states imposed an average of about eleven conditions on each parolee, whereas in 2008 the average was over eighteen.[27] Parole terms limit where the parolee can live, who he can spend time with, and so on. Some of these conditions may make sense on their own, but in the aggregate they make life very difficult for parolees, inducing stress that may increase the risk of recidivism. Parolees are often told they cannot associate with known felons (despite living in neighborhoods where as many as one in three people have criminal records); they may be denied the right to drive a car (despite living in areas without good public transportation); and, either legally or practically, they may be denied access to public housing (despite lacking resources to rent a market-rate apartment).[28] They are also often required to find a job—which can effectively "criminalize" unemployment—despite poor training while in prison.[29]

Although most parole restrictions are at least plausible, if ultimately harsh and counterproductive, some almost seem intended to lead to recidivism, although it is more likely that they are just the product of political expediency and insufficient foresight. Congress's denial of access to federally subsidized public housing as well as food stamps and similar sorts of public support applies to anyone convicted of a drug offense—but not of, say, murder or arson.[30] In New York State prisons, the single most popular training program is barber school; yet until 2008, graduates of the program discovered that the agency in charge of licensing barbershops would not, as a general rule, give a license to anyone with a prior felony record.[31] And sex offenders often face such severe limitations on where they are allowed to live that, in one egregious example, several sex offenders in Florida were forced to live under a bridge.[32] Stable housing and employment are key pathways to desistance from crime, and parole conditions can undermine these routes to successful reentry. So while it is true that nearly 70 percent of those who violate parole have been arrested for or convicted of a new offense, at least some of those "failures" are surely due to the pressures of parole itself. Even some of those who recidivate after their parole terms are over may have reoffended in part because of the lingering costs of parole stress.

Furthermore, formerly incarcerated people labor under various formal and informal restrictions after their parole terms expire. They may continue to face legal limits on where they can live, benefits they can receive, and whether they can vote. Many must "check the box" on employment forms acknowledging that they are convicted felons or remain registered as sex offenders for years, sometimes for their entire lives.[33] Restrictions need not always be formal, either. Prison undermines job skills, social networks, and social support in ways that complicate life in general, and things like employment in particular. These impediments can last for a long time; skills and community support do not magically return the day a person is released from parole supervision.

If we view these formal and informal post-parole collateral consequences as part of the person's sentence, then even if time served in prison has not grown longer, the duration of "total punishment" certainly has. Moreover, like parole conditions, many of these durable restrictions increase the risk of subsequent reoffending, contributing to at least some new (that is, not parole revocation) admissions down the line. Looking at just the number of people being admitted off parole thus understates the number of people who recidivate in part because of post-conviction restrictions.

The number of people subject to these restrictions is remarkably large. On any given day, there are about 850,000 people "free" on parole, but that significantly understates how many people struggle with formal and informal restrictions that follow time in prison. Consider that between 2000 and 2014, state prisons admitted about 9.6 million prisoners, a figure which we'll see might represent as many as 6 or 7 million unique individuals. (And we're not even considering the 10 million to 12 million who pass through county jails every year.) Many of these people will face protracted restrictions; even if these restrictions do not lead to future crime or prison terms, they certainly lead to future difficulties and challenges. Whatever the problems with her argument tying mass incarceration to the war on drugs, Michelle Alexander is unquestionably right to call our attention to this population of legally and socially stigmatized former inmates who are largely invisible in our official statistics and frequently overlooked in much of our reform discussion.

Again, however, we must not run too far with this argument. Parole helps many who are on it, and it is at least not harmful to many others. Plus, a sizable majority of those entering prison are not coming in following a prior admission; a majority, in fact, appear to be first-time admissions.[34] Nonetheless, our parole (and post-parole) system is often counterproductive, and it needlessly harms many under its control, including sending some back to prison for no justifiable reason. It demands repair and reform, we should, however, be realistic about the impact such reforms will have on prison populations more generally.

TIME SERVED, NOT TIME IMPOSED

Despite my longer-sentences-are-relatively-unimportant claim, I should be clear: cutting the time people serve in prison will reduce the prison population. Even if time served hasn't grown (much), and even if it isn't that long in the first place, prison populations will decline if we reduce it.

Consider the following results, produced by a nifty web tool the Urban Institute created to estimate the impact of time cuts on prison populations.[35] Using data from fifteen states (which hold about 40 percent of the nation's prisoners), the tool estimates the impact by 2021 of various cuts in time served today. It reports that a 25 percent reduction in time served by people convicted of violent crimes would drop prison populations by 7 percent; in time served by people convicted of property crime, 5 percent; and in time served by people convicted of drug crimes, 3 percent.[36] These are not necessarily huge drops individually, particularly for drug offenses, but they are not trivial, either: a 25 percent cut across the board would produce a 15 percent decline in the total prison population by 2021.

Yet these results overstate what legislatures can accomplish, perhaps significantly. The tool estimates the impact of a cut in time actually served—something over which legislatures actually have little control. Legislatures can only set the maximums and minimums; judges and prosecutors (and, in many states, parole boards) control how much time is ultimately served. Perhaps if legislatures adopted binding, detailed guidelines that set very specific sentences ("aggravated assault must get between five and six years for someone with two prior felony convictions") and abolished or narrowed parole, they could exert more control over the time actually served. But the US Supreme Court has made those sorts of highly specific sentencing guidelines much harder for states to use these days, and states have generally adopted approaches that give prosecutors and judges a fair amount of discretion.[37]

Moreover, as a general rule, prosecutors and judges impose sentences that are below the statutory maximum for the crime, perhaps often significantly so. For the legislature to reduce time served by 25 percent, then, it would have to cut the official statutory maximums by much more than 25 percent, more than may be politically viable, even in the current reformist moment.

For example, assume the statutory maximum for an offense is twenty years, but most defendants receive sentences of about ten years. What, then, does a 25 percent reduction in the official sentence, from twenty to fifteen years, accomplish? It surely does something, even for the sorts of cases that had received ten years before the cuts. It is unlikely, however, that by cutting the maximum from twenty to fifteen, those who had received ten years before would now get seven and a half years, which is what the Urban Institute tool implicitly assumes would happen. The prosecutor's bargaining power is somewhat weaker, true, but it is unclear how this will shape plea outcomes. A large stack of evidence suggests that people who engage in criminal conduct tend to put less weight on the future than those who do not. Dropping a threat from twenty years to fifteen therefore might not really make much of a difference to a defendant. And it's nearly impossible to predict how prosecutors or defense attorneys would respond to this change in relative plea-bargaining power, since we have no data, and no real theoretical guidance either.[38]

One last complication in cutting time served is that those who are in prison for long stretches—who are actually serving long sentences that could be most meaningfully shortened by cutting the statutory maximum—have almost all been convicted of serious violent crimes. For example, in one large-scale study of those who had been in prison for at least eleven years at the end of 2013, fully one-fourth were in for murder or manslaughter, and 65 percent had been convicted of an index violent crime; all told, 83 percent of these long-serving inmates had been convicted of some sort of violent offense.[39] These are, of course, the very sentences that legislators are least likely to cut, and in fact are the ones that they often make *longer* to justify cuts elsewhere—bad policy, as we'll see later on, but good politics.

A REVOLVING DOOR?

The Standard Story's emphasis on the role of parole violations stems in part from confusing statistics on recidivism that make the risk that someone will return to prison appear greater than it is. The impression that most people who go to prison return seems to emerge from the cold, dry statistics of the Bureau of Justice Statistics. In two separate studies, one in 1994 and a follow-up in 2005, the BJS tracked a large number of releasees (200,000 in 1994; 400,000 in 2005) for several years after they were discharged from prison. In both studies, over two-thirds were rearrested within three to five years of release (primarily for a felony or serious misdemeanor), and half returned to prison during that time for either a new crime or a parole violation.[40] These seem like fairly high, and stable, rates of rearrest and readmission. These results are not exactly wrong, but recent research shows that they also aren't measuring what most people actually want to know. If someone asks, "What is the chance that someone who is released from prison will end up back in prison?" the question he or she is really asking is, "What is the probability that someone released from prison *at some point* ends up going back?" not, "What is the probability that someone released from prison *in a specific year* ends up going back?"

These may seem like identical questions, but they aren't—although *a lot* of criminologists (including this one) didn't appreciate this for a while—

and the BJS reports are answering the less interesting question. A simple example can illustrate the problem. Assume that people can commit only one crime at a time, and it's a minor one that faces a one-year prison sentence. Every year, Bill commits the crime on January 1, quickly gets arrested and convicted, and is released on December 31. On January 1 of the next year—the very next day—he repeats the process, and he does this every year. Bill is what we would call a "high-risk offender." At the same time, each year one other person commits the same crime but never does it again. So in Year 1, someone else, say it's Carl, goes to prison for this crime, but after his release on December 31, he never returns. In Year 2, a third man, Dave, goes to prison along with Bill instead of Carl, and in Year 3 it's Ed's turn. Carl, Dave, and Ed are all "low-risk offenders."

The two BJS reports looked at just one year of releases. In the example, it would be as if the BJS looked at everyone released in Year 1 (Bill and Carl) and in Year 3 (Bill and Dave). Each report would say that half of all those released in that year ended up returning to prison. There is, however, another way to interpret the same data. Over four years, this state admitted five people to prison, and only one person—Bill—returned. He returned *a lot*, but overall only 20 percent of the people admitted to prison end up returning, even though in any one year 50 percent of all those released end up back in.

A recent study used a new dataset that allowed the researchers to see how many *unique* people return to prison: that is, to see if the person returning to prison every year was the same Bill or not. Using thirteen years of data, it found that only about one-third of all people admitted to prison at any point ended up returning at any later time—not one-half as the BJS reports suggested.[41] Furthermore, it found that two-thirds of those who did return to prison did so only once. Only about 11 percent of those admitted to prison returned two or more times. For most people, parole is not quite the revolving-door "failure" that the official statistics suggest.[42]

There is, however, a dark side to this seemingly good news. Recall that between 2000 and 2014, the states admitted a total of over 9.6 million people, or between 550,000 and 700,000 people per year. These are not all unique individuals, but the smaller the fraction of people cycling through prison, the greater the number of unique people there are being admitted to prison. The BJS studies claiming that half of all people admitted to prison return suggest that those 9.6 million admissions comprise something on the order of 5 million unique people. Our new results, however, point to something more along the lines of 6 or 7 million people.[43]

In some ways, lower recidivism rates paint a more positive (or at least less negative) picture of prison, but they also mean that a larger pool of people have come into contact with the prison system and all of its official and unofficial collateral costs. If prisons are going to admit 600,000 people per year, it is surely less socially costly for them to be the same 600,000 rotating through than for them to be a fresh group every year.

UNINTENDED CONSEQUENCES

The fact that we admitted 9.6 million people to prison between 2000 and 2014 while prison populations barely rose from 1.25 million to 1.35 million is a clear sign that most prison terms are quite short. But these numbers also point to a risk that cutting prison sentences might entail. We could cut prison sentences and see prison populations fall—while at the same time sending more people to prison.

It sounds like a paradox, but it's nothing of the sort. Assume that states cut time served for every prisoner by about six months starting in 2000, but still admitted the same 9.6 million people over the years 2000–2014. The six-month reduction would have led to hundreds of thousands of fewer people in prison on any given day, but the same number of people passing through prisons. In fact, it's possible that states could cut time served and see prison populations fall even as prosecutors sent *more* people through prison than ever before. In other words, cutting time served could mask prison *growth*: there could be fewer people in prison each day, but more people passing through each year.

This is not a thought experiment. If we exclude California, whose drop has been precipitous owing to extraordinary situations, then we are witnessing this very thing: declining prison populations, but increasing admissions.[44] Outside of California, total prison populations fell by 1.9 percent between 2010 and 2014. Total admissions, however, rose by 1.1 percent.

Now, to be fair, if we restrict our attention to those non-California states that have seen a decline in total prison populations since 2010, then both populations and admissions have fallen in the aggregate: a 4.2 percent drop in population, a slightly smaller 1.5 percent reduction in admissions. But that masks some stark outliers. Georgia saw prison populations fall by 6 percent, while admissions rose by 10 percent; in North Carolina, populations fell by 8 percent, and admissions rose by 34 percent; in Pennsylvania, the percentages are, respectively, -1 percent and 20 percent; and in Texas, a state often hailed as the miracle reformer, they are -4 percent and 2 percent. All told, ten of the twenty-six states that have seen population declines since 2010 experienced admissions increases over the same period. This is a particularly pernicious vulnerability, since it is hidden. The official prison population is going down, which looks like a success, but it hides the failure. These data highlight an unappreciated conceptual flaw with reform efforts: the primary goal should be to reduce the number of *prisoners*, not the *prison population*. Focusing on the latter allows the former to quietly rise.

It's likely that many of the collateral costs of admission max out pretty quickly. The diminished job prospects and strained familial relations that come from being in prison are probably about the same whether one spends twelve months in prison or eighteen months. It's the very act of going to prison that imposes the biggest costs. Some collateral sanctions, like the inability to apply for some jobs, don't even require admission to prison—a felony conviction is enough. All of which means that we should worry at least as much about the number of people passing through prison as we do about how long they are staying there. The current focus on cutting prison populations by cutting time served misses this point almost completely.

PROSECUTORIAL CONDUCT

If sentences aren't getting (much) longer, and if they aren't that long to start with, then what is causing prison growth? The obvious answer is rising admissions—in fact, this *must* be true, since the only changes that can drive up prison populations are changes in the number of people entering prison or changes in the amount of time they spend there once they are admitted. And the person driving up admissions is the prosecutor. To see this, we need to step back and scrutinize the institutions that drive prison admissions. As we've seen, people talk all the time about the "criminal justice system," but this is something of a misnomer. It isn't a system at all.

What we call the criminal justice system is, in practice, a mishmash of independent, often competitive bureaucracies, all attentive to different constituencies and facing different political and economic incentives. Someone who commits a crime does not just all of a sudden turn up in a prison. That person must be arrested by city police, indicted by a county prosecutor, and convicted by a county jury or by a county or state judge (though more often than not he or she will just plead guilty), all according to laws passed by state legislators. And each of these state legislators is nominally a state official but in fact represents a small—in the case of an urban representative, often quite small—part of the state.[45] Finally, the prisoner is eventually released by a state-level parole board or according to fixed release policies passed by that same sort-of state legislature.

These are *systems*, not a system. These agencies do not interact with each other smoothly, and one unintended consequence of this poor design is that prosecutors have ended up with almost unfettered, unreviewable power to determine who gets sent to prison and for how long. Over the past few decades, even well into the crime decline, prosecutors have decided to use that power more and more aggressively, and no one has stepped up to stop them. In fact, when we break the criminal justice "system" into its constituent parts, a striking fact stands out: one decision by county prosecutors—the decision about whether to file felony charges against someone arrested by the police—seems responsible for a lion's share of the growth in prison admissions since crime started dropping in the early 1990s.[46] Moreover, since time served has been fairly stable, by pushing up admissions prosecutors have been the ones who are most responsible for overall prison growth.

Our failure to understand this critical role of prosecutors is due in part to the fact that there have been surprisingly few efforts to determine which institutions have driven prison growth.[47] Those papers that have addressed the issue have generally broken the criminal justice system into four stages: trends in crime, trends in arrests per crime, trends in prison admissions per arrest, and trends in time served per admission.[48] Even the prestigious National Research Council's comprehensive 2014 report on the causes of prison growth relied on this (flawed) approach.[49]

The choice of these stages is mostly a concession to available data. There's readily available data from the FBI and the BJS on crimes, arrests, and prison admissions, but (to repeat myself) almost none on prosecutor offices. The resulting studies have claimed that growth has occurred mainly because of increases in admissions per arrest (although some have argued that in more recent years time served has played an increasingly important role). Pointing to "admissions per arrest" as the primary source of growth, however, is somewhat confusing, because it implicates a lot of different agencies. Are police making better arrests? Are prosecutors filing more aggressively? Are judges sentencing more aggressively on their own—or being compelled to by mandatory sentencing laws?

This concession to data limitations, however, was premature. It turns out that there *is* data on what prosecutors do, although, tellingly, it is gathered by state judiciaries, not by prosecutors. Since 1994, the National Center on State Courts (NCSC) has collected annual data from state courts on the number of felony cases filed in those courts.[50] This dataset, sitting in plain view on an NCSC server but apparently overlooked by all the studies before my own, provides a rare window into how prosecutorial behavior has changed over a period of declining crime and still-rising incarceration.[51]

The results tell a very clear story. In short, between 1994 and 2008:

- Reported violent and property crime both fell steadily.
- Arrests for all violent, property, public order, and non-marijuana drug offenses fell as well.[52]
- The number of felony cases filed in state court rose significantly. Fewer arrests but more felony cases meant that the probability of any particular arrest leading to a felony charge rose sharply.
- Once a felony case was filed, the probability of it resulting in a prison admission remained almost perfectly unchanged.

When I first saw my own results, I stared at my computer for a few minutes in disbelief. I had expected to find that changes at every level—arrests, prosecutions, admissions, even time served—had pushed up prison populations. Yet across a wide number and variety of states, the pattern was the same: the only thing that really grew over time was the rate at which prosecutors filed felony charges against arrestees.

Let's take each of these claims in turn.

The crime decline since 1991 has been dramatic. Nationwide, between 1991 and 2008 violent crime fell by 36 percent and property crime by 31 percent. By the end of 2014, both violent and property crime had declined another 14 percent.[53] The benefits of this decline are tremendous. Had crime rates remained at their 1991 level until 2014, there would have been about 250,000 more murders, 8.5 million more aggravated assaults, and 54 million more thefts.

While crime rates fell, police "clearance" rates—the percentage of each type of crime that results in an arrest by the police—remained relatively flat, and in some cases declined.[54] As a result, as violent and property crimes fell, so too did arrests for those offenses. Arrests for non-marijuana drug offenses also fell, at least through the early 2000s, before rising in the latter half of the decade. All told, the number of arrests for violent, property, non-marijuana drug, and "public order" offenses fell in the states I examined by about 10 percent between 1994 and 2008.[55]

Yet while arrests fell, the number of felony cases rose, and steeply. Fewer and fewer people were entering the criminal justice system, but more and more were facing the risk of felony conviction—and thus prison. Between 1994 and 2008, the number of felony cases in my sample rose by almost 40 percent, from 1.4 million to 1.9 million. Given the drop in the number of arrests during this time, the implications of this rise are striking, with the chance that an arrest would lead to a felony case growing from about one in three to about two in three.[56]

That was the only thing that really changed. Once a felony charge was filed, the probability that it would lead to a prison admission remained flat, at about one in four. In short, between 1994 and 2008, the number of people admitted to prison rose by about 40 percent, from 360,000 to

505,000, and almost all of that increase was due to prosecutors bringing more and more felony cases against a diminishing pool of arrestees. It's important to be wary of "one thing explains it all" theories for anything, especially for a phenomenon as complex as prison growth. These results, however, certainly support a claim of "one thing explains most of it"— and they rely on simple accounting, not complex statistics with all the risks and assumptions they entail.

Nonetheless, there are three reservations to keep in mind. First, even here I am eliding a crucial stage in the process. I looked at "admissions per felony case," not "convictions per felony case" and "admissions per felony conviction." This choice was due to yet another gap in data, in this instance for convictions.[57] What little data we have on convictions, however, does suggest that the conviction rate has been fairly stable over time, which would imply that the decision to file really is the main driver of growth.[58] Second, it is unclear what would have happened to these new felony cases in the past: Would these cases have been dismissed or dropped altogether, or are prosecutors simply "upcharging" more cases that in the past might have been tried as misdemeanors instead of felonies? The only data addressing this issue is sufficiently vague that its results are equally consistent with either option or anything in between.[59] Third, although it is clear that the number of cases filed has risen even as arrests have declined, it's still difficult to identify what sorts of cases have received more attention from prosecutors. The data I have on case filings, for example, don't give any information about what the felony cases were (i.e., violent, property, drugs, or something else).

We can, however, shed some indirect light on this last issue. Table 2.2 looks at the ratio of admissions to arrests for several crimes in 1991, 2001, 2006, and 2011.[60] Three patterns stand out: increasing toughness against violent crimes, generally steady (and perhaps surprisingly low) toughness against property crimes and drug possession, and rising (through 2001) and then declining toughness against drug trafficking. Although these patterns are informative, note that they do not tell us why any of these ratios have changed. Maybe police are doing a better job investigating certain types of crimes, maybe prosecutors are being more aggressive in charging them, maybe judges are more willing (or compelled) to send

Table 2.2 Fraction of Admissions to Arrests, 1991, 2001, 2006, and 2011

	1991	2001	2006	2011
Murder/Manslaughter	0.50	0.91	0.87	1.13*
Robbery	0.28	0.46	0.38	0.46
Aggravated Assault	0.06	0.11	0.14	0.16
Burglary	0.17	0.23	0.24	0.26
Theft	0.03	0.04	0.04	0.03
Fraud	0.04	0.08	0.12	0.14
Drug Possession	0.05	0.04	0.04	0.04
Drug Sales, etc.	0.28	0.42	0.41	0.38

*It's not impossible to admit more people in a year than are arrested for that crime, if the courts are clearing out back cases. And of all case-types, murder trials usually take the longest. This figure could also just reflect discrepancies in the data, which come from different bureaucracies. The upward trend in the ratio for murder is likely more reliable than the specific values.

Sources: Data from E. Ann Carson and Daniela Golinelli, "Prisoners in 2012: Trends in Admissions and Releases, 1991–2012," US Department of Justice, Bureau of Justice Statistics, December 2013, accessed August 24, 2016, www.bjs.gov/content/pub/pdf/p12tar9112 .pdf; US Department of Justice, Bureau of Justice Statistics, "Arrest Data Analysis Tool," accessed August 24, 2016, www.bjs.gov/index.cfm?ty=datool&surl=/arrests/index.cfm.

defendants convicted of them to prison. But they are consistent with the idea that an increasing prosecutorial focus on violent offending has played a big role in real prison growth.

A FLOW, NOT A STOCK

The most concise takeaway from this chapter is simply that despite so much "throw away the key" rhetoric, and despite the nearly automatic assumption by so many that prison growth is due to ever-longer sentences, the main driver of growth, at least recently, has been steadily rising admissions for fairly short terms. Even if we take a more sophisticated view of time served, such as treating parole reentries as extensions of the initial term in prison, initial admissions remain the key source of prison expansion. It's critical to understand the centrality of prosecutor-driven prison admissions, because if we do not, we simply cannot solve the problems we face.

Here's an example. Between 1993 and 2013, the number of "older" prisoners, defined as inmates fifty-five years and above, rose from about 26,000, or 3 percent of all state inmates, to 131,500, or 10 percent of state inmates.[61] Given concerns about the vulnerability of these inmates, the difficulty that prison poses for them, and the increased medical costs of caring for older, sicker people in prison, reining in the "graying" of the US prison population is an issue that has been getting a lot of attention. To address their situation, however, we must first ask why they are there.

Not surprisingly, the conventional wisdom is that longer sentences have led to older prisoners. Shorter sentences, the argument goes, would result in fewer people needlessly growing old in prison. We need to cut sentences, expand parole, and so on. But recent studies indicate that much of the aging of our prison population is actually due to the fact that we are admitting more and more older people to prison.[62] In general, an older inmate is less likely to be a younger admission who has aged in prison than to be an older admission: someone who is offending, and thus being admitted, in his older years. This finding is counterintuitive. As we'll see in Chapter 8, there's a sizable body of evidence showing that people generally "age out" of crime in their thirties or forties, for various biological and social reasons. Right now, however, there is an unexpectedly large cohort of older people committing crime later in life. One study ties it to the effect of excessive drug abuse when these individuals were younger and to their persistent drug abuse later in life.[63]

Now, of course, some of the older inmates are people who were admitted when they were younger and are still serving very long sentences. This appears to be the case in particular for those who are over sixty-five, a third of whom in 2013 had been sentenced to life in prison or had received a death sentence; half of these inmates aged sixty-five and up had been in prison for over ten years. Even with these inmates, though, fully one-third had served less than five years as of 2013, indicating that they had been admitted when they were already over sixty; even those who had already served ten years were at least fifty-five when admitted. In the end, if we want to cut back on the number of older inmates in prison, we need to focus much more on the root causes of their later-in-life offending (for instance, drug abuse) and how prosecutors respond to it, and much less on the length of time they will spend behind bars. Which is the exact opposite of what the Standard Story reformers suggest.[64]

GOOD NEWS, BAD NEWS, AND THE POWER OF COUNTIES

That prisons are driven more by admissions than by time served should give reformers reason to be both optimistic and pessimistic. On the one hand, it suggests that the size of our prison population could change surprisingly quickly once we start to focus on the real cause. Prison admissions are a flow, not a stock: they depend far more on choices made today than on the lingering effects of thousands of past decisions. We can change the admission rate today simply by admitting fewer people to prison today.[65] On the other hand, the actors in control of admissions—the police and prosecutors—are hard to regulate. Courts are loath to second-guess their decisions, and legislatures are unlikely to rein in enforcement of serious crimes, which are what a majority of the current prisoners have been convicted of. Later on we'll explore some legislative reforms that we can enact if we want prosecutors to send fewer people to prison, but we will also see that changing the attitudes of prosecutors, not their options, will likely have the biggest impact. That's a much harder task.

Furthermore, once we think about prisons as being driven by admissions, not time served, we are forced to rethink the very way in which we discuss where prison growth is booming. The standard question is something like, "Why do we see different outcomes in New York and Florida?" That's a valid question to raise—but perhaps not the most important one. The flow into prisons is driven more by county-level factors than state-level ones. We've already seen this with New York. New York *State* didn't decarcerate. The five counties of New York *City* did, along with a few other more urban counties, while the rest of the state sent more people to prison. The city declines were simply big enough to offset the increases. A study of California made a similar finding, showing that differences in the number of people that counties send to state prison have little to do with differences in those counties' crime rates and more to do with county politics.[66] High-crime but liberal areas like Los Angeles and San Francisco send relatively few people to prison, given their crime rates, while more rural, more conservative counties are inherently more punitive. There is no single, coherent "California" story.

Admissions, then, are primarily a county issue, not a state one. Although it is true that prisons are run by the states, and that state criminal codes define the conduct that can result in prison time, the number of people in those prisons is effectively determined at the county level. It's becoming increasingly clear that many of the divides we see nationally are less across states than within them. New York City and Austin, Texas, for example, probably have more in common with each other than either does with the more conservative suburbs that surround them.[67]

Yet almost every reform effort, whether targeted at sentencing law or other factors thought to drive mass incarceration, has focused almost solely on state-level policies. Few have addressed county incentives, and fewer still have addressed the coordination problems raised by the way authority is divided between state and local agencies. We will return to this disturbing issue in the pages ahead.

CHAPTER THREE

PRIVATE PRISONS, PUBLIC SPENDING

T HE THIRD MAJOR THREAD OF THE STANDARD STORY, AFTER
the war on drugs and longer sentences, is its emphasis on the amor-
phously defined "prison industrial complex." The prison industrial complex is a somewhat nebulous collection of private-sector actors that,
driven by the desire to profit off the immiserization of prisoners, push for
tougher sentencing laws and larger prison populations. Reformers' primary targets usually are private prison firms such as the Corrections Corporation of America (CCA) and the GEO Group, which build or operate
prisons holding state or federal prisoners under government contracts.

So disliked are these firms that early in the 2016 Democratic presidential primary both Hillary Clinton and Bernie Sanders felt the need to
explicitly distance themselves from them. Sanders's first act in trying to
put together a criminal justice platform for his campaign was to propose
a (clearly unconstitutional) law banning the use of private prisons at the
state and federal levels, and shortly thereafter Hillary Clinton returned
what few campaign donations she had received from private prison firms.[1]
However, like the attention paid to drug offenders (rather than violent
offenders) and to longer sentences (instead of admissions), this dislike

of private firms misses the point. It's not the private sector that should concern us. It's the public sector.

The power of private firms is overhyped at every turn. Yes, there are a lot of inmates in private prisons—but vastly more in public ones. Yes, private prison firms donate to candidates—but so too do public-sector officials, and private donations are not that large by comparison. Yes, private prison firms lobby for tougher laws—but alongside public-sector groups, too, so the impact of the privates is hard to separate out. Yes, private firms have incentives to maximize the number of prisoners—but so do public-sector actors, and they often have *stronger* incentives to do so, not to mention easier access to the politicians.

Moreover, the critique of private prison groups actually misses the real source of the problem. Public prison officials, when given the same basic incentives that privates often contractually face, act *exactly the same way* as the privates. Conversely, private actors with "better" contracts (a term I'll define below) may very well outperform public prisons. It's not the profit motive. It's the contracts.

Ultimately, the attack on privates for their privateness isn't only misguided, but likely harms reform. It's not just that reformers are spending time fighting relatively minor players. More seriously, the focus on privates prevents reformers from seeing how the very defects that concern them about private firms exist equally in the public sphere as well. In fact, public prisons suffer from every pathology attributed to private prison firms. Every one, and likely in costlier ways. These public failings, however, get less attention, despite the fact that public prisons hold almost all the prisoners. So once again, the Standard Story focuses on marginal but emotionally salient topics—people profiteering off the misery of others—and in doing so distracts us from the far more important causes of prison growth.

Before looking at the relative importance of the private and public sectors, however, I should raise an important caveat. The prosecutor, of course, is the most important actor shaping prison population size—and there are plenty of examples of prosecutors both ignoring tougher sentencing laws and circumventing efforts to scale them back. So it is possible, indeed quite easy, to overstate the impact of *both* private- and public-sector lobbying for tougher laws and more prisons. My point here is simply comparative: *to the extent* that legislative changes matter, these changes are shaped far more by the public sector than by the private sector.

PRIVATE PATHOLOGIES?

Throughout the 2016 presidential campaign, private prisons were often at the heart of discussions about criminal justice reform. They didn't come up just in the bill Sanders introduced in the Senate (the Justice Is Not for Sale Act) or Clinton's refunds to donors. The candidates discussed these institutions in almost every debate, they were a key topic in the first formal meeting between Clinton and Black Lives Matter activists, and academics and journalists wrote pages and pages of analyses on them. Yet it is easy to see, almost immediately, that their importance is consistently overstated. In 2008, both the number and the percentage of inmates housed in private prisons nationwide hit its all-time peak.

Of about 128,000 and 8 percent, respectively.[2]

To break the second figure down, private prisons held 7.2 percent of state prisoners and 16.7 percent of the prisoners in the much smaller federal system. Yet people still talk about privatization becoming "the norm."[3] Now, to be fair, 128,000 people in private prisons represents a noticeable increase from the 7,800 (or 1 percent of all prisoners) held in such prisons in 1990, when privatization started to pick up steam.[4] Still, 8 percent is a small fraction of the total prison population.

Moreover, most private prisoners are held in just a handful of states. In 2014, half of all private prisoners were held by the federal government and just two states (Texas and Florida); setting aside the federal government, only five states held half the private prisoners who were in state systems.[5] Interestingly, although these states held most of the private prisoners, most of their prisoners overall were in public prisons. Texas, for example, held 16 percent of all state prisoners in private prisons in 2014, but those prisoners made up less than 9 percent of Texas's total prison population.

In the end, as of 2014 only seven states had more than 20 percent of their prisoners in private prisons. Most of these were states with small populations, such as Montana and North Dakota, where a small absolute number of prisoners in private facilities can make up a large percentage of the overall prison population. All told, these seven states (which also included Hawaii, Oklahoma, Mississippi, New Mexico, and Vermont) held only about 5 percent of the nation's prisoners; only Mississippi and Oklahoma had more than 10,000 people in prison. It's also worth pointing out that twenty states—including states with large prison populations like Illinois, Michigan, and New York—have no private prisoners at all. Other states with large prison populations, such as California, Maryland, and North Carolina, have less than 2 percent of their prisoners in private prisons. There are plenty of states that have put a lot of people behind bars without relying on private prisons.

Put another way, banning private prisons tomorrow would drop state prison populations by no more than 7 percent, but only if every inmate in a private prison were immediately paroled instead of transferred to a public prison—and that definitely would not happen. The states would surely find a way to rehouse their inmates in public facilities (or buy out the private prisons from the current owners), because despite rhetoric to the contrary, it's unlikely that states are relying on private prisons for the (alleged) cost savings. As a number of scholars have pointed out, in the final analysis private prisons do not appear to be noticeably cheaper than public ones.[6] Their use likely reflects more an ideological interest in relying on private contractors to handle tasks that were once the sole domain of the public sector. All of which suggests that if private prisons were banned, states would find other places to put some, if not most or all, of the prisoners.

In fact, the decarceration trends of the past six years have likely further weakened any impact of banning private prisons. Many states now have unused public prison beds they would love to fill, in order to preserve the public-sector guard jobs in those prisons. So any state forced to close its private prisons could simply transfer those inmates to public prisons in states with unused capacity. This is just the first example of how private pathologies ("Keep the prison filled!") are just as apparent in the public sector as in the private sector.

Maybe, though, we should focus less on the numbers in private prisons and more on the conditions in which these prisoners are held. Even if private prisons do not hold a lot of prisoners, if the ones they hold are treated exceptionally worse than the inmates of public prisons, then these institutions may still merit a disproportionate share of our attention. What little data we have on conditions often suggests—although by no means unequivocally—that conditions are generally worse in private facilities than in public ones, since private prison contracts often incentivize cutting every possible corner when it comes to food, guard training, safety, and more.[7] One study, for example, found that in Mississippi, assault rates in private prisons were three to five times higher than those in public prisons.[8] The US Department of Justice also recently said that it would likely not renew contracts with private prison firms over concerns about safety and conditions.[9] On the other hand, in Florida every private prison has air conditioning, while only some of the public prisons do, and then usually only in certain areas.[10] Regardless, even if we assume that all private prisons are in general five times more violent than publics, which is likely an overestimate, these results imply that there are still more than twice as many assaults in public prisons than in private ones, given how many more people are in public prisons.

If we want to minimize assaults against inmates, we should by all means improve the incentives that private prisons face—but we should be sure to make similar demands of public prisons too. A conversation about the dangerous conditions at CCA's Lake Erie Correctional Facility in Ohio that doesn't also raise the utterly brutal conditions at the public Pelican Bay State Prison in California or Rikers Island Jail in New York City is missing a significant part of the picture.[11] In fact, given that political capital and attention are both scarce resources, if we are going to focus on conditions in either the private or the public prisons, then public prisons likely deserve our attention first.[12]

There are still other arguments people raise for targeting private firms. If not the sheer number, and if not the conditions, then perhaps what matters is how private prison firms lobby to toughen sentencing laws that apply to all inmates. The privates themselves may hold a small number of prisoners, but they also may have played an outsized role in pushing for mandatory minimums, three-strike laws, and other tough policies that result in a lot more people spending time in private and public prisons alike. There are certainly anecdotes that support this line of thinking. Private prison firms, for example, have long contributed to the American Legislative Exchange Council (ALEC), a lobbying group—frequently described as conservative—that drafts model legislation on a wide range of topics for states to adopt, including several tough-on-crime initiatives, such as truth-in-sentencing laws and mandatory minimums.[13]

But the idea that private lobbying for tougher laws, either on its own or through groups like ALEC, directly leads to more people in prison runs into two practical problems. First, the effectiveness of private prison lobbying is often overstated. Private prison corporations lobby in only a handful of states, and those states do not appear to have experienced above-average prison growth. Moreover, the private prison groups in these states have suffered some surprising—but telling—defeats. Second, to the extent we see tougher sanctions in states with private prison lobbying, it's hard to separate out the impact of that lobbying from concurrent lobbying efforts by the public sector. As we'll see, public-sector actors often have very strong incentives to push for tougher laws too, which makes it hard to estimate the incremental impact of private prison lobbying. Particularly confounding is that most private prison lobbying has occurred in fairly conservative states, where public officials may already face above-average pressures to be tough on crime.[14] There's almost no data at all on this issue, but I would confidently wager that prison populations in states with sizable levels of private prison lobbying would look pretty much the same in the absence of that lobbying.

A PAPER(ISH) TIGER

Let's start by scrutinizing private prison lobbying. Between 1986 and 2014, private prison firms spent slightly more than $13 million on lobbying activities.[15] Although this is often presented like a lot of money, context is critical. During that time, all interest groups spent a total of $36 *billion* lobbying state governments. That $13 million comes to about 0.03 percent of the total.

This argument, however, may be somewhat unfair. Like the private prisons themselves, private prison lobbying is concentrated in a few states.

Almost 40 percent of private prison lobbying money was spent in Florida, 12 percent in California, and about 5 or 6 percent each in Georgia, New Jersey, and Tennessee. But even then, these efforts came to just 0.3 percent of all lobbying expenditures in Florida, 0.03 percent in California, 0.1 percent in Georgia and New Jersey, and 0.2 percent in Tennessee.

Yet even these figures make for a potentially unfair comparison. Low spending could reflect an incredibly efficient lobbying machine that has a high rate of return. It could also reflect the weakness of the opposition. Why spend much if the other side isn't spending anything at all? In fact, the claim that the private prison lobby, like other tough-on-crime groups, faces no real political opposition is a common component of the Standard Story. In most policy areas, it's easy to define antagonist groups: labor versus management, industry versus environmental groups. Yet in crime policy, things seem much more one-sided. There's "tough on crime" on one side, but on the other? There's never been a successful soft-on-crime group (under any name), and until recently "smart-on-crime" wasn't much of a political force.

At first blush, the politics of crime really do appear to be different from politics-as-usual. Perhaps the private prison groups simply don't need to spend that much. This account, however, mischaracterizes the political arena in which private prison groups operate. Most research on interest-group competition focuses on the federal system, yet the private prison battle is a distinctly state-level issue—and state-level interest groups face something much closer to a zero-sum game than do the lobbying groups at the federal level, at least when it comes to funding. States cannot print money, and they generally borrow at less favorable rates than the federal US government, which has the most sought-after debt in the world. State-level groups compete for slices of a pie that cannot grow nearly as easily as the federal "pie."

So although it is true that tough-on-crime groups generally do not face opposition from explicitly "soft-on-crime" organizations, they surely face intense competition from other bureaucracies and advocates struggling to get their hands on the same limited pool of dollars, such as schools and universities, hospitals, and transportation providers, not to mention tax cutters who prioritize shrinking budgets and taxes over spending more broadly. A dollar that goes to a prison is a dollar that doesn't go to a school or a hospital; even if hospitals don't directly lobby against prison expansion, if they are more effective at saying "This dollar should go to us," they will, in effect, push back against expanded prison spending.

These other groups have a lot of money, and frequently much more clout. For example, while private prison groups spent $13 million on lobbying efforts between 1986 and 2014, educational groups (mostly primary and secondary education, like the American Federation of Teachers and the National Education Association) spent over $256 million, medical groups over $360 million, and—perhaps most importantly—public employee groups (which include, but certainly are not limited to, prison guard unions) over $132 million.

Now, these groups have spread their money across a lot more states than the private prison firms have, so this comparison exaggerates the differences in the states where private prisons actually compete. Yet again take Florida, where prison groups focused almost half their spending. They were still outspent there five to one by medical groups and two to one by education groups. If private prison groups are trying to "buy" tougher sentencing laws, we should expect other, better-funded groups to try to outdo these efforts to make sure the funds go to them instead. Even if the politics of law enforcement favor the pro-prison groups—it's easier to demand tougher laws than laxer ones—the power of the groups that are opposed to private prisons should impose real limits on what the privates (and often the publics) can accomplish.

The 2008 financial crisis provides more evidence that there are very real limits to private prison campaigning. Private prison firms apparently thought the crisis would work in their favor: they expected states to quickly close public prisons to save money, only to turn to privates when ensuing overcrowding became too hard to manage and public capacity could not be revived quickly enough.[16] Yet between 2008 and 2014, the private share of state prisoners stayed flat, at about 7 percent, as the number of people in private prisons dropped in lockstep with the numbers in public ones. Despite their optimism, private firms failed to capitalize on the fiscal emergency. In short, although private lobbying certainly isn't making things better, private prison donations are a very small part of whatever forces are pushing states to invest heavily in prisons despite opposition from educational, medical, and other major lobbies.

THE POWER OF THE PUBLIC SECTOR

In overemphasizing the importance of private prison lobbying, the Standard Story commits another major error, namely, understating the power of public-sector lobbying. One bit of supporting evidence that public groups have a significant influence is that when private prison companies confront public-sector unions, the privates frequently lose. In 2012, for example, GEO Group—which is headquartered in Florida—attempted to privatize 27 prisons in Florida and take responsibility for about 14,000 inmates.[17] The bill to do so had the support of Rick Scott, the state's Republican governor at the time, and the state's strongly Republican Senate (28 Republican senators to 12 Democratic ones). Yet the bill died in the Senate by a vote of 19–21. Faced with the prospect of losing 3,000 public prison guard jobs, the public employees' union managed to get nine Republicans to join all the Democratic senators to defeat the bill. Similarly, in 1998, the legislature in Tennessee attempted to pass a bill to put the entire state prison system under the control of CCA, the nation's largest private prison firm, which is headquartered in the state. Yet despite at first winning broad bipartisan support in both chambers of the state legislature, the bill was eventually scuttled when the public-sector union realized how many jobs were at stake and have lobbied against it aggressively.[18]

Looking beyond these sorts of head-to-head conflicts between the public and private sector over who should manage prisons, there are many other reasons to assume that the public sector is more likely to push for tougher laws in general and to do so more effectively. In fact, the incentives of public-sector actors are strong enough that I imagine prison policies would be almost exactly the same today if private lobbying had not taken place. There are four main reasons for this.

First, public-sector unions representing prison guards have an incentive to fight for more prisoners to ensure job security, if not job growth. The California Correctional Peace Officers Association (CCPOA), perhaps the most famous guard union in criminological circles, is well-known for campaigning for tough-on-crime laws, such as California's notoriously harsh three-strikes law.[19] The unions also ensure that prison closures do not result in lost jobs. In Pennsylvania, the state laid off only three guards when it closed two entire prisons in 2013.[20] Similarly, New York has struggled to close prisons despite seeing its prison population drop by about 25 percent since 1999, owing in no small part to fierce opposition from the New York State Correctional Officer and Police Benevolent Association (NYSCOPBA).[21] And when Michigan announced plans to close a major prison in 2016, the state Department of Corrections was suspiciously cagey about layoffs.[22]

Second, many legislators and citizens believe that prisons provide vital economic support, even beyond guard salaries, to the disproportionately rural communities in which so many are located. Although empirical studies suggest that such benefits are minimal to none, local politicians and their constituents certainly *believe* they exist.[23] And so they will also fight hard to keep the prisons open. Consider New York again. NYSCOPBA by itself did not keep half-empty prisons open; it had to enlist the aid of local politicians. Moreover, when New York did close prisons, the closures were disproportionately *not* in rural areas, which tend to be overrepresented in state legislatures and whose politicians may fight harder against closure than their urban counterparts.[24]

In fact, when it comes to legislators fighting to save their local prisons, lobbying isn't even necessary. There's no need for lobbyists to educate legislators about the (perceived) importance of those facilities in their districts or to encourage them to defend them. Politicians are typically already in favor of "their" prisons, and they are also likely immune to counter-lobbying. Importantly, over the past several decades the number of smaller counties with prisons has grown substantially (even if a majority of prisons still seem to be in fairly urban or adjacent suburban areas).[25] To the extent that rural economies are struggling, legislators from these counties represent a bloc that will push for tougher laws and against reforms in order to preserve a rare source of local jobs, even without any outside lobbying.[26] Looking just at lobbying dollars therefore understates the ability and inclination of the public-sector actors to be tough on crime.

Third, beyond wanting prison-guard jobs, more rural counties may have an incentive to fight for tougher sentencing laws because of the US Census. This is one of those dry-as-dirt administrative issues that can have profound implications and costs. The shape of a representative's district, perhaps even the very viability of his or her seat, depends on the number of people who live in it. But where should prisoners be counted—the county where they last resided before incarceration, or the county where they are locked up? In almost every case, these are not the same places. Outside of four states, prisoners count as living in the area where they are imprisoned.[27] Politicians in rural areas with prisons will therefore fight reform efforts, if only to prevent their districts—and thus their party's power—from shrinking.

Besides voting power, rural politicians also believe that prisoners help bring in state and federal grant money, although this is likely more myth than reality. Some state and federal grant programs allocate money proportional to the number of people in the county; in theory, more prisoners would translate into more funds, even if in most cases the prisoners would not have access to the resulting programs. In reality, most funding programs use models that are not easily duped by prison populations (these include looking at, say, the number of school-aged children, not the total number of people), but the perception that funding can turn on total population is yet another factor that encourages rural politicians to resist reform.[28]

And fourth, the politics of punishment are such that legislators, judges, and prosecutors all have strong incentives to remain tough on crime, even when the electorate itself is pushing for more leniency. Broadly speaking, the electorate is more sensitive to a failure to punish hard enough than to the costs of overpunishing those who don't pose a risk: the recidivist who commits a crime is far more salient than the person who poses no risk languishing needlessly in prison. Knowing this, politicians persistently err on the side of being too tough, and the electorate rarely—a few recent examples aside—punishes them for it. We will return to this problem, as well as to the US Census, later on.

It should be clear by now that public-sector actors don't need much outside support or encouragement to remain tough on crime. Combine this fact with the relatively small amounts of money that private prison groups throw at politicians, and we can see that the overall incremental impact of private prison firms, compared to that of public-sector actors, is likely pretty small. And the data seem to support this: prison populations in states with expanding private prison populations did not appear to grow any more quickly than prison populations in other states during the 1990s and 2000s.[29] Prison populations in the more private-friendly states appear to have *contracted* somewhat less quickly during the post-2008 recession, but that could just reflect the more conservative ideological preferences of states that are inclined to rely more on privatization than on the power of the privates themselves.

THE PUBLIC AND PRIVATE PRISON INDUSTRIAL COMPLEX

Although I have focused in this chapter on private prisons, reformers often take aim at the broader "prison industrial complex" (which I'll refer to from here on as the "PIC"), which includes not just the private prisons themselves but also the firms that provide food, clothing, and phone calls to inmates. For example, the Bob Barker Company—which is not owned or named after the *Price Is Right* host, although people apparently often think so—is a private, family-run company that makes upward of $100 million per year supplying prisons with soap, deodorant, and other commissary items that prisoners increasingly need to purchase.[30] The food-services behemoth Aramark runs the dining services for many prisons, and numerous other smaller companies manage the often exorbitantly expensive collect-call services that inmates must use to maintain contact with family and friends outside of prison.[31]

Privatization extends beyond incarceration as well. The United States is one of only two countries that relies on private firms to provide bail to people detained in jail (the other is the Philippines).[32] In recent years some states have also effectively privatized probation and parole by turning them into bail-like systems.[33] Potential probationers and parolees need to post a bond before release, often obtained from a private broker, and the broker is repaid only if the parolee or probationer avoids some sort of easily identifiable "failure" (like rearrest or reconviction), which encourages the private company to monitor the parolee or probationer. These sorts of privatization efforts are controversial, and they deserve much more scrutiny than they often get.[34] Here, however, I want to keep the focus on privatization in the prison context.

It's true that there is a fairly extensive network of private firms that service public prisons. But, again: How important are these firms in *driving* growth? To start, note that the PIC clearly did not cause prison growth; rising incarceration was well underway before the private firms started appearing. The PIC, in other words, developed in response to rising incarceration rates. If the PIC matters now, it is not because it caused the growth but rather because it resists reform. Moreover, although states can easily avoid relying on private prisons—many states don't use them at all—the broader PIC is perhaps simply unavoidable. In fact, it makes almost no sense to talk about a PIC-free world. States are not going to start making deodorant, managing farms, and sewing clothes. There will always be private actors supplying many of the goods that prisons need to function.

It's certainly fair to ask how much we should rely on private contractors; not everything that is contracted out needs to be. For example, phone calls could be monitored by prison guards instead of private firms. State employees could sell commissary goods rather than contracting that service out, and instead of relying on firms like Aramark to provide food, prisons could train prisoners to make it. Doing these things, however, would require hiring more prison guards, more store clerks, and new employees to supervise and train the food preparers, purchase the food, plan the menu, and so on. And then those (non-inmate) public-sector employees would push even harder against reforms in order to protect these jobs. The pathologies of the private sector are just as present in the public sector.

In other words, reformers should not really be concerned with the privateness of the PIC. They should worry that as prisons grow, the supporting bureaucracies—private and public alike—will grow as well, and they will fight against anything that jeopardizes their power and pay. How different is the world with Aramark running the food services from one where food is prepared (or at least ordered and delivered) by public employees? Will Aramark lobby more effectively than the public-sector unions fighting to maintain the same contracts? Perhaps a nationwide firm like Aramark will be better at lobbying and negotiating, but that seems like a much less important difference than the ones usually raised by reformers and critics.[35]

In a perverse way, maybe having big firms provide these services actually helps reform. There's no data to point to, but it's possible that prison contracts aren't as important in the grand scheme of things for bigger companies. Aramark, after all, is a lot more diversified than NYSCOPBA. A few years ago, for example, Aramark entered into a three-year, $145 million contract with the Michigan Department of Corrections to provide food to inmates. Put aside that Aramark performed so poorly that the contract was canceled two years in—although Aramark's shoddy performance could indicate how much it valued the contract.[36] What matters here is that Aramark's annual revenues are about $15 billion per year; a three-year, $145 million deal, while large in most contexts, comes to about 0.3 percent of Aramark's annual revenue.[37] The incentive for Aramark to fight for prison growth (or against prison shrinkage) might be smaller than the incentive for a smaller direct provider who has more (relatively) at stake.

Moreover, it may be politically riskier for nominally non-penal companies like Aramark to lobby for tougher sentencing laws than it would be for public-sector groups to do the same thing. Florida's Stand Your Ground law provides an interesting example. After George Zimmerman shot and killed Trayvon Martin on February 26, 2012, many media accounts mistakenly thought that Zimmerman would rely on this somewhat notorious law, which expanded the situations in which people could use deadly defensive force.[38] Although this assumption was incorrect—Zimmerman relied on Florida's more conventional self-defense law—these accounts caused people to dig into the history of Stand Your Ground, and they reported that the American Legislative Exchange Council, the lobbying group, had played a big part in spreading the law nationwide.[39]

The reaction against ALEC was swift, and in response many companies quickly cut their ties with it to avoid bad press.[40] The comment from Coca-Cola is representative: "We have a long-standing policy of only taking positions on issues that impact our company and industry," it said as it tried to distance itself from a criminal justice controversy. Compare Coca-Cola's response, however, to the actions of groups like CCPOA, NYSCOPBA, and the National Association of Assistant United States Attorneys (NAAUSA, the lobbying arm for federal line prosecutors). These organizations openly embrace their connections to the criminal justice system, and they actively and proudly—and publicly—push for tougher laws and against reforms. In other words, firms that we do not associate with being "criminal justice firms" fear the backlash from criminal justice failures. Groups more directly tied to the system do not have that fear. Quite the contrary.

It is undeniable that the PIC exists. Yet if it didn't, the same phenomena would still be at work—just in the public sphere rather than the private one. As long as someone, public or private, is benefiting from servicing prisons, that person will push back against reforms. Focusing on privateness distracts us from what really matters: who is gaining, how much are they gaining, and how hard will they fight to keep those gains? A debate framed as "public *versus* private" effectively gives the public prisons an undeserved pass. The real question we need to ask isn't "What is wrong with the privates?" but "Are the pathologies of the privates worse than those of the publics?" This is actually a fairly tough question to answer.

Take a controversial part of many private prison contracts: the minimum occupancy requirement. These require that a minimum percentage of beds (70 percent, 90 percent, sometimes even 100 percent) be "filled."[41] Those opposed to private prisons attack such provisions as driving states to focus on keeping prisons filled, or as a form of "low-crime tax."[42] Yet similar provisions effectively exist for the public prisons as well. They aren't spelled out in contracts, which likely explains why they get so much less attention, but just as private prisons get paid for empty beds, so too do state prison guards. As I've mentioned, New York State has kept numerous half-empty prisons open because NYSCOPBA and local legislators don't want to lose guard jobs, and Pennsylvania closed two prisons and somehow managed to lay off only three guards.

What is the difference, then, between a state paying a private contractor for an empty bed and the same state paying a guard for guarding an empty bed? Neither the CCA nor the NYSCOPBA really cares about how many people are in prison. They just want to make sure their flow of money doesn't decline.[43] Contractual terms for the CCA and political pressure by the NYSCOPBA accomplish the same goal in roughly the same way. Moreover—given that between half and three-quarters of state prison spending is for wages, so closing a prison saves very little unless guards are laid off—the costs to the state budget are probably comparable as well. Yes, the destination of the money is different, since the spending on wages stays in-state while a much greater share of the money given to, say, CCA will flow to Tennessee, where CCA is headquartered, and to CCA's shareholders. But that's not the difference that reformers are pointing to. What they are pointing to, though, is not much of a difference at all.

It's worth asking why the private sector seems to get so much more criticism for defects that are just as rampant on the public side.[44] This could reflect the generally left-leaning nature of those who are fighting against mass incarceration: their politics lead them to distrust the private sector but think favorably of the public sector. Mass incarceration, however, is primarily—indeed, almost entirely—a public-sector project, and its continued durability as well as any future reduction will necessarily be the result of public efforts.

HOW FISCAL HEALTH PERMITTED PRISON GROWTH

One aspect of the public sector that has gotten a fair amount of attention is the rise in what we spend on criminal justice in general, and on incarceration in particular. At first blush, the increase is dramatic: by 2013, state and county governments were spending nearly $80 billion on prisons and jails, up from under $30 billion in the early 1990s (or under $50 billion in 2013 dollars), and up from about $6 billion in the early 1980s (or about $17 billion in 2013 dollars).[45] Overall criminal justice spending rose from under $10 billion in the early 1970s (about $50 billion in today's dollars) to over $200 billion by the early 2010s.[46]

In recent years, reform advocates on the Left and the Right alike have pointed to these (seemingly) large expenditures to justify policy changes.

Figure 3.1 State Real per Capita Revenues and Expenditures, 1952–2012

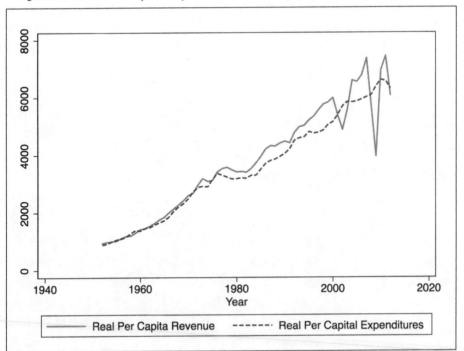

Source: US Cenus Bureau, "State and Local Government Finance," www.census.gov/govs/local.

On the Left, some argue that prison spending crowds out spending on more socially productive programs like education, while others suggest that tight state budgets create the opportunity for the federal government to use grants to incentivize decarceration efforts. On the Right, groups like Right on Crime argue that trimming correctional spending in an era of low crime is an efficient way to rein in government budgets. All these arguments, however, have significant shortcomings. There are relationships between correctional spending and prison growth, as well as between the fiscal crisis of 2008 and the push for reform, but they are substantially different from the ones we usually hear.

To start, it's true that criminal justice spending, including correctional spending, rose significantly in the second half of the twentieth century. This increase, however, took place in the context of overall growth in government spending. As shown in Figures 3.1 (for the states) and 3.2 (for the counties), between the 1950s and the 2000s, with a short break in the

Figure 3.2 County Real per Capita Revenues and Expenditures, 1952–2012

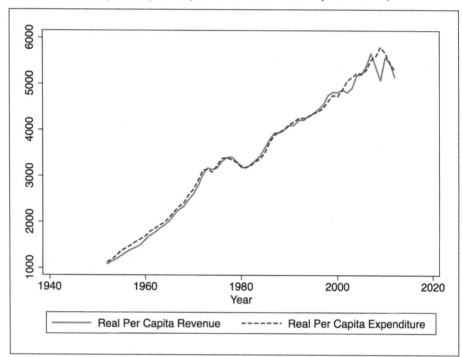

Source: US Cenus Bureau, "State and Local Government Finance," www.census.gov/govs/local.

mid-1970s, real per-capita revenue grew steadily at both state and local levels, and total expenditures moved nearly in lockstep with revenues. In the 2000s, thanks to two serious recessions, revenues were more erratic, but spending continued to grow, in part because of large federal infusions of cash.

These data provide some much-needed context for the 1990s and 2000s, periods when crime began to fall but incarceration—and thus correctional spending—continued to rise. The rise in criminal justice and correctional spending during the crime decline coincided with rising spending more generally. In fact, as crime began to fall, the *share* of state budgets given over to criminal justice and corrections remained fairly stable, rising slightly in the 1990s before leveling off and declining in the 2000s, as shown in Figure 3.3.[47] For counties, the results are less dramatic, with the share of spending on criminal justice and corrections rising slightly over the 1980s (detailed county data isn't easily available

Figure 3.3 Correction and Criminal Justice Spending
as Share of State Budgets, 1952–2012

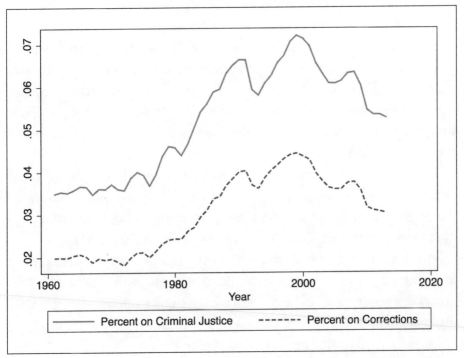

Source: US Cenus Bureau, "State and Local Government Finance," www.census.gov/govs/local.

before 1977) and then leveling out in the 1990s. As always, of course, any sort of single US story masks important differences across states. The bumpiness of state shares from 1991 to 2000 in Figure 3.3 reflects differences across states more than changes within states. About half the states saw corrections' share flatten around 1991, and another half around 2000 (although some of those slowed briefly around 1991, then picked up again through 2000). So Figure 3.3 flattens out some state differences, but by 2000 the share spent on criminal justice had stabilized in almost all states.

What's notable in these results is that even at the late 1990s peak, states dedicated only about 7 percent of all spending to criminal justice, and 4 percent to corrections; for counties, it was about 8 percent to criminal justice and 2 percent to jails. These are not outsized amounts. The $50 billion that states spent on corrections in 2013 came to barely

3 percent of the $2 trillion they spent on everything. As we'll see, this has important (and potentially favorable) implications for the connection between austerity politics and prison reform.

It is important to keep cause and effect straight here. At first blush, Figures 3.1 to 3.3 seem to tell a simple story: as state and county budgets grew, states and counties spent more money on everything, including prisons. This increased prison spending led to more prison capacity, which in turn led to more prison admissions.[48] In reality, it is less likely that increased fiscal capacity *drove* prison growth than that it *permitted* the prison growth to take place. To argue that more spending led to more prisoners glosses over important institutional issues. Although states build the prisons, it is primarily the choices made by county-level prosecutors that send prisoners to them. And these prosecutors likely don't worry too much about state issues, including the costs of running prisons.

In a time of rising budgets, when everyone is getting more money from the state government, we should expect less of the opposition that otherwise tends to arise in the fairly zero-sum game of state budgeting. As a result, legislators may have felt little pressure to restrict the tough-on-crime options available to prosecutors, and perhaps even felt comfortable passing tougher ones. Expanding state fiscal capacity most likely helped drive prison growth less by incentivizing prosecutors to be tougher on crime and more by disincentivizing legislatures from reining in prosecutorial power. However, a conundrum now comes into view. If states are spending relatively little on corrections and criminal justice, why has so much of the post-2008 reform effort focused on the seeming necessity of cutting back on correctional spending?

TOO LITTLE MONEY

It's common to hear politicians, especially conservative ones, ground the need for criminal justice reform in cost-savings terms. We spend too much on corrections, they say, and in this time of fiscal austerity and low crime rates, cuts to corrections are an easy way to save money. Dig a little deeper, though, and this story starts to crumble.

First, as we just saw, we don't really spend that much on corrections. It's true that $50 billion is a lot of money, but it's only about 3 percent of overall state budgets, and perhaps twice that of the discretionary budget.[49] That's real money, but even shutting down corrections completely, a utopian idea, would not yield massive savings. Second, and more problematically, politicians overstate, often by significant amounts, the savings we should expect from decarceration. It's not just excessive optimism about how many people we can really let out of prison; it's that politicians—and activists, and academics, and journalists—are using the wrong number. Almost every discussion of the cost savings from decarceration uses the average cost of incarcerating a single prisoner, which is simply the total amount spent on corrections divided by the total number of prisoners. In 2010, these averages ranged from slightly below $15,000 per prisoner in Kentucky and Indiana to more than $60,000 per prisoner in New York; the national average was about $31,000.[50]

So we often hear statements such as, "Each prisoner we release will save the state about $30,000." But this is simply wrong. Releasing one inmate from prison in New York will not save the state $60,000. It will save the state about $18,000 at best, or less than one-third the number that is so often cited.[51] The discrepancy comes from the frequently overlooked difference between average and incremental (or marginal) costs. Many—indeed most—of the costs of running a prison do not change when a single prisoner is admitted or released. Set one prisoner free, and there is no change in wages, in the heating bill, in the electricity bill, even (really) in the food and laundry costs. In general, the marginal costs of prisons seem to range from about one-third to as little as one-seventh the oft-cited average costs of $16,000 to $60,000.[52]

In fact, wages alone often make up approximately 50 to 75 percent of all correctional spending in the states, so in the absence of layoffs, there are very little savings from releasing inmates. A state would have to release enough prisoners to close an entire wing of a prison *and* have the power (or perhaps the courage) to actually lay off personnel to generate savings closer to the average cost per prisoner. Unfortunately, inmate reductions, and even prison closures, are more common than layoffs.

It strikes me as unlikely that politicians do not understand all of this—that they are unaware that corrections make up such a small share of the state budgets, and that marginal savings are substantially below average costs. Perhaps the calls for budget-inspired reform are all just political theater, allowing politicians to look fiscally responsible while they actually do little about spending. Or maybe there is another dynamic at work: perhaps politicians are using the budget crisis as political cover to be less tough on crime, not so much for financial reasons as for moral or personal ones. As I noted earlier, the (inattentive) way in which voters follow crime policy leaves politicians much more afraid of seeming too lenient than too harsh. The political costs of leniency resulting in a shocking act of recidivism are much greater than the costs of needlessly locking someone up for too long. The financial crisis, however, provides political cover for mistakes. A politician can now say, "We just couldn't keep all the inmates in prison, we just couldn't afford it." A subsequent recidivist's failure is no longer the result of undue leniency, but the consequence of a fiscally difficult choice foisted onto the official by the economy. This need not be a conscious decision that governors and legislators and judges are making. But they surely feel safer cutting back on prison populations when they can claim, or genuinely believe, that they had no real choice.

If I'm right—that the economic arguments for reform are more political than financial—then an improving economy need not derail reform efforts. The fiscal crisis helped politicians push down prison populations, and crime has not really gone up in response. At least for now, that could create momentum for further cuts, and further savings, regardless of the state of the economy.

Of course, there are always caveats to good news. In this case, two deserve particular attention. First, the fiscal crisis can probably serve as cover for cutting back punishment only for people convicted of nonviolent crimes. "I had to make a hard fiscal call" is a viable excuse when the recidivist was originally found guilty of theft. It is a harder argument to make when the original crime was aggravated assault or attempted murder. This is a real limitation to reform: as we've seen, large-scale reform will require us to think more carefully about how we punish people convicted of violent crimes. Second, although an improving economy alone may not derail reform, an improving economy alongside rising crime may. We may not even need that large of a rise in crime for it to do so. Alarmingly, a one-year uptick in violent crime in 2015 quickly led some commentators and policymakers to start worrying about a new "trend" in rising crime, even though one year is hardly a trend. Violent crime has gone up several times since 1991 only to resume dropping shortly thereafter, and violent crime rates remained at near-historical lows by the end of 2015.[53] But the reaction showed just how quickly "fear of crime" arguments can resurface, even after years of dormancy. It's also worth keeping in mind that, at least according to official crime statistics, for all the decline since 1991 the violent crime rate in 2014 was still 100 percent higher than it was in 1960, and the property crime rate was about 50 percent higher. Americans may not be too fixated on crime now, but it likely won't take much of an increase to bring their attention back much more strongly (although they still seem committed to reform, despite modest rises in violent crime in 2015 and the tough-on-crime rhetoric of Donald Trump's presidential campaign throughout 2016).

TOO MUCH MONEY

I've just argued that corrections and criminal justice budgets appear to be too small to explain the amount of cost-cutting attention they receive. I now want to suggest that however little states spend, it is still enough to thwart another avenue of reform that many have raised: federal grants.

The Brennan Center for Justice at New York University Law School, for example, recently proposed the "Reverse Mass Incarceration Act," calling on the federal government to give $20 billion over ten years to states that reduce prison populations by at least 7 percent over three years without seeing any real increases in crime.[54] That sounds like a large program, but again, state and local governments spend over $200 billion per year on criminal justice, and about $80 billion on prisons and jails alone; at about $2 billion per year, the Brennan proposal comes to less than 1 percent of criminal justice expenditures and 2.5 percent of corrections spending. It doesn't seem likely to move the policy needle much. And the Brennan proposal is about on the same scale as some of the federal criminal justice grant programs already in effect. Between

1993 and 2012, eight major grant-making arms of the US Department of Justice awarded about $38 billion to state and local governments.[55] As a percentage of annual criminal justice spending, these grants consistently hovered (in total) around 2 percent for the states and under 1 percent for local governments.

I don't want to be too pessimistic. Federal grants may fund pilot programs that otherwise would have languished; if those programs succeed and can then be scaled up, smallish grants can have outsized returns.[56] As a general matter, however, state and local governments are already spending so much money that attempts to change criminal justice policy by just paying them to be less punitive will likely fail. With a total budget of a little less than $30 billion, the Department of Justice simply lacks the resources to ratchet its grants up high enough.[57]

There's other evidence to warrant skepticism. Consider a prominent funding failure: the Violent Offender Incarceration and Truth in Sentencing (VOI/TIS) Incentive Program, part of the sprawling and controversial federal Violent Crime Control and Law Enforcement Act of 1994, which set aside over $10 billion for states that adopted restrictive "truth-in-sentencing" laws. These laws mandated that people convicted of specific violent crimes had to serve at least 85 percent of their sentences before becoming eligible for parole. Congress and the president lack the ability to directly change state laws; VOI/TIS was an effort to bribe states to change. By all measures, it did not succeed (although many seem to refuse to accept this).[58] A Government Accounting Office report on the impact of VOI/TIS noted that although twenty-seven states adopted truth-in-sentencing laws, only four said the grants really shaped their decision, and eleven said they had a partial effect.[59] For thirteen states, the grants were irrelevant, and twenty-three more never adopted the laws at all. All told, despite the federal government authorizing about $10 billion for the program, states claimed only around $3 billion, leaving 70 percent of the money unclaimed.[60]

It's also hard to see any evidence that truth-in-sentencing laws had any real impact on prison growth, although the 2016 Democratic primary campaign was rife with people accusing Hillary Clinton of "causing" mass incarceration by supporting her husband's 1994 crime bill.[61] There's been little rigorous work done examining the impact of these laws, but it's hard to find any noticeable differences in incarceration trends among the states that did not adopt truth-in-sentencing laws, that had such laws independent of the grant, that were moderately influenced by the grants, or that were seriously influenced by them.[62] Furthermore, the nationwide rate of prison growth *declined* steadily from the year before the VOI/TIS grants became available through the 2000s.

Perhaps most striking is the case of New York, one of the four states that said it was heavily influenced by the program to adopt truth-in-sentencing laws. Between 1996 and 2001, New York received over $100 million in VOI/TIS money, more than any other state. Yet its prison population began to steadily decline in 1999, right in the middle of getting millions of dollars from the VOI/TIS program. Even as the legislature was taking money to make laws tougher, prosecutors simply started sending fewer people to prison (in part due to New York's sharp drop in crime).[63]

A rather different approach to incentivizing states, which, like VOI/TIS, has yielded disappointing results, was used in the federal Sex Offender Registration and Notification Act (SORNA), which was part of the broader Adam Walsh Child Protection and Safety Act of 2006. SORNA required states to adopt a fairly punitive sex offender registration law or face a loss of 10 percent of the funds they received through the Edward Byrne Memorial Justice Assistance Grants program, a major federal program—although one that awards only about $400 million per year. According to the agency in charge of monitoring SORNA, as of early 2016 thirty-three states had declined to adopt the standard, despite a compliance deadline of 2011.[64] In general, states felt that the costs of losing the grant money were less than the costs of implementing the program, so they just ignored it. Once again, the amount at stake just didn't measure up to the amounts state governments were already spending.

AN OPEN WINDOW

The Standard Story bemoans the nefarious influence of private money and private profit motives on prison policy and prison growth. But these critiques take too narrow a view of what really drives our incarceration policy. There are plenty of public actors who benefit from prison growth,

too, and who thus have an incentive to fight for tougher correctional policies and to oppose reform efforts. And it seems likely that these actors are
consistently stronger and more influential than their counterparts in the
private sector. As a result, the emphasis on private prisons distracts reformers from the people and groups who really shape our criminal justice
policies and laws. This misplaced attention is not without cost.

The fiscal crisis has opened the window for real reform. Yet that opportunity will be squandered if reforms focus on the factors that are less
important. As we've seen, the Standard Story frequently puts its attention
in the wrong places. It overemphasizes the war on drugs, it cares more
about long sentences than it does about admissions driven by prosecutorial aggressiveness, and it worries more about the private sector than the
public. The issues taking center stage are not irrelevant, but they are not
the issues that matter most.

So after a brief but closer look in Chapter 4 at the specific problems
with reform proposals being made today, I will demonstrate exactly how
and why prosecutors, politics, and the problem of violence drive mass
incarceration, and I will lay out an alternative set of reforms that confront
these issues directly.

CHAPTER FOUR

COSTS OF THE STANDARD STORY

A s crime rose during the 1980s, the politics of punish-ment was simple: no one—prosecutor, judge, legislator, governor, or president—could go wrong by being tough on crime. States passed harsher laws, and prosecutors filed more charges. Even as we entered the 1990s, and crime began to decline, the politics and rhetoric of crime remained aggressively tough.

With hindsight, it's easy to accuse politicians in the 1990s of overre-acting to a waning problem. Throughout much of the early part of the decade, however, the decline in crime looked very much like a similar, transient decline that had occurred from 1980 to 1984. The crack-related violence that had spiked in 1984 was still on everyone's mind, especially with several prominent criminologists warning of a rising cohort of "su-perpredators" who were going to create an even more dire crime wave.[1] Compared to 1981–1990—the peak of the crime boom—the decade from 1991 to 2000 actually saw nearly 3,000 more murders, over 100,000 more rapes, over 60,000 more robberies, and nearly 2.5 million more ag-gravated assaults. Crime had begun to decline, but only slowly, and from such a high peak that its costs were still significant over the 1990s.

Nevertheless, as crime declined, public fear of crime seemed to slowly subside as well, even in the early 1990s.[2] In fact, although state prison populations grew over the 1990s, the rate of growth started to slow almost as soon as crime rates began to drop. The causes of this slowdown are poorly understood—if only because many commentators seem to incorrectly assume that prison growth accelerated in the 1990s—but changing attitudes surely played some role.[3] As a result, the year 2000 seemed to present an opportunity to stop the rise in incarceration rates. Crime was still steadily declining, and the post-dot-com recession hurt state economies, leading to talk of cutting prison and other criminal justice budgets. Yet the economy recovered fairly quickly—and then 9/11 happened, shifting the policy focus away from criminal justice reforms, and the moment passed.[4] Being tough on crime remained the norm.

After years of little change, the reform effort found itself revitalized around 2008. Crime had continued to decline, prison populations had continued to rise, and the country was hit with another, even deeper financial crisis. One study found that between 2000 and 2007, legislatures passed laws making sentencing and punishment tougher three times as often as they passed more "progressive," decarcerative reforms, only to see progressive reforms outnumber harsher new laws by the same three-to-one ratio between 2007 and 2012.[5] This transformation in policy has excited reformers, who regularly tout the latest "significant" reform bill working its way through a state legislature. It is certainly a change in attitude that we should embrace.

With criminal justice reform, however, there is always a caveat. Here, there are three in particular. First, these reforms will likely yield disappointing results. By and large, reforms have focused mostly on the two main pillars of the Standard Story: making it harder to send "nonviolent drug offenders" to prison, and cutting "long sentences," often by expanding parole options, usually just for people convicted of the same drug and other nonviolent offenses. (There has also been a lot of discussion, but much less action, concerning private prisons.)[6] As reformers frequently tell me, these reforms may reflect the limits of what is politically feasible. Aiming at prosecutors is risky, and changing policies for violent crimes may be almost impossible. That's quite likely true (at least for now). None of that, however, changes the fact that such a focus will ultimately produce disappointing results.

Second, as we touched on before, it's possible that the tactics used to pass the reforms of today will actually complicate more substantive reforms in the future. Several reform laws combine leniency for nonviolent offenders with tougher sanctions for violent crimes. Even when reform efforts do not do this, the rhetoric that reformers employ—we need to save prison beds for "those who deserve them"—promotes a tough-on-(violent)-crime mentality. It would be surprising if states that raised sanctions for violent crimes when lowering them for nonviolent offenses then turned around and lowered the punishments for violent crimes shortly thereafter. If they have argued that they need to free up prison space for people convicted of violent offenses, they may later find it difficult to cut back on sending people to prison for those very sorts of crimes.

Third, one likely reason for the anemic natue of the reform results is that politicians and reformers alike are understandably worried that reforms could lead to an increase in crime, and that that increase would then make future reforms unlikely. However understandable, there are some serious, often unaddressed problems lurking in this position. If nothing else, it overstates the risk of the reforms leading to an increase in crime. More fundamentally, though, it may be that some reforms are justifiable even if they *do* lead to more crime. It's true that crime is costly—but so, too, is punishment, especially prison. The real costs are much higher than the $80 billion we spend each year on prisons and jails: they include a host of financial, physical, emotional, and social costs to inmates, their families, and communities. Maybe reducing these costs justifies some rise in crime. This argument may seem politically impossible, and that may be true, at least today; I certainly get told that often enough. More thoughtful reforms, however, could make this notion seem more viable down the road. For now, however, this sort of deeper debate about values is completely off the table, to our detriment.

This last point touches on what are perhaps the most important issues here: What exactly is the relationship between punishment—prison, in particular—and crime? And how should we balance the costs of crime against the costs of punishment? These are the sorts of issues where people often have very firm beliefs, despite data that are actually quite complex, nuanced, and contingent. It is impossible to understand what reforms make sense without first understanding what we know—and, even more importantly, do not know—about what causes crime to rise and fall. It is also impossible to know what reforms are desirable without carefully thinking through all the various benefits *and costs* of enforcement.

Let's start by looking at the reforms that have been proposed so far, to see more clearly what they may get right and what they probably get wrong. Then we'll turn to the more fundamental question: How, in ways both small and large, should we think about the impact of decarceration on crime?

THE REFORMS SO FAR

For the past several years, The Sentencing Project has published an annual review of state-level sentencing reforms.[7] Given the fact that hundreds of new laws have been passed since 2010, it may be helpful to look at a single year. Here we'll examine the prison and sentencing reforms that took place in 2013.[8]

Most of the 2013 reforms, unsurprisingly, focused on nonviolent crimes and drug offenses. The most common reforms, adopted in nine states, softened sentencing laws for drug crimes; three states raised the dollar threshold for property crimes (following in the wake of six other states having done the same thing in prior years). Some reforms expanded parole opportunities for people serving time for nonviolent crimes, and one increased the amount of time that those nearing release could spend in transitional programs—but excluded all of those convicted of index violent crimes (murder or manslaughter, forcible sexual assault, aggravated assault, and robbery) as well as some other types of violent crimes. A handful of other reforms, however, apply to violent and nonviolent offenses alike, or at least did not explicitly exclude all violent crimes from their reach. One state, for example, didn't exclude people convicted of some violent crimes from an expansion of parole, and another permitted courts to divert people convicted of both nonviolent and some violent crimes to alternative sanctions. Another required all new criminal law proposals, for both violent and nonviolent crimes, to come with racial impact statements—reports detailing how enforcement of the new law would change the racial composition of those arrested, convicted, or incarcerated by the state.

Finally, a few reforms focused explicitly on the treatment of violent crime. One state repealed its death penalty—although for all the media attention the death penalty gets, it impacts a vanishingly small fraction of cases (just 0.3 percent of all state prisoners, and 0.04 percent of all people under state correctional observation, are on death row). More significantly, another state launched a task force to look into reforming its truth-in-sentencing law for violent offenders, which it did, fairly dramatically, the next year. This last reform, however, remains a very distinct exception, and all told, nearly 70 percent of the 2013 reforms either completely or primarily excluded those convicted of violent crimes.

One clear feature of these reforms is that they focus more on the back end than the front end of the system: on hastening release through parole reform, for example, rather than preventing admission (or even conviction) in the first place. Most of the drug reforms, for example, cut mandatory minimums and expanded judicial discretion over how much prison time to impose; only two effectively cut back on admissions by raising the drug-weight bar for felony offenses. The two reforms directed at violent crime also focused on time served. Even some of the reforms that raised the threshold for property crimes just made adjustments *within* the various felony categories, rather than raising the cutoff between misdemeanor (jail time) and felony (prison time) offenses.

The same patterns appear in the other editions of The Sentencing Project's annual reports as well as in a parallel series of reports produced by the Pew Charitable Trust's Public Safety Project. The review of state legislation from 2000 to 2008 discussed at the beginning of this chapter makes similar findings.

I don't want to seem overly pessimistic. For those who get released early, the reforms matter. At the same time, the impact of back-end reforms will likely disappoint, because they're missing the real heart of prison growth, namely admissions. My concerns here are not theoretical. We have had several years of reforms now, and their impact remains unimpressive. Take Mississippi, which in 2014 implemented a spate of reforms that raised the cutoff for felony theft (from $500 to $1,000), made probation presumptive for thefts of under $1,000, expanded parole options for nonviolent offenders, and increased access to drug courts.[9] At the time, only 43 percent of Mississippi's inmates were in for violent crimes, so focusing on nonviolent offenses should have mattered more there than in other states. It was also the one state that cut the minimum time that those in prison for violent crimes had to serve, from 85 percent of their maximum sentences to 50 percent.

First, the good news. In 2013, Mississippi's prison population was almost 22,000. Without reforms, that population was expected to rise to almost 24,500 by 2024; the Pew Public Safety Project predicted that the reforms would push the population down to about 20,500 by 2016, followed by a rise to 21,000 by 2024. So far, declines have beaten the forecasts, as the prison population fell to under 19,000 by 2015, where it remained as of early 2016.[10] That's a decline of almost 14 percent since 2013, to a level more than 22 percent below what was predicted for 2024 without reforms—nothing to scoff at. But 19,000 gets Mississippi back to where it was in 1999. In 1990, after years of prison growth and at the peak of the crime era, Mississippi had just over 8,000 people in prison. In 1978, it had just under 3,000. So 19,000 is still 137 percent higher than the state's 1990 prison population, and 533 percent higher than its 1978 population. By most standards, then, Mississippi remains a mass-incarceration state despite the reforms. With 19,000 people in prison, its incarceration rate is still 635 per 100,000, above the current national average and higher than that of almost any other country in the world. And for now, Mississippi's prison population appears to be holding steady, a seemingly common occurrence in reform states, which often experience short-run declines followed by stasis.

Zooming out from specific states, we can easily see the limited impact so far of reforms in the national numbers. It's true that the US prison population dropped for the first time in over forty years in 2010.[11] We should,

Figure 4.1 Rate of Prison Growth: 1979–2014

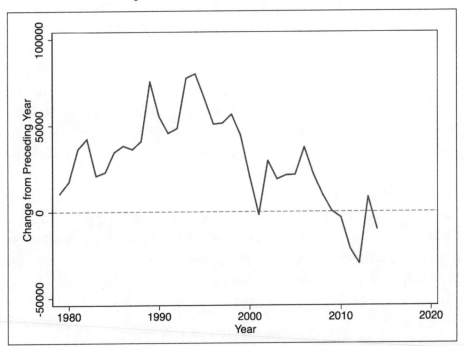

Source: US Department of Justice, Bureau of Justice Statistics, "Data Collection: NPS Program," www.bjs.gov/index.ctm?ty=dcdetail&idd=269.

however, take a closer look at that decline. First, it has been pretty small. From their 2010 peak to 2014 (the last year for which there is data), state prison populations fell by about 4 percent. That's a reduction of about 56,000 people, bringing state prison populations down from 1.41 million to 1.35 million. An improvement, but not a sharp one. And there's a catch: about two-thirds of the decrease—35,000 of the 56,000—is due *solely* to California, whose path to decarceration is highly idiosyncratic, and whose precipitous decline in prison populations also appears to have stabilized pretty quickly.[12] Excluding California, state prison populations since 2010 have seen a drop of just under 2 percent. At this rate, it will take more than thirty years, until 2049, for prison populations to return to where they were when crime rates peaked in 1991. To return to 1978 levels, it would take almost ninety years.[13]

Second, it isn't clear how much credit the spate of post-2008 reforms deserve for these drops. Figure 4.1 plots the annual rate of change of state prison populations over time. Prison populations grew faster and faster through the early 1990s, at which point the rate of change immediately slowed. The results shown in Figure 4.1 are consistent with two fairly distinct stories. One is that there were two periods of slowing growth, 1993 to 2001 (likely fueled by falling crime and the dot-com bust, which began in early 2000) and 2010 to 2014 (driven by current reforms and economic austerity). The other, however, is that prison growth generally slowed down over the entire period between 1993 and 2014, just not consistently every year. We can't be sure which story is correct. Quite likely, both are. Declining crime, which persisted from the 1990s through the mid-2010s, diminished the urgency of locking people up. At the same time, the 2008 crisis and the subsequent reforms likely encouraged further declines. Regardless, Figure 4.1 suggests that even the small decreases we've seen since 2010 are not entirely attributable to reforms, but are partially the continuation of a preexisting trend tied to falling crime.

THE VULNERABILITY OF REFORMS

The reforms that the states have passed so far have focused on highly salient but ultimately less important issues, and their impacts have been slight, especially when we look beyond California. If this were just a slow start, there may not be much to be concerned about; we would do best, in that case, to give these reforms more time.

This may not just be a slow start, however. As I've already stressed, the rhetoric and actions of reformers today may make deeper reforms tougher to get approved in the future. Furthermore, there are still many ways in which the current reforms can falter or be reversed. For instance, prosecutors, never the target of reforms themselves, often retain enough discretion to undermine reforms if they want to. And reforms have not targeted any of the political problems that caused us to overreact to rising crime in the first place, leaving us vulnerable to similar responses in the future.

That's the state of current reforms. Progress has been slow and inconsistent, and whatever gains there have been remain vulnerable. Whether the results are good or bad, however, turns on what we think the optimal level of incarceration should be. How deep do we want these cuts to go? To answer that, we need to think a bit more about the costs and benefits of prison.

A CONSISTENT STORY

One thing that is clear from the rhetoric of policymakers on all sides of the reform debate is that everyone remains haunted by the precipitous rise in crime from the 1960s through the 1980s. However bipartisan the push for decarceration is, so, too, is the claim that "we can cut prison populations *without causing crime to rise*." This formulation makes clear that whatever the costs of large-scale incarceration, the costs of higher crime are worse.

The sentiment is understandable, given the magnitude of the crime drop since 1991. Had murder and manslaughter, forcible sexual assault, robbery, and aggravated assault rates remained at their 1991–1992 peaks, then between 1993 and 2014 there would have been about 250,000 additional murders, 700,000 more forcible sexual assaults, about 7.7 million more robberies, and 8.5 million more aggravated assaults. That would have been more than 10,000 additional murders per year, and more than 1,000 additional aggravated assaults per day—for twenty-two years. The numbers for property crimes are even larger: there would have been 31 million more burglaries, 54 million more thefts, and 17 million more car thefts. That's an extra 3,800 more burglaries and 6,700 more thefts per day—again, for twenty-two years.

We have made remarkable gains. And for all these reductions in offending and victimization, official violent and property crime rates are still high compared to the early 1960s, suggesting that we could push the crime rates down further still.[14] People will understandably resist policies that threaten the gains we've made, or that seem to prevent us from reducing crime even more. To understand the costs and benefits of prison, then, we need to start by tackling the question of what role exactly soaring incarceration played in the drop in crime. It's not just a question of how much of the post-1991 crime decline resulted from rising incarceration, but of how much worse things would have been in the 1970s and 1980s without it.

DID MASS INCARCERATION CAUSE CRIME TO DROP?

There is little middle ground in the debate over the impact of rising incarceration on crime. On the one hand, defenders of imprisonment point to the fact that the drop in crime occurred at the same time that prison populations kept rising. On the other hand, reformers point to a large number of empirical studies that seem to show little relationship between falling crime and rising prison populations; they also note that both incarceration rates and crime rates rose together over much of the 1970s and 1980s, further suggesting that incarceration can't stop crime.[15]

There are many reasons for this disagreement. Some of it is surely ideological: knowing a person's view on the impact of prison on crime provides a lot of information about other political views. Some of the disagreement, though, reflects the fact that data here are messy. The problem is that a major statistical challenge bedevils most efforts to measure how prison influences crime—in a way that causes most studies to *under*state the impact that prison has on it.[16] There are some studies that address this defect better than others, however, and these stronger studies indicate that rising prison populations played an important role in restraining crime growth over the 1980s, but that the effect of incarceration weakened as prison populations continued to grow into the 1990s and 2000s. The returns on locking one more person up were much greater when crime was high and prison populations were low (the 1980s) than when the opposite was true (the 1990s and, especially, the 2000s and 2010s). Furthermore, even though prison "worked", we could have achieved the same decline in crime more effectively by investing in other, less costly, less brute-force solutions.

Steven Levitt (of *Freakonomics* fame) estimated that as much as 25 percent of the crime drop, at least during the 1990s, came from higher incarceration rates.[17] Two sociologists in turn found that between 1978 and 1990, each additional prison-year (i.e., locking one more person up for one more year) prevented 2.5 violent crimes and 11.4 property crimes, which is consistent with Levitt's results; between 1991 and 2004, however, those numbers fell to 0.3 violent crimes and 2.7 property crimes.[18] So prison was important, but it is much less important now. In fact, it's quite likely that the remaining crime-fighting effect incarceration still has is sufficiently slight that the costs of incarceration—not just the fiscal costs to the state, but the various collateral costs to inmates and their families—exceed these gains. Whatever it did before, prison growth now almost certainly imposes a net social loss.

This declining impact of prison on crime is both good and bad news for reformers. The good news is clear. Reforms that cut back on prison populations should not lead to an increase in crime, because if current increases in prison populations aren't really reducing crime—if other factors are driving that change—then modest decreases in incarceration levels shouldn't increase crime either. Furthermore, as prison cuts get deeper, the risk of rising crime can be tempered by spending the savings on more efficient alternatives.

The bad news is a bit more speculative. As prison populations shrink, prisons appear to become more effective; their current ineffectiveness is partly due to scale. So while we have room to cut back, there may be a point at which cuts in prison populations do lead to perceptible rises in crime, which as a political matter may end or even reverse reforms.[19] Yet prison is by no means the only thing that drove crime rates down from the 1990s to the 2010s. Besides prison, crime is shaped by the number of police, the unemployment rate, wage levels, the number of crime-aged young men in the population, immigration levels, cultural attitudes toward violence, technological improvements, and so much more.[20] All these factors have changed since the 1980s as well, many in ways that helped reduce crime. If all these other crime-shaping factors remain where they are now, then the bad news may not be so bad. None of these factors operates in a vacuum: the effectiveness of and need for rising prison populations in the 1980s may have been due in part to some of these other factors being "worse." People exposed to lead when they are young, for example, are thought to be more likely to engage in criminal conduct when older and those who were in their teens and twenties in the 1970s and 1980s had been exposed to much more lead than today's young people.[21] Now that lead exposure (and many other such factors) are at "better" levels, prison may be less necessary than before, making even deeper cuts more possible.

There is certainly reason to believe that the overall proclivity of people to engage in crime is lower today than it was just a few decades ago. We have just weathered a severe recession, along with a Baby Boomer–sized cohort of Millennials aging into their peak crime years, without any apparent faltering in the decline in crime.[23] This is a somewhat simplistic analysis, but it at least suggests that we may be less vulnerable to rising crime than we were before. In fact, one researcher has suggested that asking, "What caused the decline in crime?" is the wrong question. What we should be asking is, "What caused the surprising *rise* in crime?," treating the increase between 1960 and 1991, not the decrease from 1991 until today, as the anomaly that needs explaining.[24] Viewed in this way, we may have even more room to be aggressive in rolling back prisons.

One challenge that we face is that while social scientists have a long, generally accepted list of the factors (besides prison) that shape crime, there is little agreement on how much each factor matters, how the factors interact with each other, and how their impacts vary over time.[22] Everyone, for example, agrees that having more police generally reduces crime. The size of that effect, however, is subject to intense disagreement. Moreover, we have almost no idea how that effectiveness changes in the presence of other factors: Does the effectiveness of policing vary with, say, the age of the population, or the level of poverty? Most models just report the average effect over time, not how it changes over time.

In the end, our predictions are limited by just how little we know about the complex ways in which all the causes of crime have interacted in the past and the ways in which they will interact (perhaps differently) in the future.

It is also imperative to understand the limited nature of the claim about prison's effectiveness. To argue that prison growth contributed to 25 percent of the drop in crime does not mean that it was an efficient use of resources: perhaps we could have achieved an equally large decline in a way that was less fiscally and socially costly. In fact, the evidence does not tell an encouraging story about the effectiveness of prison. It appears as though rehabilitation programs outside of prisons do a much better job of reducing crime, and there's little evidence of "specific deterrence," the "scared straight" idea that going to prison itself prevents future offending.[25] The evidence also suggests that the threat of prison generally fails to significantly deter those who have not been locked up before (what is called "general deterrence").[26]

Of course, perhaps the goal of prisons is neither rehabilitation nor deterrence, but simply to incapacitate the person until he no longer poses a threat, or to lock offenders up for purely moralistic, "retributive" goals. As we'll see in Chapter 7, if the goal of prison is to incapacitate, we do it very poorly. In fact, it's possible that many of the gains from incapacitating someone are offset by the person committing more crimes than he otherwise would have after he is released—the exact opposite of deterrence.[27] As for retribution, it isn't really focused on what prison accomplishes, so the sorts of policy issues raised here are largely irrelevant. It is, however, a powerful cultural value that permeates punishment today.

Even studies claiming that prison played a significant (short-term) role in reining in and reversing the crime rate often acknowledge that other approaches would have worked better. Hiring a police officer is probably about as expensive as hiring a prison guard, for example, but investing in police has a much bigger deterrent effect and avoids all the capital expenditures of prisons. Steven Levitt has estimated that $1 spent on policing is at least 20 percent more effective than $1 spent on prisons.[28]

In sum, cutting prison populations need not expose us to rising crime. Reformers likely have room to be more aggressive than they have been so far. Or, to put the blame where it more properly belongs, politicians have room to be more daring. The impact that each additional admission to prison will have on the crime rate is surely weak at present, given how large the prison population is. As the prison population shrinks, any risk of increased crime would ideally be addressed through smarter, more efficient approaches. That said, even though non-incarcerative alternatives may be more efficient, they carry more political risks. Unfortunately, as we'll see in Chapter 6, no one is proposing ways to minimize these risks, which will ensure that politicians generally won't *be* more adventurous, even if they could—and should—be.

BEYOND THE $80 BILLION

Up to this point, I have argued that we can likely cut prison populations without pushing crime up. This approach implicitly accepts the view of reformers and politicians that crime reduction is paramount. Whatever good it may do, a reform that risks an increase in crime is unacceptable under this formulation. This is a troubling position for reformers to take: the idea that lower crime is the only acceptable goal simply isn't true. There are other, competing goals that are also desirable.

We don't spend all our money on crime control, despite non-zero levels of crime. We don't, for example, insist that everyone serve as a police officer. Nor, contrary to what some libertarians may think, have we gutted the constitutional protections that hinder policing and pre-serve fundamental personal rights. We could have less crime—but we also want more schools, more privacy, and lower taxes. There's a level of crime we're willing to accept. No politician will say this publicly, but it's inarguably true.

Yet people often miss or downplay this point, ignoring the fact that criminal justice goals have to be balanced against other ones. For exam-ple, the Supreme Court's 2004 decision in *Blakely v. Washington* forced many states to weaken guidelines they had adopted to constrain judges at sentencing.[29] A few years later, one scholar purported to find the opin-ion's "silver lining": states with guidelines saw crime grow faster in the 1980s and drop more slowly in the 1990s than states without guidelines, so by invalidating these states' guidelines, *Blakely* "saved them" from their seemingly higher-than-necessary crime rates.[30] Perhaps it did. Maybe the guidelines reflected ignorance, or problematic penny-pinching, or some sort of interest-group manipulation. Or maybe the impact of guidelines on crime reflected a rational tradeoff. Some states may have been willing to accept higher levels of crime in exchange for better-funded schools, better hospitals, or lower taxes. Less crime is better than more, of course, but that's not a decision made in a vacuum.

The current debates over criminal justice reform suffer from similar myopia. There is no discussion, even by those outside of politics—who have more freedom to ask such questions—about what the optimal level of crime should be, or about the other things we could gain if we directed criminal justice spending elsewhere. Why is crime control inherently more important than education or medical research or public health? Even in the few moments when these tradeoffs do come up—like when Vermont senator Bernie Sanders argued that we should invest more in schools and less in prisons—it is often in the context of reducing crime more efficiently, not because investing more in education should be prioritized over crime control on its own terms.

Here, however, I want to focus on a narrower issue—not on the costs that prison spending imposes on other government programs by "crowding out" funding, but on the costs that incarceration imposes on offenders, their families, and their communities. These costs alone, too frequently overlooked, should make us rethink our emphasis that the costs of crime are the "only" ones that matter, although most cost-benefit analyses of prisons tend to omit these. What if a reduction in prison populations would allow 100,000 children with at least one parent in prison to now have both parents at home, but at a cost of a 5 percent rise in aggravated assaults (or even some number of additional murders)—is this a fair tradeoff, even assuming no other criminal justice benefits (like lower future offending rates among these children)? According to our current rhetoric, the answer seems to be no. But isn't this a debate worth having? Given the magnitude of mass incarceration and our historically low crime rates, isn't this a debate we *need* to have now? As long as the narrative is that "we can lower prison populations without lowering crime," "lowering crime" remains the primary goal. All the other costs associated with prisons are secondary. Before simply accepting that framework, let's at least look at what these other costs are.

Most immediately, there are the costs to the inmate while in prison. Prisons are less violent than shows like HBO's *Oz* suggest, yet they remain dangerous places.[31] Although data are scarce, assault rates appear to be higher in prisons than in the general population (perhaps even after controlling for the elevated levels of violence in the neighborhoods that inmates disproportionately lived in prior to their convictions).[32] Levels of sexual assault are high enough that Congress, which has generally taken a fairly unsympathetic, tough-on-crime stance toward prisoners, passed the Prison Rape Elimination Act in 2012 to try to reduce its incidence. Prisons are known to cause mental health problems in some prisoners and to exacerbate preexisting mental health issues in others, and the overall health effects of being in prison are alarming: some studies suggest that for each year an inmate spends in prison, he or she ages the equivalent of two years, at least in the short run.[33] Of course, counting these harms as "costs" is not universally accepted. At least in the United States, many feel that one of the goals of prison is for the prisoner to suffer. This is not how most other Western countries now view prison, but it is still the reality here.[34] To many, then, the suffering the prisoner experiences isn't really a cost, and it may even be a benefit.

Then there are the costs to the inmate outside of prison. Even putting aside the various legal impediments former prisoners face, people who have been released from prison encounter a wide range of costs and risks. They are more likely to overdose on drugs (since drugs outside of prison are cheaper and more potent, and a person's tolerance declines while incarcerated); they leave prison less healthy than when they went in; their family ties are weakened, if not broken; they find it harder to get jobs; and the jobs they do find provide fewer hours, are less secure, and pay less per hour than the jobs they could have landed without a prison record.[35] Some of the employment harms come from losing skills while in prison, as well as the loss of contacts that everyone relies on to find jobs and discrimination by employers who are not willing to take a chance on formerly incarcerated people. Some of these costs are then exacerbated by legal barriers, like being barred from certain jobs, being forced to declare prior convictions on job applications, being banned from public housing and denied welfare support, and so on. All of these obstacles increase stress, decrease income and family stability, contribute to future recidivism, and simply make life less enjoyable and more difficult.

These are not just costs for the prisoner; many of them are costs to society. People who are sicker after their release will put more demands on health-care services, including public health-care programs like Medicaid. Unemployed and underemployed former prisoners pay less in taxes than they would have if they had not gone to prison and had held down jobs, and they need more government support. We all end up paying for their diminished health and opportunity levels—although it is the former prisoner who certainly pays the most.

Beyond the costs that fall on the prisoner (and indirectly, everyone else) are those borne by the prisoner's family. Even if one thinks that *none* of the costs to the inmate should count—that committing a crime effectively removes the prisoner from "counting" at all, a harsh and unforgiving view of offending that nonetheless often seems politically popular—the costs to his or her family seem harder to ignore. There are financial costs, like the loss of the income the inmate used to bring home, as well as the exorbitant charges imposed on the collect calls that prisoners make, and the costs in time, money, and inconvenience and discomfort of having to travel to visit a family member at a far-flung institution (over half of all people in prison are housed one hundred to five hundred miles from home, and over 10 percent are more than five hundred miles away).[36] Some costs are emotional, including the stigma that comes from being married or related to someone in prison, the private sense of loss that comes from being separated from a loved one, and the anxiety of worrying about a family member or partner being mistreated or lonely in prison.[37] And even if the impact of incarceration on divorce appears slight, it surely weakens and undermines marriages.[38]

The costs to the inmate's community are also significant. In this context, incarceration can be thought of like chemotherapy or radiation treatment: it targets a disease, but in a blunt way that causes a lot of collateral damage and if not properly calibrated it can do more harm than good. It may reduce crime, to the benefit of those who live in the community, but if imposed too broadly, real costs emerge. Returning prisoners, for example, may spread diseases they contract in prison, such as sexually transmitted diseases (STDs) or tuberculosis (TB). Incarcerating too many people, especially more minor offenders, can make a neighborhood less safe by undermining its "social control," the extent to which the neighborhood can police itself.[39] Obviously, serious violent offending undermines social control, but those who commit lesser offenses may provide more pro-social functions than their minor offending offsets.

Large-scale incarceration can even change how people date and marry. "Dating markets" work best when the sex ratio is as close to fifty-fifty as possible. Mass incarceration, however, can skew this ratio—in one study of high-incarceration neighborhoods in Washington, DC, the ratio dropped as low as forty men for every sixty women.[40] The result, perhaps ironically, is that the remaining men have more leverage in the dating market, since men are in scarce supply. In one series of interviews, people said they felt the imbalance led to more men having multiple partners, to women agreeing to engage in riskier sexual behavior, and the like.

Thus the question isn't simply, "Will a reduction in the prison population raise crime?" It's also, "Will a reduction improve relationships, mitigate exposure to TB and STDs, improve the wealth and stability of individuals and neighborhoods?" Framed this way, a rise in crime should not automatically trigger an immediate stop to reforms. Obviously rising crime, like rising incarceration, can undermine relationships, cause real physical and emotional harms, and weaken neighborhood functioning. But we need to think carefully about how to balance the costs of crime against the costs (and benefits) of enforcement.

The current nature of the prison reform movement provides some provocative evidence about whether we are achieving this sort of balance. Both crime and punishment are geographically concentrated, and they are disproportionately higher in poorer areas whose residents are more likely to be members of minority groups. Some who are wary of reforms thus point out that poor minority communities have been the biggest beneficiaries of the crime drop, and so we should oppose reforms out of a sense of racial justice.[41] Yet many of these supposed beneficiaries are leading reform efforts like Black Lives Matter. I suppose one could argue that they just don't "get it," that out of ignorance or something else they are protesting the very thing that made their communities safer. The reality, of course, is that those who are protesting are those who have seen both the benefits and costs up close, and have decided that the costs now are simply too great.[42]

FEAR

The current slate of reform policies does not seem to be driving down prison populations as quickly as many people hoped it would. People's faith in the Standard Story is surely one reason why expectations were high. But fear could also help explain the anemic state of prison reform. The increase in crime from 1960 to 1991 was real, and it was profoundly destructive. And although prison may not have been responsible on its own for the decline that started in 1991, it seems as though it played a major role; indeed, many people credit it with stopping and reversing the rise. Pushing back too hard against incarceration is surely risky for politicians, who are not willing to take a chance on society ending up back where it was in the 1970s and 1980s, or even to appear to be willing to take that chance. The statistics are on the side of reform, but there are real risks for policymakers who rely on them. The rise in violent crime in 2015—reported as this book was going to press—certainly adds to that risk, even if reforms are not responsible for the increase.[43]

Yet while incarceration "worked," it worked in a brute-force manner. There were other, more efficient routes we could have taken but didn't, for structural and political reasons that reformers are not really addressing. Furthermore, the crimes that prison prevented have to be weighed against the personal, familial, and community costs it has imposed in the process. Crime is not the only societal outcome that incarceration implicates.

I don't know what the optimal size of our prison population should be. No one does, in part because no one is really asking. But it's almost certainly true that no matter one's views on the goals of the criminal justice system, cuts far deeper than what current reforms are producing are needed. So it's worth asking what our prison reforms should actually aim to achieve.

PART II

A New Narrative

CHAPTER FIVE

THE MAN BEHIND THE CURTAIN

F EW PEOPLE IN THE CRIMINAL JUSTICE SYSTEM ARE AS POWER-
ful, or as central to prison growth, as the prosecutor. Recall that over
the 1990s and 2000s, crime fell, arrests fell, and time spent in prison
remained fairly steady. But even as the number of arrests declined, the
number of felony cases filed in state courts rose sharply. In the end, the
probability that a prosecutor would file felony charges against an arrestee
basically doubled, and that change pushed prison populations up even as
crime dropped.

Yet here's the remarkable thing. For all their power, prosecutors are
almost completely ignored by reformers. No major piece of state-level
reform legislation has directly challenged prosecutorial power (although
some reforms do in fact impede it), and other than a few, generally local
exceptions, their power is rarely a topic in the national debate over criminal justice reform. They are essentially invisible.

Perhaps the most revealing example of this invisibility comes from a
report by the National Research Council on the causes of prison growth.[1]
The NRC is the branch of the prestigious National Academy of Sciences
tasked with producing expert reports on important public policy issues.[2]

Yet when called on to explain the causes of soaring incarceration rates, it barely discussed the role of prosecutors at all.[3] In this chapter I confront this startling blind spot in our national conversation on prison reform.

A LITTLE HISTORY OF THE PROSECUTOR

American prosecutors have not always operated as they do today: politically powerful, directly elected and independent of almost any oversight, and substantially better positioned than defense attorneys. Public prosecutors have existed since the colonial era—although at that time they were appointed, not elected—but they were generally not viewed with much respect; even well after the American Revolution, victims often preferred to hire private prosecutors to try their cases, even when public prosecutors were available.[4] Public prosecutors were generally younger, less skilled, and less well-financed than private defense counsel.

The office of the public prosecutor underwent two major changes during the Jacksonian era (1828–1850). First, Americans came to view appointing officials like prosecutors and judges as a process potentially riddled with corruption. Elections, they believed, would ensure that control rested with the people, not with insiders.[5] Second, states started pushing back against private prosecutions, which increasingly struck people as morally dubious. Prosecutors, many felt, should focus on doing justice, not solely on winning. Across the country, a wave of legislation and state court opinions eliminated or constrained private prosecutions.

Some aspects of the old system nonetheless endure. In certain states, victims can still retain private prosecutors, although their scope is limited and they are rarely used.[6] Some jurisdictions also hire private lawyers to serve as public prosecutors, an arrangement that can actually remind us why states moved away from this model; in Ferguson, Missouri, for example, the local prosecutors were known for being particularly (if ineffectively) aggressive, in part because they were private lawyers who charged the city by the hour and faced no cap on how much they could bill.[7]

As a general matter, however, prosecutors are now government officials. Forty-six states call for the election of prosecutors (in Alaska, Connecticut, Delaware, and New Jersey prosecutors are appointed), and

85 percent of district attorneys are full-time public officials—a notable rise from 1974, when only 44 percent of them were full-timers.[8] In the 15 percent of jurisdictions around the country still without full-time district attorneys, he or she remains a public official, albeit one with a separate private practice who has signed a contract with the county to handle its prosecutions.

Prosecutor offices tend to be fairly small. In 2007, almost 60 percent of full-time prosecutor offices served communities with fewer than 100,000 people, and the median number of lawyers in these offices was three: one elected DA and two assistant prosecutors.[9] Yet while most offices are small, most of the cases take place in larger counties with more professional departments. Barely 11 percent of prosecutor offices were in communities with more than 250,000 people in 2007, but these offices processed almost 60 percent of all felony cases; the 2 percent of offices in districts with over 1 million people alone handled over 20 percent of all felony cases.[10]

Two features of the modern prosecutor's office demand particular attention. The first is that the number of line prosecutors (those who actually try cases) has grown significantly over the past forty years, but in a somewhat peculiar way. From 1970 to 1990, the number of prosecutors rose by 3,000, from 17,000 to 20,000. From 1990 to 2007 (the last year of reliable data), the number of line prosecutors grew more than three times as fast, to 30,000. This is the opposite of what one would expect. Between 1970 and 1990, violent crime rates rose by 100 percent, property crime rates by 40 percent, and the number of line prosecutors by 17 percent. From 1990 to 2007, violent and property crime rates both fell by 35 percent, but the number of line prosecutors rose by 50 percent—a faster rate of growth than during the crime boom.

Given the data we have, measuring changes in the productivity of these prosecutors is tricky. Table 5.1 attempts to estimate it using four different proxies: index crimes per prosecutor, index arrests per prosecutor, index and drug arrests per prosecutor, and prison admissions per prosecutor.[11] Although none of these is a perfect measure of caseloads and productivity, all four show the same general pattern, namely that prosecutors worked harder and harder as crime rose throughout the 1980s, but then output per prosecutor held steady or declined throughout the crime drop. This

Table 5.1 Various Measures of Prosecutorial Productivity,
1974, 1990, and 2007

	Index Crimes per Prosecutor	Index Arrests per Prosecutor	Index + Drug Arrests per Prosecutor	All Arrests per Prosecutor	Prison Admissions per Prosecutor
1974	588	141	176	617	9
1990	725	145	200	710	25
2007	377	73	133	473	23

Sources: Data from John M. Dawson, "Prosecutors in State Courts, 1990," US Department of Justice, Bureau of Justice Statistics, March 1992, accessed August 24, 2016, www.bjs .gov/content/pub/pdf/psc90.pdf; Steven W. Perry and Duren Banks, "Prosecutors in State Courts, 2007—Statistical Tables," US Department of Justice, Bureau of Justice Statistics, December 2011, accessed August 24, 2016, www.bjs.gov/content/pub/pdf/psc07st.pdf; US Department of Justice, Bureau of Justice Statistics, "Arrest Data Analysis Tool," accessed August 24, 2016, www.bjs.gov/index.cfm?ty=datool&surl=/arrests/index.cfm; US Department of Justice, Bureau of Justice Statistics, "Data Collection: National Prisoner Statistics (NPS) Program," www.bjs.gov/index.cfm?ty=dcdetail&iid=269.

pattern could provide an important explanation for why felony filings rose as crime rates fell: there were simply more prosecutors. Even if individual prosecutors were no more aggressive than prosecutors in the past, the increase in staff size would lead to more cases even as crime declined.

The second is the magnitude of the discretion they wield. For example, prosecutors have the unreviewable ability to decide whether to file charges against someone who has been arrested, and they face almost no oversight about what charges to file if they decide to move ahead with a case. The US Supreme Court has made it clear that it will not regulate these sorts of decisions: in 1985, the Court said this bluntly in *Wayte v. United States*, calling the "decision to prosecute" something "particularly ill-suited to judicial review."[12] So while this power is not new—public prosecutors have had substantial discretion since their offices were founded—prosecutors appear to be using it in increasingly aggressive ways these days.

Over the years, legislators have expanded this discretion by giving prosecutors a growing array of often-overlapping charges from which to choose. For example, the Model Penal Code, drafted by the prestigious American Law Institute in 1962 as a framework to help states modernize their criminal codes, included exactly two degrees of assault: simple assault (for "bodily injury") and aggravated assault (for "serious bodily injury"). New York State, however, now has twenty-three or so assault offenses, many of which overlap. Take "Assault on a Judge," which is simply "Second Degree Assault" with the additional fact that the victim is a judge trying to perform his official duties.[13] Second Degree Assault is a Class D felony; on a judge, Class C. A prosecutor in New York facing a case that qualifies for Assault on a Judge can nonetheless charge the case as Second Degree Assault if he wishes. No one can review this, and the difference matters. The statutory maximum for a Class D felony is seven years, compared to fifteen for a Class C. By the choice of charge, the prosecutor can more than double the potential sentence a defendant faces.

While in New York the choice of charge only affects the ceiling (at one year, the minimum for a Class C felony is the same as for a Class D), in many states the choice of the charge can determine both the minimum and the maximum, which means that prosecutors can restrict judges to narrow sentencing ranges.[14] I once heard a retired DA tell a conference that he and his colleagues would figure out what the "just" sentence for a defendant was, and then try to pick the right set of charges to make sure the judge had to impose something close to that. One observer has gone so far as to joke that "one premise of mandatory minimums is that prosecutors are competent to decide appropriate sentences until they become judges."[15] We trust no one, except the prosecutor.

Prosecutors can use their discretion to be lenient, but there is basically no limit to how prosecutors can use the charges available to them to threaten defendants as well. Take the landmark 1978 Supreme Court case of *Bordenkircher v. Hayes*.[16] Paul Hayes wrote a fraudulent check in Kentucky, where the routine sentence at the time was two to ten years in prison. Owing to his prior criminal history, however, he qualified for a now-repealed repeat offender enhancement, which carried a sentence of life. The prosecutor offered Hayes a deal: plead guilty to the fraud, and he'd recommend a sentence of five years, but if Hayes insisted on going to trial, the prosecutor would invoke the repeat felon law and seek life. Hayes gambled, went to trial, lost, and received a life sentence. He appealed, arguing that such a disparity between the offer and the threat was coercive to the point of violating his due process rights. The Court disagreed, and the lesson of *Bordenkircher* is clear. No matter how unjust or uncommon the charge, if the facts fit, the prosecutor can charge it, or even just threaten to charge it.[17]

This is a tremendous amount of power for one official to have, and it is made all the more powerful by the fact that prosecutors generally wield it out of public view. Nearly 95 percent of the cases that prosecutors decide to prosecute end up with the defendant pleading guilty.[18] For all the courtroom drama we see on *Law & Order*, nearly everyone in prison ended up there by signing a piece of paper in a dingy conference room in a county office building, or in a dingier room in a local jail.

This lack of a public record actually makes it easy for prosecutors to look less aggressive than they are. A striking example comes from the federal system, where a single criminal act can implicate numerous overlapping statutes, some of which carry vicious mandatory minimums while others do not. Congress has recently set about trying to roll back some of these mandatory minimums, but the lobbying organization for federal trial lawyers, the National Association of Assistant United States Attorneys, has pushed back strongly. One of the NAAUSA's arguments is that the mandatory minimums should not be repealed because they are almost never used, but instead are saved only for the worst of the worst defendants.[19] At a simple level, the NAAUSA's argument appears correct, since few federal inmates have been sentenced to these mandatory minimums. But federal prosecutors often wield the threat of the mandatory minimum to persuade a defendant to plead guilty to a charge that doesn't carry such a stiff sentence. Using a gun during a drug deal can result in a mandatory minimum of up to thirty years under a particular statute.[20] A prosecutor, however, can tell a defendant that if he pleads guilty to just the drug charge, the prosecutor will make the gun disappear. The threat of thirty years is enough to terrify most defendants into agreeing.[21] So even if the mandatory minimum is rarely imposed, it is *used* much more often. But thanks to the plea process, the public almost never sees how prosecutors actually deploy it. If the public were able to observe how often federal prosecutors threaten relatively minor defendants with these mandatory sentences, there would (perhaps) be a backlash.

Plea bargaining not only shields prosecutors from accountability, it also makes them more powerful by allowing them to process more cases per year. Pleas can be resolved in a matter of days, compared to the weeks or months that would go into a trial. Most commentators admit that the criminal justice system in the United States would grind to a halt if plea bargaining were banned.[22] The handful of jurisdictions that have attempted to abolish plea bargaining have quickly given up, if they ever really stopped it at all.[23] Furthermore, plea bargains help prosecutors work around weaknesses in their cases. Even if the main case is weak, a prosecutor can come up with a set of charges and sentences that are more appealing to the defendant than the risk of something worse at trial. Given that defendants have almost no constitutional right to discovery during the plea process, prosecutors are often able to convincingly bluff with weak hands, especially given the sorts of threats that *Bordenkircher* allows and harsh sentencing laws facilitate.[24]

Taken together, these attributes and tools make prosecutors the most powerful actors in the criminal justice system. While the police determine who "enters" the criminal justice process, prosecutors have complete control over which cases they file and which ones they dismiss. If prosecutors decide to move a case forward, their choice of what charges to bring is limited solely by what they think they can prove—or what they think they can convince defendants they can prove. These charges in turn often place significant limitations on the sentences that judges can impose. Prosecutors are free to threaten whatever severe sanctions legislators have passed, and legislators have been happy to enact tougher and tougher laws. It's true that judges are required to sign off on pleas and can thus reject those they find unsatisfactory, but in general, they will acquiesce to the deals struck by the prosecutors and defense attorneys.

Prosecutors, as we've noted, have used this power to drive up prison populations even as crime has declined over the past twenty or so years. To date, however, no state- or federal-level proposal aimed at cutting prison populations has sought to explicitly regulate this power.[25] Everyone else in the criminal justice system currently faces reforms, such as efforts to change interactions between civilians and police, or to amend sentencing laws and parole policies. But prosecutors have remained untouched.

In a few cases, the ballot box has been used to try to regulate prosecutors, and voters have recently deposed a few individual prosecutors over concerns about excessive aggressiveness or other bad decisions. In 2016, Anita Alvarez lost her primary campaign to remain the state's attorney for Cook County, Illinois (Chicago), in part because many saw her as needlessly punitive, and more immediately because her office refused for over a year to file charges against Chicago Police Department officer Jason Van Dyke, who shot Laquan McDonald sixteen times.[26] In 2015, Scott Colom, a black Democrat, unseated longtime district attorney Forrest Allgood (a white independent) in northeastern Mississippi, running on a platform that Allgood was too tough on crime.[27]

These are among a handful of isolated examples, however; by and large, district attorneys are reelected with unfailing regularity. It's hard to view elections as a way to systematically regulate prosecutorial behavior. Yet other than a joint proposal by the American Bar Association and the NAACP Legal Defense Fund on how prosecutors can better address racial inequalities in the criminal justice system, few groups have proposed ways to systematically regulate the unreviewable power prosecutors possess.[28]

THE BLACK BOX

If we hope to rein in this increased prosecutorial aggressiveness, then it is essential to understand how it operates. Here, however, we hit a wall. Despite the power of prosecutors, there is almost no data or research on what drives them. Few scholars study prosecutors with any regularity, surely in no small part because of the lack of data we have on them.[29] Unlike the other branches of the criminal justice system, prosecutor offices are almost entirely "black boxes." So it is impossible to say with any strong empirical support why prosecutors filed more and more charges over the 1990s and 2000s, but there are certainly some plausible hypotheses that deserve our attention. Here are a few.

Increased Staffing

As we've seen, prosecutorial staffing rose more quickly during the crime decline than during the crime boom. It's unclear why this happened (in fact, I've never seen anyone even mention it), although the rise could be tied to the expansion in state fiscal capacity we saw in Chapter 4. That said, dig a little deeper and this story gets somewhat more confusing. The increase in staffing was likely concentrated in larger counties. Most offices are small, and thus lack either the resources or the need to add more prosecutors. Although a majority of cases are filed in the districts with larger offices that have more room to add staff, new evidence shows that incarceration has been growing the fastest in the smallest counties—those with populations under 100,000, which have the least capacity to take on new staff.[30] In other words, much of the increase in staffing since the 1990s likely took place in counties whose incarceration rates grew the slowest or declined, which complicates a "more prosecutors means more prisoners" story.

Perhaps more relevant was the rise in the number of offices with any full-time prosecutors, which as we saw before went from under 50 percent in the early 1970s to 85 percent by 2007. Unlike staffing increases, the shift from having a part-time to a full-time prosecutor's office almost surely took place entirely in rural counties, where we now see the most rapid prison growth. No one has rigorously examined this effect at this point, so we can't do more than speculate, but the theory is certainly a plausible one.

Tougher Sentencing Laws

Strike laws, other repeat offender laws, mandatory minimums, gun enhancements, long maximum sentences: all these make the prosecutor's threat to go to trial riskier for the defendant, and they serve as additional cards the prosecutor can offer to drop during the plea process in exchange for a deal. William Stuntz has argued that legislators likely pass tough sentencing laws *hoping* that prosecutors will use them only as threats to get (less-harsh) plea deals rather than imposing them with any regularity.

If prosecutors actually sentenced most defendants to the maximums the legislatures make available, the political and financial costs could be too high. As long as prosecutors simply use the tough laws as bargaining chips, not real punishments, legislators can reap the political benefits of looking tough on crime while avoiding difficult financial decisions. At the same time, in those cases where someone receives something less than the maximum and then recidivates in a particularly bad way, legislators can blame prosecutors for not using the tougher laws the legislature had passed. Moreover, many statutory maximums are harsher than what prosecutors themselves think is generally just.[31] If that is true, prosecutors will gladly offer pleas below the maximum they could seek at trial, as it allows them to resolve cases more quickly *and* impose sentences they think are more appropriate.

Longer Criminal Records

Crime rose significantly over the 1970s and 1980s, and the decline was slow enough that more crimes were committed during the first decade of the decline than in the last decade of the boom. As a result, from the 1970s through the 2000s there was a growing cohort of people with criminal histories, perhaps extensive ones.[32] Furthermore, even though crime and arrests have declined since the 1990s, the number of felony cases, and thus the number of felony convictions, has continued to rise, implying that the number of people with such records has grown even as crime has fallen. If prosecutors tend to be more aggressive against defendants with longer criminal histories—less likely to drop charges, more insistent on higher bail amounts, more likely to seek prison time, and so on—then prosecutorial charging decisions could have become harsher without much change in overall attitudes.

A Weakened Opponent

The American legal system is built on the belief that truth and justice are best achieved adversarially, with strongly partisan advocates fighting hard for their clients in front of relatively neutral and passive judges and juries. Who is the prosecutor's "adversary"? In almost every case, it's a lawyer provided by the state or county government.

In *Gideon v. Wainwright* in 1963, and in *Argersinger v. Hamlin* in 1972, the US Supreme Court held that anyone facing prison or jail time is entitled to a lawyer.[33] The *Miranda* warning line used in a thousand TV and movie police procedurals has made this idea famous: "You have the right to an attorney; if you cannot afford an attorney, one will be provided to you." This is a critically important right, since about 80 percent of defendants in serious criminal cases need a state-provided lawyer.[34] States vary in how they meet this requirement, but the solutions tend to fall into two broad categories: appointed counsel and public defenders. Appointed counsel are lawyers with their own private practices who are also paid by the government, often at remarkably low hourly rates, to represent indigent defendants.[35] Public defenders are lawyers for whom defending indigent clients is a full-time job; some are government employees, and others work for private contractors who are hired by the government.

The striking thing about public defense is that even though almost all defendants need it, state and local governments spend relatively little on it. In 2008, state and local governments spent $4.5 billion on indigent defense—about 2 percent of the over $200 billion they spent on all criminal justice activities.[36] That $4.5 billion is almost 30 percent less than the $5.8 billion that went to state prosecutors in 2007.[37] Moreover, prosecutor budgets understate prosecutors' competitive advantage, since unlike defense attorneys, prosecutors do not have to pay for their investigative services, which are provided directly by the police, sheriffs, and other law enforcement agencies. A study in North Carolina found that accounting for these sorts of services effectively tripled the amount spent on prosecution in that state.[38]

While real spending on indigent defense did rise over the 1990s and 2000s, by about 4 percent per year, it apparently wasn't enough to keep up with the 40 percent increase in felony case filings that occurred over the same period, and we now face a crisis in indigent defense. Caseloads for public defenders nationwide exceed what is manageable; in some jurisdictions, defenders spend only minutes with their clients before deciding whether to accept a plea deal.[39] Counties around the country are now embroiled in lawsuits about inadequate indigent defense.[40] The situation has gotten so bad that the public defender office in New Orleans simply stopped taking certain serious cases—including murders—on account of its inability to represent the defendants adequately. The American Civil Liberties Union immediately sued the state to provide more resources, which might have been the public defender's goal in declining cases in the first place.[41]

Public defenders are thus increasingly overwhelmed, while prosecutor caseloads appear fairly stable. Prosecutors also have the advantage of being able to regulate their caseloads more than public defenders can. A prosecutor's office can simply start dropping minor cases, while the public defender must take whatever cases the prosecutor decides to file. In such an environment, it isn't surprising that prosecutors would be able to convince more and more people to plead guilty. Public defenders simply lack the time and resources to explore whether their clients have viable defenses. They may not be able to effectively argue against cash bail or for a lower bail amount, they may not have the time to stand firm long enough to get a better deal, and so on, all of which works to the prosecution's benefit.[42]

In *Ordinary Injustice*, the lawyer and journalist Amy Bach provides a disheartening account of the failures of indigent defense. She writes about the time she spent watching criminal cases in Greene County, Georgia, a county of about 20,000 people. Greene County had one public defender, Robert Surrency, who also had a private practice on the side. Surrency was all about speed: at one point, Bach watched him plead out forty-eight clients in a row. In later interviews with various defendants, she realized that in his haste Surrency had missed critical mitigators and defenses. This was not entirely, or even mostly, Surrency's fault. His caseloads were unmanageable—he even privately contracted with a second lawyer to handle some of the formal pleas so he could meet with other clients at the same time—and his budget didn't pay for expert witnesses or even investigators. In the end, a prosecutor in Greene County went so far as to admit that, "You can mete out a lot more mercy as a prosecutor than as a defense attorney."

Improved Policing

Perhaps prosecutorial toughness is not just driven by the prosecutors. While police clearance rates haven't budged that much over the years, perhaps the arrests the police are making are now of a higher quality. This improvement could have taken place for several reasons. Perhaps police have become more professional, so prosecutors are less likely to receive cases marred by shoddy investigations, by evidence that can't be used because of unconstitutional searches, and so on. It could also be that police simply have better evidence now, such as DNA test results and more extensive camera footage (police car dash-cams, body cameras, security cameras, cell-phone cameras). It's easy to imagine that defendants presented with security camera footage of the crime will plead out far more quickly than those who think they are only facing one or two unreliable witnesses. Unfortunately, there's simply no data on the quality of arrests or of the cases that prosecutors file.

Changing Political Ambitions

This is a speculative theory, but an intriguing one. Almost all prosecutors are elected, but those elections often seem like foregone conclusions. Incumbents rarely face challengers, and when they do they usually win. One scholar has gone so far as to say that we've come to view district attorneys like civil servants, voting them in regardless of whether crime is going up or down.[43] This practice would seem to make them relatively insensitive to electoral pressures.

What if, however, we're thinking about the wrong election? What if prosecutors aren't tough on crime to retain their seats as district attorneys, but in order to win something bigger, such as state attorney general, governor, US representative, senator? There is almost no data on this, but there are suggestive anecdotes of political ambition. Dan Donovan, the former district attorney for Staten Island, ran unsuccessfully for state attorney general in 2010, and successfully for Staten Island's open House of Representatives seat in 2014. The former governor of Pennsylvania, Ed Rendell, started as the district attorney for Philadelphia, serving for two terms until he ran unsuccessfully for governor in 1986; he later became mayor of Philadelphia and eventually governor. Going further back, both Earl Warren and Thomas Dewey ran high-profile campaigns—for governor of California and president of the United States, respectively—in part based on their accomplishments as prosecutors.[44]

Of course, district attorneys have been elected officials in most states for over a century now, so we need to ask what changed in recent years that may have made them *more* ambitious. The obvious answer is rising crime. The surge in crime from the 1960s to the 1990s surely elevated the social and political status of prosecutors. Just think of how popular culture generally valorizes prosecutors, such as in the long-running *Law & Order* franchise (which premiered at the peak of the crime wave, in the fall of 1990). It could be that as the officials spearheading the war on crime, district attorneys have seen their political options expand, and this has encouraged them to remain tough on crime even as crime has fallen. After all, a scandal resulting from being too lenient could derail a career; being too punitive (within reason) has traditionally been much less likely to do so. A tough stance on crime could also preserve political support from groups such as police unions that could help turn out the vote for the next campaign.

This is the sort of theory that makes studying prosecutors both exciting and infuriating. On the one hand, we can come up with provocative ideas that point to fascinating explanations for prosecutor behavior. On the other hand, we have so little information on prosecutors that in the end we can do little more than that: speculate, offer a few anecdotes, and move on.

This lack of data, by the way, should not just infuriate scholars who want to peer inside a black box. It should alarm all of us as a case of democratic failure. Prosecutors are profoundly powerful. We should not be forced to guess why they do what they do, or why their behaviors or attitudes have changed over time. Prosecutors should be as closely studied, examined, pushed, and prodded as any other government official. That they have not been is deeply troubling.

INCENTIVES ARE EVERYTHING

The unfettered nature of prosecutorial discretion is to some extent unavoidable. Prosecutors' jobs may be almost unmanageable without a substantial degree of discretion.[45] At the same time, discretion always raises concerns, and prosecutors are the only actors in the criminal justice system who have successfully held on to almost all the discretionary power accorded to them. Fears of racially motivated behavior and excessive leniency, for instance, have led to substantial restrictions on judges and parole boards, and similar fears of racial bias and misconduct have led to (lesser) restrictions on the police as well.

There is no real reason for prosecutors alone to avoid regulation. In fact, several options available to policymakers and voters to regulate prosecutorial discretion have all proven inadequate. It is worth examining why.

What If You Held an Election and No One Showed Up?

Originally, prosecutorial elections were intended to reduce the risk of corruption that came with appointments and to make sure prosecutors were more accountable to the public. It's unclear if elections ever accomplished these goals; for our purposes, we can say with certainty that there are real problems with elections today.

One of the only studies to look at prosecutorial elections yielded fairly bleak results.[46] Prosecutors running for reelection win about 95 percent of their primary and general election campaigns, owing in no small part to the fact that 85 percent of the races are unopposed in both the primary and general elections. When incumbents face challengers, their prospects fade a bit, but they are still likely to win; they come out ahead in 64 percent of their contested primaries and 69 percent of their contested general elections. In larger jurisdictions, which process more cases, the contested-election win rate for incumbents is even higher, at around 80 percent.

Even in contested races, turnout is often low. In 2013, Brooklyn's twenty-year incumbent district attorney, Joe Hynes, faced a bitter primary challenge amid allegations of wrongful convictions and the under-prosecution of sex crimes among Brooklyn's insular Hasidic community (which voted consistently for Hynes). Hynes lost the primary election, becoming the first sitting Brooklyn DA to run for reelection and lose in over a century.[47] Yet despite the high stakes, only about 20 percent of the borough's registered Democrats turned out to vote.[48] Meanwhile, in Cleveland in 2012, there was a race for an open district attorney's seat during a fairly close presidential election, when turnout should be high. About 482,000 people in Cuyahoga County voted, but 165,000 of them, or over 34 percent, simply left the prosecutor ballot blank.[49]

Given apparent voter apathy, we shouldn't be surprised that prosecutors serve long terms in office. Few perhaps serve as long as Henry Wade in Dallas (thirty-six years) or Robert Morgenthau in Manhattan (thirty-four years), but a 2005 survey by the Bureau of Justice Statistics reported that 72 percent of district attorneys had served at least five years (implying at least two four-year terms), and 40 percent had served at least twelve.[50] Turnover is slightly higher in larger jurisdictions, but that does not reflect a stronger electoral check, just that there are more reasons for these prosecutors to leave office voluntarily, such as for higher office, or for more lucrative private-sector jobs.

Making matters worse, when there are contested races, they rarely focus on broad penal policy. Because voters lack information on general outcomes, elections turn on a few big cases or a particularly shocking (and thus likely nonrepresentative) scandal. There are a few instances where challengers appear to win based on broad claims about how the office should be run, but these appear to be rare.[51]

Prison Beds for Free

Perhaps if electoral checks fail us, budgetary ones can save us. After all, even if prosecutors face little direct political oversight, they have to get the money to operate from somewhere. Whoever controls the purse strings should be able to exert at least some influence over the prosecutor.

Yet even here prosecutor offices manage to escape regulation. Prosecutors exploit, perhaps not even always intentionally, a gigantic moral hazard problem that arises from the way legal authority and financial responsibility are (poorly) allocated in the criminal justice system. Like jails and probation, prosecutor offices are either entirely or predominantly funded out of county budgets—unlike prisons, which are paid for by the state.[52] The reason for this division is not immediately clear, but the implications are readily apparent: there's no real financial limit on prosecutors' ability to send people to prison.

In fact, it's worse than that. Prosecutors get all the tough-on-crime political benefit of sending someone to prison, but the costs of the incarceration are foisted onto the state as a whole. This alone should make a prosecutor overuse prison, even if unintentionally. That the alternatives—misdemeanor probation or jail time—are paid for by the county only exacerbates the problem. For the prosecutor, leniency is actually more expensive than severity, and severity is practically free. This problem has likely persisted for so long because, until recently, state legislatures had little incentive to address it, if they even noticed it at all.[53] As we've seen, prior to the 2008 financial crisis, prison costs weren't large enough to justify the costs of reining in spending. Even now, prison costs—especially marginal costs—are not that large a share of state budgets, which could help to explain why this issue still gets little attention.

Even if legislators wanted to tighten the purse strings to rein in prosecutors, they may not have sufficiently precise tools to truly punish overly aggressive prosecutors. In Oregon, for example, the state legislature sets the district attorneys' salaries, while most other budgeting matters are left to the counties. Yet the salary "stick" is a very crude one, since the legislature has only two options: setting one common salary for the district attorneys in the ten "urban" counties (currently $116,868) and one common salary for the remaining twenty-six less urban counties (currently $99,288).[54] So if one or two rural county prosecutors become particularly aggressive, the state cannot single them out for reactive salary cuts. To do so, they would have to revamp the budgeting statute, and that would surely result in strong prosecutorial pushback.

Now, this moral hazard problem didn't cause the surge in incarceration, since it existed long before prison populations started rising in the 1970s. But it certainly facilitated whatever other factors made prosecutors more aggressive. This problem is also a good reminder that we miss a lot when we think about prisons as state-level institutions. It is true that *prisons* are run by the states, but *prisoners* come from the counties. The goal is not to reduce the number of prisons, but the number of prisoners; to do that, we have to understand what is happening at the county level far more than the state level. Incarceration, like politics, is local.

The Executive Hydra

For all its dysfunction, one thing can be said in favor of the federal system: it has a unitary structure. In the end, everyone reports back to a single person, the president. The president appoints the attorney general; and all US attorneys, the head of the Bureau of Prisons, the director of the FBI, and the heads of all the other federal criminal justice agencies report to the attorney general, another cabinet secretary, or the president. In practice, many of these officials have a lot of autonomy, but the president can nonetheless exert a certain amount of direct control over the federal criminal justice system as a whole.

By contrast, in the state systems almost no one is in control. The police respond to a directly elected city mayor. The prosecutor is directly elected by the county. The governor is elected by state voters and often controls the parole process, but state-level law enforcement is run by the state attorney general—who in most states is directly elected by state voters as well, and thus not under the control of the governor (and perhaps is even antagonistic toward the governor, if he or she has eyes on the governor's mansion).

Even within counties, authority is diffuse. Since the prosecutor is directly elected, the county executive and other county officials cannot tell him or her what to do. This leads to situations like the following:

> In Sierra County, California authorities had to cut police services in 1988 to pick up the tab of pursuing death penalty prosecutions. The County's District Attorney, James Reichle, complained, "If we didn't have to pay $500,000 a pop for Sacramento's murders, I'd have an investigator and the sheriff would have a couple of extra deputies and we could do some lasting good for Sierra County law enforcement. The sewage system at the courthouse is failing, a bridge collapsed, there's no county library, no county park, and we have volunteer fire and volunteer search and rescue." The county's auditor, Don Hemphill, said that if death penalty expenses kept piling up, the county would soon be broke.[55]

This reads as if a death penalty case is a natural disaster, an unavoidable financial hurricane that leaves shattered county services and infrastructure in its wake. But, of course, it isn't. The prosecutor *decides* whether to seek the death penalty. Yet no one, even among county officials, can force him to take into account the costs he imposes—and here, even the DA tries to make it seem like the decision to seek the death penalty is out of even his hands, which is rather disingenuous.

Even more centralized states exhibit peculiar fiscal fractures. In New Jersey, for example, prosecutors are appointed by the attorney general, who is appointed by the governor—which is as close as any state gets to a unitary executive. Yet in New Jersey the county pays for the state-appointed prosecutor's budget, and if the prosecutor feels like the budget is too small he can go to (state) court to sue for more funds.[56] As a result, counties admit that they try to accommodate the demands of their locally funded, state-appointed prosecutor.

This is a dispiriting state of affairs. Spending on prosecution crowds out spending elsewhere, but it is probably unreasonable to expect a prosecutor to ask for a smaller budget in the name of better schools, or for someone to run against an incumbent on a platform of fewer prosecutions in order to improve the sewer system. Nor should we expect voters, already poorly informed about what the district attorney is doing, to vote based on complicated budgetary tradeoffs.

A centralized executive exists to decide how best to allocate limited funds across various bureaucracies. The lack of centralization, or even coordination, within the states' criminal justice systems is the sort of boring "structural" issue that gets far too little attention in the reform movement, despite the fact that budget constraints can be powerful tools of control, and their absence an all-too-eager accomplice to severity.

PROSECUTING RACE

So far we've examined how prosecutors have used their discretion to push up the prison population. Let's now pivot to look at how they can (mis)use that discretion in other problematic ways, particularly when it comes to race.

We need to start with an important concept from psychology called the "fundamental attribution error," which refers to the fact that we tend to define people we don't know by their actions. If someone I don't know gets in a fight in a bar, it's because he *is* aggressive; if I get in the same fight, however, it's not a reflection on my character but is instead the product of stresses in my life, like problems at work or home. It's an easy mental shortcut, because I know what's happening in my life, but not in his.

In his incredibly important *The Condemnation of Blackness*, the historian Khalil Gibran Muhammad does not use this exact term, but in effect he describes how the fundamental attribution error plays out when it comes to race and crime.[57] Charting how Americans have discussed crime from the immediate post–Civil War era to the present day, he points out that when a white person commits a crime it is often seen as an individual failing, but when a black person commits a crime it is viewed as an indication of the broader failings of black Americans in general. This is the fundamental attribution error writ large, operating at both an individual and social/racial level (that is, at the level of how one racial group classifies the behaviors of another group).

These racial biases need not be conscious, as is made clear by the extensive literature on "implicit racial bias," which refers to the way people—whites and blacks alike—often harbor unconscious biases toward minorities. It is easy to see how these biases, conscious and intentional or not, can shape the way prosecutors allocate their time and energy. Prosecutors may view crimes committed by black people as more serious than the same offenses committed by otherwise identical white people, for the reasons that Muhammad illuminated: they interpret them as indications of deeper community-wide social pathologies that need to be "controlled." They may see their more aggressive response in minority areas, if they are even aware of it, as a social good, even if it is anything but. This effect may also explain why, as some studies demonstrate, police appear to concentrate enforcement efforts in black neighborhoods with seemingly fewer social ills than other equally dangerous—or more dangerous—predominantly white neighborhoods.[58]

Elsewhere in the criminal justice system our concerns about these sorts of biases in enforcement have led to restrictions on discretion, such as sentencing guidelines for judges or consent decrees restricting police stops. Prosecutors, however, face no such constraints, despite the fact that they surely suffer from similar biases. In fact, that whiter, wealthier suburbs exert significant influence on who gets elected as district attorney likely amplifies the impact of the problem. The selection process almost ensures more social distance between prosecutors and the neighborhoods where they handle most of their cases, which increases the risk that prosecutors will exhibit the biases Muhammad describes and thus be overly aggressive in minority communities.

ON PROSECUTORIAL REFORM

While prosecutors may need some, perhaps a fair amount, of discretion in order to do their jobs, some sort of regulation is clearly needed. So far, however, almost none is being proposed. It's therefore time to start focusing more directly on what such regulations should look like. In this section, we'll start by looking at two reform options that have actually been adopted, although each by just a single state. One receives almost no attention at all, despite the fact that most states could adopt it; the other is the subject of constant attention, even though it would be much tougher for other states to implement. We'll then look at a few more possibilities, even if right now they are nothing more than theories.

The Prosecutor's Guidebook

Alone among the states, New Jersey has imposed guidelines on prosecutors, at least when it comes to pleading out serious drug cases. In the 1990s, as part of a decades-long dispute with the legislature over how much sentencing power the legislature was effectively giving prosecutors, the New Jersey Supreme Court limited prosecutors' almost wholly unreviewable power during plea bargaining to set a defendant's minimum prison sentence under the state's Comprehensive Drug Reform Law. Arguing that lower courts had to be able to ensure that such decisions were not made "arbitrarily and capriciously," the Court ordered the state attorney general to develop guidelines for prosecutors that defined acceptable plea bargains for certain parts of the drug code; trial judges could then review pleas for compliance.[59]

After several years of trial and error and relitigation, the state attorney general eventually drafted a comprehensive set of guidelines. Called the *Brimage* Guidelines, they run over one hundred pages and look almost exactly like sentencing guidelines that many states use to regulate judicial sentencing.[60] The guidelines provide a grid, with the charged offense on one axis and the defendant's prior criminal history on the other, and each square on the grid provides an approved range of sentences the prosecutor can offer during the plea process.[61] The guidelines also list aggravating and mitigating factors that allow (and sometimes require) the prosecutor to offer less or more generous plea deals, and they discuss how to handle cases where the evidence is particularly weak or where there are extraordinary reasons to depart from the guidelines' approved range.

These guidelines appear to have received almost no attention outside of New Jersey.[62] Perhaps people just assume that what works in a state with appointed prosecutors could never work in a state with elected ones. But that line of reasoning does not convince. The guidelines should work as long as the judges are willing to enforce them, and as long as defense attorneys have enough time and resources to complain to judges when prosecutors fail to follow them. Unfortunately, there seems to be little rigorous data on how well the guidelines are working even in New Jersey. The New Jersey attorney general, however, has since issued plea guidelines for offenses beyond drug crimes, including sexual assaults, DWIs, and shoplifting, which suggests that they are viewed as effective, although none of the other guidelines exhibit nothing close to the rigor and detail of the *Brimage* guidelines.[63]

There is, however, at least one reason to be concerned about the impact of such guidelines. For all the good that judicial sentencing guidelines have done, one persistent criticism of them is that they transfer significant power to prosecutors.[64] By choosing the specific offense to charge, how many offenses to charge, and how many prior crimes to invoke, prosecutors have often been able to confine judges to very narrow ranges of possible sentences. At first blush, plea bargain guidelines do not appear to solve this problem. Prosecutors still seem free to choose the charges and thus the ranges of acceptable plea bargains to offer. In fact, one can see how prosecutors could use the guidelines aggressively: "I'd like to offer you a better deal, I really would, but look what the guidelines say . . . "

This criticism, however, is less about prosecutorial guidelines in general than it is about how they may be written in practice. If guidelines set the default ranges for most offenses below what prosecutors had been demanding before, require that certain additional facts must be shown for borderline cases to result in prison admissions, and establish a generous set of mitigators that defense attorneys can raise before judges, then they will be able to push down prison populations. They may also be able to ensure that pleas are more consistent across race, age, and other factors we think shouldn't be taken into account when imposing sentences.

The risk is that poorly designed guidelines may make things worse. If the mean sentence is set higher than before, for example, punishments may become more severe. This happened in New Jersey. Before the guidelines went into effect, prosecutors in urban counties had been offering much more generous deals than those in suburban or rural counties; when the guidelines were adopted, the ranges available to prosecutors were more in keeping with the harsher suburban deals than with the more lenient urban ones, effectively "suburbanizing" plea offers.[65]

Guidelines can also unintentionally exacerbate racial disparities, as New Jersey also discovered at first. The initial, pre-*Brimage* version of the guidelines made it harder for urban prosecutors to plead around "school-zone" enhancements, which elevate the sanctions for selling drugs close to a school (usually within about 1,000 feet). These laws are generally viewed as having disparate racial impacts. Minorities are more likely to live in denser urban areas—in no small part because of redlining and exclusion from more suburban areas—and the denseness of cities means that school zones cover a greater fraction of cities than they do nonurban areas. Seventy-six percent of urban Newark, for example, falls within a school zone, compared to just 6 percent of rural Mansfield Township.[66] Members of minority groups who sell drugs are thus more likely to do so within a school zone than (less urban) whites are, even if they are not trying to sell to schoolchildren. It soon became apparent that restraining urban prosecutors' ability to avoid the enhancement in cases where it seemed inappropriate was exacerbating racial disparities with New Jersey's prison population.

Neither of these problems, however, was impossible to fix. While the guidelines remain somewhat controversial, subsequent revisions have addressed concerns both about general severity and about racial disparity.[67] New Jersey thus demonstrates that it is certainly possible to regulate how prosecutors perform one of their most influential and least transparent tasks.

California's Experiment

California's effort to regulate prosecutors has been quite different from New Jersey's, focusing on budgetary incentives rather than targeting prosecutorial behavior directly. These reforms appear to have been quite successful at scaling back incarceration, at least in the short run; the long-run prognosis remains unclear.

At the start of the 2010s, California faced a correctional crisis. Between 1980 and 2006, its incarceration rate quintupled, from around 100 per 100,000 to nearly 500; with its prison population at over 175,000 people, its share of US prisoners had risen from below 8 percent to above 11 percent. The state opened twenty-one prisons between 1984 and 2005 to handle the increase, but by 2005 its capacity was only up to about 80,000—less than half the number of people the system was actually holding.[68]

Conditions in California's overcrowded prisons were deplorable. Inmate litigation eventually led a panel of three federal judges to find that overcrowding so reduced physical and mental health coverage that there was one preventable death about every five to six *days*. The panel ordered California to reduce the number of prisoners to below 137.5 percent of the system's capacity—through new construction, out-of-state transfers, large-scale releases, or whatever else the state could come up with. The US Supreme Court ultimately upheld the order, and California moved to make serious changes.[69]

The state's answer was to adopt the Public Safety Realignment Act of 2011 (or just "Realignment"), one of the most dramatic criminal justice reforms in the United States in decades. Realignment sought to ensure that only serious offenders ended up in state prison by making counties responsible for incarcerating low-level offenders. Though not framed as such, it was a direct strike at the budgetary moral hazard problem of free prison space. The core idea behind Realignment is fairly straightforward. A defendant classified as a "triple non"—someone convicted of a crime that is not violent, nor serious, nor a sex offense that requires registration as a sex offender, and who has no violent, serious, or registration-requiring prior offenses—has to serve his time in a county jail, even if his conviction is for a felony.[70] Realignment also shifted some parole supervision to county probation, stated that parole violators could be returned to prison only if they committed a new crime (a major change in a state that had unusually high rates of parole violators returning to prison), and required judges to give defendants even more credit for pre-conviction time spent in county jail when setting a post-conviction sentence.[71]

Some of the offenses that fall within Realignment's jail-not-prison list are not ones that immediately seem "less serious," such as vehicular manslaughter while drunk, involuntary manslaughter, possession of an assault weapon, and brandishing a firearm and causing serious bodily injury, among others.[72] By necessity, there are exceptions throughout each of the major provisions, but Realignment nevertheless represents a major shift of obligations onto the counties. Under Realignment, the prosecutor remains free to seek out the statutory maximum for these less serious offenses—which for many is three years, although some carry maximum sentences as high as at least nine—but in theory the county picks up the tab. The hope is that prosecutors will start to ask if incarceration is really worth it for these lower-level cases.

There are, however, two reasons to worry about Realignment's ability to really make prosecutors pay attention to these budgetary issues. First, counties argued that their jails were ill-equipped to handle increases in inmates and that they needed assistance from the state government to expand them. So far, at least twenty-eight of California's fifty-eight counties have received a total of $1.7 billion in state aid for this purpose.[73] Unfortunately, following a similar move by the legislature, the voters in California approved a referendum making these state subsidies permanent.[74] Which, of course, undermines a lot of the potential moral-hazard-solving effects of Realignment. The state is still picking up at least some, if not most, of the cost of housing prisoners. Second, as we've seen, it isn't always so clear how much prosecutors even care about county budgets, despite being county officials. If prosecutors simply storm ahead, then counties will likely just incur increasing costs unless they vote such prosecutors out of office.

These caveats aside, Realignment appears to have produced at least a significant one-time shock to California's prison system. Within the first year of the program, prison populations dropped by about 30,000, at which point they held steady, and even rose slightly, until November 2014, when voters approved Proposition 47. That proposition reclassified certain drug and property felonies as misdemeanors, causing another decline in the state prison population. Jail populations rose a bit during the first year of Realignment as people who previously would have been sent to prison ended up in jail instead, but ultimately California's overall prison and jail incarceration rate appears to have declined, at least for now.[75]

So far, Realignment does not appear to have led to any real increase in California's crime rates. One sophisticated study showed that Realignment did not change California's violent crime rate at all, and there was only a small increase in property crime (compared to what it otherwise would have been), which was almost entirely due to a relative increase in auto theft; a follow-up study a few years later by other social scientists suggested that even auto-theft rates had leveled off.[76] Fewer prisoners, and no real increase in crime, especially in serious crime.

As with prosecutorial guidelines, there is no reason other states could not attempt to "localize" punishment in much the same way that California has. It appears, however, that only one other state has tentatively followed in California's footsteps, and only to a small degree. Indiana recently passed a law holding that those convicted of the lowest-level felony could not be sent to state prison, but had to be sent instead to local jails or community programs.[77] But this appears to be the lone effort to copy Realignment. The conditions that induced California to adopt Realignment were fairly distinctive: it was a response to exceptional overcrowding and exceptional federal judicial oversight. Moreover, California's state political system was completely controlled by Democrats during this time; Democrats have held the governor's mansion since 2011; they controlled 62 percent of the Senate and 65 percent of the House in the 2011–2012 term, and they then won supermajorities in both chambers in the 2013–2014 term. This unified power likely gave California more freedom to act on such a sensitive issue than more divided state governments might have.

Prior to Realignment, California (again) experimented in the 1970s with another way to tackle this moral hazard problem, offering counties subsidies for diversion. The Probation Subsidy Act of 1965 offered counties $4,000 for each defendant who was supervised by (county) probation rather than sent to (state) prison.[78] The program was discontinued in 1978 for a host of reasons, but before its end it was thought to have encouraged counties to divert as many as 45,000 people.[79] Its spirit survives today in the form of justice reinvestment grants, which similarly try to reward local governments for policies that save the state government money.

To the extent that prosecutors pay attention to county budgets, efforts that make them pay attention to the costs they externalize onto the state, whether by making them feel those costs more directly (like with Realignment) or rewarding them when they avoid the costs (like with probation subsidies), should help rein in incarceration, at least somewhat. But that caveat is far more important than it should be

The *Brimage* guidelines and Realignment appear to be the only two major state-level efforts to directly regulate prosecutor behavior (although individual counties may have tried other approaches). So let's think instead about other options that states could consider to rein in prosecutorial aggressiveness.

Mocking the Constitution

If nothing else, states (as well as the federal government) could attempt to regulate prosecutorial behavior by making sure that public defenders and other lawyers for the indigent can do their jobs.

In many ways, this may be the most logical solution. It may be hard to ever really rein in prosecutorial discretion, and not just because legislators will consistently have incentives to give them a lot of power. If powerful prosecutors with wide discretion are going to remain a fixture of American criminal justice, then perhaps we should at least make sure that our nominally adversarial system is in fact adversarial. As things stand now, however, those who defend the indigent simply lack the resources to do their jobs.

While Americans appear to generally believe that all people are entitled to counsel, we don't want to pay for it. In a 2000 survey, only about two-thirds of respondents agreed that the state should pay for poor people's lawyers, and initially only 17 percent thought we should increase funding for indigent defense, a number that rose to only 33 percent after some discussion.[80] Public defense is so poorly funded that in forty-three states, poor defendants are required to pay some or all of their defense lawyer's costs: state provided, defendant funded.[81] The result can be truly unjust. In South Dakota, poor defendants are required to pay $92 an hour for a public defender, and payment is due even if the defendant is found not guilty. Failure to pay is itself a crime that can result in the defendant getting locked up.

So a poor person is arrested, and the public defender convinces the prosecutor that the arrestee was across town at the time of the crime; the defendant is factually innocent. The prosecutor drops the charges, but if it took the public defender ten hours to make the case, the defendant—by definition quite poor—now owes the government nearly $1,000. The very act of acquiring the lawyer needed to establish innocence can result in the defendant committing the crime of not paying that lawyer back.

Making the poor pay for their own constitutionally required lawyer is a mockery of everything the constitutional right to counsel stands for. But in our era of austerity, it is likely that states and counties are even less willing to increase spending on indigent defense than before. This is one area where the federal government could make a big difference. In light of local resistance to funding indigent defense, the federal government could be the agency best able to push through more spending for it. Doubling national spending on public defense would require a grant of about $4 billion per year from the federal government—about 0.4 percent of the $1.3 trillion discretionary federal budget. In other words, a rounding error, but one that could transform how most indigent defendants are represented.[82]

Threat Mitigation

Another way to limit prosecutorial aggressiveness would be to restrict the threats they can make during plea bargains. The easiest way to do this would be to cut statutory maximums. This type of reform may not change time served much, since prosecutors regularly bargain around the maximums anyway, but it could weaken their bargaining power somewhat. The effect of cutting statutory maximums, however, is hard to predict. It's true that threats based on the draconian mandatory minimums in the federal system certainly seem to have some impact, but states often lack laws nearly so harsh even before the recent reforms. As always, the distinct lack of data on the plea bargaining process makes it difficult to say anything more.[83]

There are other, less direct ways to regulate the threats of long sentences made during plea bargaining. Stuntz, for example, proposed a way to target "pretextual" threats that a prosecutor makes during the plea process but that the prosecutor himself likely doesn't think are right or fair or just. Stuntz suggested that prosecutors be required to make public the sentences they have threatened to seek if a defendant did not take the plea.[84] If a threatened sanction is the sort that is rarely, if ever, imposed in similar cases—if the prosecutor threatens to seek twenty years for a crime that almost always faces no more than five years when taken to trial—then a judge could refuse to accept the plea on the grounds that it is too coercive.

The appeal of such a reform is that it doesn't require the legislature to cut the statutory maximum, something that could be politically difficult to do. Of course, the obvious risk is that prosecutors might seek tough sentences at trial *more often* just to preserve the threat for plea bargains. Still, it is a reform worth considering.

Crimes and Misdemeanors

Rather than changing the back-end sentence lengths, another way to restrict who prosecutors send to prison is to change the front-end admission rules. States can simply redefine offenses that were once felonies as misdemeanors, and misdemeanors as violations, making it impossible for defendants charged with the crimes to end up in prison (for felonies turned into misdemeanors) or perhaps even jail (for misdemeanors turned into violations).

Some states have, in fact, started implementing changes such as these. California's Proposition 47 in 2014 raised the dividing line between misdemeanor and felony for various property crimes to $950, up from as little as $450 or even lower.[85] Now, if someone steals a single $600 iPhone, it is simply impossible for a prosecutor to send him to prison, even in the absence of Realignment.[86] South Carolina similarly raised the minimum for felony theft from $1,000 to $2,000, and Mississippi raised the same minimum from $500 to $1,000. Many states have revised their drug codes to raise the quantity of drugs that trigger felony convictions too.[87]

These sorts of front-end reforms may have a bigger impact than reforms aimed at time served, especially since most prisoners already serve much less time than the current statutory maximums allow. Moreover, by keeping people out of prison entirely, rather than shortening the time they spend there, this type of reform reduces the collateral costs that come from going to prison, like lost jobs, frayed relationships, reduced health, and so on.

So far, however, this strategy has been limited to property and drug crimes, since those are the easiest areas of reform for politicians and the general public to accept. These offenses also have the advantage of having clear, objective cut-off points. It's easy to adjust quantitative lines for "how much was stolen" or "how many grams were sold." It's less clear how that might be done for violent crimes. Many criminal codes differentiate among death, serious bodily injury, and bodily injury, but it is hard to see how to draw more precise lines than that. States could, however, still redefine some violent felonies as misdemeanors. This idea is not as implausible as it may sound. New York State's definition of second-degree assault, for example, overlaps significantly with Illinois's definition of aggravated assault, yet in New York second-degree assault is a felony, while many aggravated assaults in Illinois are misdemeanors.[88] Such low-level reclassifications will only get us so far, however, since many violent crimes will clearly remain felonies.

Finally, a related reform issue that is discussed far more than it should be is the "overcriminalization" debate, which argues that instead of reclassifying felonies as misdemeanors, we should eliminate entire sections of the code that criminalize conduct that shouldn't be criminal at all.[89] Some reformers often point to ridiculous laws, like those making it a crime to fail to pick up a dog's waste in some national parks in Minnesota, to label pasta that is more than 0.11 inches thick as "spaghetti," or to sell a toy marble without a label stating that it is a toy marble.[90] Obviously, these things should not be crimes, and if unnecessary laws can be eliminated easily and quickly, we should repeal them. But for all the attention they might receive, such changes would do little to change the realities of incarceration and punishment generally. Especially at the state level—which has far fewer of these sorts of criminal laws than the federal system—local prosecutors have their hands full dealing with politically "mandatory" crimes like murder, arson, assault, rape, theft, and so on. These are the crimes that grab voters' attention, and that are used to measure how "safe" a city is.[91] Stripping the code of "crazy" crimes will have almost no impact on arrests, prosecutions, convictions, and prison populations.

Flying Blind

Even if legislatures are unwilling to directly regulate prosecutors or curtail their power and discretion, they could at least help us better understand how prosecutors wield the authority they have. We have extensive data on crimes, arrests, and prison populations, but when it comes to prosecutors we have next to nothing. We have no reporting systems for prosecutors similar to the Uniform Crime Reports for the police and the National Prisoner Statistics for prisons. We have no comprehensive data on such basic issues as the number of cases resolved by plea bargaining, the number of cases dismissed by prosecutors or judges, or the demographics of line prosecutors—and how those might interact with the demographics of defendants or defense counsel. The data that we do have on prosecutors, such as the number of felony cases filed in state courts, generally come from other bureaucracies, such as the court systems. The Bureau of Justice Statistics has a few datasets that examine the prosecutorial process, but they are surveys of only some jurisdictions, and sometimes cover only a small part of the year. It is, in short, impossible to know what is consistently happening across counties over time.

It's unclear why prosecutors remain such black boxes. One reason could be their relative invisibility. Police are highly visible at all times, and their interactions with the public, for good or ill, frequently grab our attention. Judges, in turn, are the ones we often see actually imposing sentences, with TV perhaps making their role seem more central than it is in a world dominated by plea bargaining. Prosecutors sneak through unnoticed.[92]

The lack of information about prosecutorial decision making could also be more intentional. For example, many states currently use or are working to adopt some sort of uniform ID number that a person would receive upon arrest, which would allow observers to link the records of his arrest, prosecution, trial, sentencing, and parole. A state corrections official once told me that his state had tried to adopt such an ID number, but that the bill had died due in no small part to opposition from the state prosecutors' lobby. He provided no more detail than that, but I have to assume it was at least in part to thwart transparency.

There are also more mundane reasons for our ignorance, such as the fact that a majority of prosecutor offices have only two or three lawyers and a few support staff; nearly 15 percent of all offices do not even have a full-time prosecutor.[93] Smaller, understaffed offices, some of which are not yet very computer-savvy, will not be able to generate much rigorous data. But while most prosecutor offices are small, a majority of *prosecutions* take place in large offices based in large counties—the sort of offices that do make sophisticated use of computers and already gather extensive data for internal use.[94]

Whatever the reasons for it, the lack of data makes it nearly impossible for scholars, policymakers, and voters to understand what prosecutors are doing, why they are doing it, and what we can do to change problematic behavior. An obvious, though ultimately tricky, way to reform the system would be to insist that prosecutors provide more data to the public, or at least to have the BJS gather such data and to produce reports comparable to what is done with the Uniform Crime Reports and the National Prisoner Statistics.

Once it has been collected, the information produced could help reformers and legislators identify more precisely what prosecutors are doing improperly and why they are doing it, and thus help them address the problems effectively. Statistics could also provide a powerful impetus for self-regulation. Take fiscal or racial impact statements: simply producing such reports could make prosecutors more aware of problematic outcomes.[95] Even if they are already aware of (and perhaps indifferent to) various problems, being forced to make such reports public could lead prosecutors to adopt preemptive reforms, if only to avoid bad press.

By now, it should be clear that there is a rather shocking gap at the heart of the Standard Story's take on criminal justice reform. Although some reforms limit prosecutorial power to at least a small degree, there have been no efforts, certainly not at the state level, to comprehensively control prosecutors' ability to send people to prison. Promisingly, discussions of the power of prosecutors and the need to regulate their behavior seem to be coming up with greater frequency of late, but we have yet to see any meaningful reforms. That must change.

CHAPTER SIX

THE BROKEN POLITICS OF PUNISHMENT

E VER SINCE THE COLONIAL PERIOD, AMERICANS HAVE HELD punitive attitudes toward crime.[1] The rising crime rate of the 1960s through the 1980s served only to harden this tendency, and as a result Democrats and Republicans have competed for years to appear as tough on crime as possible. California's notoriously harsh three-strikes law, until recently the most severe in the country, was a bipartisan effort.[2] Bill Clinton lobbied for and signed a raft of tough-on-crime laws during his eight years as president. And there's plenty of evidence that elected judges from both parties tend to be harsher than appointed judges, and that they become harsher still as elections near.[3]

The assumption that politicians must always be tough on crime, however, is now faltering. A few tough-on-crime prosecutors have lost elections, and surveys of even staunchly conservative voters, suggest that Americans increasingly favor "smart" responses to crime, such as diversion programs, treatment for nonviolent offenders, and greater use of parole.[4] Legislatures, too, have been passing more and more reforms. As states watch both prison populations and crime rates decline together, the political opportunity to roll back harsh criminal and sentencing laws grows stronger. But at least two major political threats loom, and they are either underappreciated or almost completely ignored by reform groups.

First, as we've touched on many times, responsibility is fractured across various city, county, and state agencies, and it is often hard for these different bureaucracies to coordinate their actions. Reforms at one level can be thwarted by parties at other levels, or one agency may not undertake effective reforms if the bulk of the benefit goes to a different one. There have been only a few steps taken to address these schisms.

Second, and more problematically, reforms are not confronting the political defects that encourage overly aggressive enforcement in the first place. When examined closely, the American political system has been built (albeit unintentionally) to overreact to increases in crime and to underreact to decreases. No one, however, seems to be trying to fix the system's design flaws. Instead, reformers are just relying on the fact that legislators are open to reforms right now due to the unique circumstances in which we now find ourselves (falling crime rates, tight budgets). If crime starts to really rise again, which almost certainly will happen at some point, there's nothing to prevent legislators from rolling back the current reforms and overreacting once more.

In fact, there is historical precedent for this kind of cyclical overreaction. In 1970, Congress passed the Comprehensive Drug Abuse Prevention and Control Act, which, among other things, abolished almost all the existing federal mandatory minimums for drug crimes. One of the law's defenders, who emphasized the need to abolish these mandatories, was a Republican representative from Texas: George H. W. Bush.[5] Later, as both vice president (1981–1989) and president (1989–1993), Bush helped reintroduce and expand federal mandatory drug sentences. And in 2016, Congress is working hard to abolish many of those same mandatory minimums for drug sentencing that Bush opposed and then supported. If we fail to change the broader political controls over how criminal laws are passed, we should expect Congress to bring back again whatever mandatory minimums it eliminates now. In fact, concerns over opioid abuse have already led some senators to introduce new mandatories even as their colleagues try to abolish others.[6]

This analysis does not just apply to legislators. Prosecutors, judges, and police face equally skewed incentives to take punitive approaches and to shun "smarter" ones. Current low crime rates have provided these officials with the same breathing room that legislators have, but the risk of future overreaction remains. Still, there is reason to be optimistic. Legislators and others can make changes today that will help limit excesses down the road. There is even some intriguing empirical evidence that legislators may *want* to tie their hands in this way. This is the time to fix the underlying causes of this (predictable) overreaction, but there has been little or no effort along these lines. This, too, needs to change.

A CULTURAL AND IDEOLOGICAL SHIFT

As we've seen throughout this book, the term "criminal justice system" is a misnomer; criminal justice is, at best, a set of systems, and at worst it is a swirling mess of somewhat antagonistic agencies. A person's path from crime to prison to release passes through a sprawling, poorly co-ordinated web of competing bureaucratic actors, each responding to different incentives put in place by different sets of constituents: city police, county prosecutors, state or county public defenders, state or county judges (who may be elected or appointed), parole boards appointed by the governor, and so on, each operating under laws passed by state legislators elected in local districts, and each usually paying only a portion of the costs they impose. It's hard to imagine that anyone would have created a system that looks like this on purpose. Unless we think carefully about the various cracks that run through these systems, we will overlook important defects that have caused, or at least facilitated, the steady expansion of prisons.

We've seen a lot of these problems already: legislators who pass tough sentencing laws in order to look tough on crime while trusting prosecutors to plea bargain around them; richer, whiter suburbanites with control over law enforcement in poorer, disproportionately minority neighborhoods; county prosecutors who can avoid dealing with the costs of incarceration by sending people to state prison; and, as we'll see shortly, cities that take advantage of this moral-hazard problem by hiring too few police officers. These sorts of problems permeate criminal justice in the United States, and they are generally unremarked upon.

There are at least two steps that reformers can take to mend these sorts of schisms. The first step would be to regulate the discretion of the local actors, such as by adopting plea-bargaining guidelines or enacting Realignment-like policies that push some of the costs back onto the counties. These types of reforms would limit the ability of county actors to undermine reform efforts or to exploit the fissures that exist. These risks of circumvention are real. Take South Dakota, which in 2013 passed a reform bill that aimed to reduce prison populations. The law did lead to prison declines in 2014 and 2015, yet at the same time prosecutors responded by charging more people with generally low-level felonies, and over these two years total felony convictions rose by 25 percent. As the one major study of the bill makes clear, these convictions put the prison reductions at risk.[7] Even if prosecutors in South Dakota are not actively seeking to undermine the reform bill—the report is silent as to why prosecutors have been filing more felony cases—their unfettered discretion essentially enabled them to do so.

The second step would be to incentivize agencies to adopt policies that save resources overall, even if the agency that establishes the policy does not benefit directly. That agencies receive only a fraction of the benefit (or bear only part of the cost) of their own policies is in fact one of the few structural defects that has garnered attention. The Justice Reinvestment Initiative (JRI), a program spearheaded by the US Department of Justice's Bureau of Justice Assistance and Pew Charitable Trusts, has attempted to rectify this problem by rewarding agencies for the benefits they create, or the costs they save, for other criminal justice bureaucracies, thus encouraging them to implement more efficient policies. In the absence of such a program, resources will be consistently squandered. A dollar spent on police, for example, is far more effective at reducing crime than a dollar spent on prison and likely causes fewer collateral costs, and yet we have increased spending on prisons far more than on police.[8] This hasn't happened because city officials are unaware of the impact of policing; it's that the prospect of hiring police officers is unattractive to towns and cities because it is expensive. Pension commitments can last for decades, and local finances can be quite variable year to year. It's cheaper for cities to skimp on policing and rely more on incarceration, because the cities can foist that cost onto the state. This is particularly so given that policing seems to take up a bigger share of city budgets than incarceration does of state budgets.[9]

As things stand, cities and counties will continue their overreliance on state-funded prisons, undersupplying the local crime prevention programs they are expected to fund, such as probation regimes, drug courts, substance abuse treatment programs, diversion options, and police training. The local jurisdictions may make some efforts, but as long as a chunk of the benefit goes to the state in terms of lower prison costs, they certainly won't do enough. The JRI program thus attempts to return some of the cost savings that cities and counties generate for the states back to these more-local governments. Oregon, for example, used JRI to reinvested $58 million that it saved in reduced incarceration into, among other things, county-level public safety programs. All told, as of 2014, the seventeen states involved in the initiative had reinvested more than $165 million to improve various state and local programs.[10]

The JRI is a promising development, even if its scale is still quite small.[11] It is not, however, without its drawbacks. JRI savings are almost always reinvested in other criminal justice agencies, for example, even though sometimes—maybe often—it would be better to invest in schools, mental health services, public health agencies, and the like.[12] Crossing such institutional lines surely would entail serious bureaucratic and administrative challenges, but if we think about the solutions to crime solely in terms of "criminal justice," we significantly limit our options. Outside of the JRI, however, there have been few, if any, efforts to really bridge the fissures running through the myriad criminal justice systems across jurisdictions. Coordination is all too rare, to the point that the *New York Times* had a headline in 2014 grimly stating, "In Unusual Collaboration, Police and Prosecutors Team Up to Reduce Crime."[13]

ALL PUNISHMENT IS LOCAL

Current reform efforts have typically taken a top-down approach, trying to change at the state level the official rules under which criminal justice actors operate. This approach, however, may be backward; perhaps we should take a more bottom-up approach, focusing less on the formal legal rules and more on changing the political incentives of prosecutors and others to use the tools already at their disposal. If, say, prosecutors faced sufficient political pressure to be less punitive for some crimes, we wouldn't need state-level reforms to force them to change.

Of course, changing the political incentives of prosecutors and judges yields improvements that are much more tentative than a major reform bill and that are vulnerable at every election. The successes would be scattered and local, and they would not offer a clear "moment of victory" like a bill-signing. Moreover, these "attitudinal" reforms would require constant monitoring and prodding. But for all these weaknesses, the impact of bottom-up changes would likely be much greater than that of top-down legislative reforms. To understand how to change political incentives, though, we need to look more carefully at the (local) politics of punishment.

There are two somewhat contradictory strands in most discussions of the politics of crime and punishment. One attempts to explain why the American public became so much more punitive starting in the 1970s or so; the other laments the disconnect between the American public and its elected leaders, pointing out that the former tends to embrace rehabilitation, while the latter favors punishment.[14] Unfortunately both of these accounts of the politics of crime have taken too grand a perspective. Most of the discussions about the criminal justice system and the attitudes of the American electorate have focused on broad, cultural struggles, tying them to a more general conservative shift that came about in reaction to feminism, civil rights, and other social upheavals of the 1960s and 1970s.[15] These claims get a lot right. But to understand the politics of crime, we also need to think smaller—perhaps a lot smaller. Viewed more locally, these two perspectives—which produce an increasingly punitive public that isn't really that punitive—are not as contradictory as they may initially seem. Americans did become more punitive, but politicians also overcompensated in response, going further than the public really wanted them to.

Rather than focusing on what has changed, we should look instead at some things that haven't. Specifically, there are four interrelated—and admittedly hard-to-repair—defects in the politics of crime that predate the rise in incarceration and that explain why elected leaders are consistently, predictably harsher in their attitudes than the people who vote them into office. Taken together, these four defects impede efforts at reform, and if left unaddressed they almost certainly ensure that any future increase in crime will cause an overreaction similar to the one that seems to finally be receding.

Defect 1: The False-Positive Problem

No amount of reform will seriously curtail police and prosecutorial discretion; it probably shouldn't even try to. Substantial decarceration will always need these officials to use their discretion in different ways. Yet police, prosecutors, judges, and parole boards all face skewed incentives that encourage them not to show leniency even if they want to. I'll focus on prosecutors here, but the problems apply equally to all these officials.

When deciding whether or not to charge someone with a crime, or whether to seek prison time or something less restrictive, prosecutors can make two types of errors. In some cases, they will fail to send someone to prison who should have been sent there, and that person will commit a future crime that could have been prevented if only the prosecutor had been more aggressive. Call this a "false-negative" result (the person was incorrectly identified as not being a risk, with "not risky" being a "negative" result).[16] Conversely, they will treat some people as high risk who are not, and thus lock up some low-risk people who could have successfully remained in the community. These outcomes are "false positives." The goal of the criminal justice system is to balance, in some way, the costs from both of these types of mistakes.

In theory, we should be more concerned by false positives (being overly harsh) than false negatives (being too lenient). As Voltaire, William Blackstone, and Ben Franklin all said, in slightly different ways, "it's better that ten guilty go free than that one innocent person be convicted."[17]

In practice, however, even if a prosecutor personally subscribed to this view, the realities of politics push him in the opposite direction. A false negative—diverting or not charging someone who goes on to reoffend—is potentially much more costly to a prosecutor than a false positive. It's easy to see why. The costs of a false negative are immediate and salient. Those of a false positive are nearly invisible and abstract. In the case of a false negative, there is an identifiable offender and an identifiable victim of the resulting crime, as well as an identifiable official at whom voters can direct their anger. The media and political opponents can ask, "Why did you release Bob? Why did you expose Mary—here's a picture of her with her two cute children—to the risk of victimization?"

This is no hypothetical. The *Washington Post* ran an article in 2016 on a man in Washington, DC, who had served time for robbery and committed a serious sexual assault after absconding from parole. A comment by a local resident demonstrated the political problem:

> "I want to know why he was out. He has a violent background. He has clearly targeted women in the past," said Denise Krepp, an advisory neighborhood commissioner who lives half a block from the scene of the crime. "So who made the decision that he should be out on the streets?
>
> "And I want a name. Because someone is responsible for this."[18]

The head of DC's Metropolitan Police Department echoed this concern: "Sometimes, we just scratch our heads," DC police Chief Cathy L. Lanier said. "We feel like there's a revolving door for violent offenders. It's very frustrating for us because we see the victim, and we see the impact on the victim." The false-positive cases are so much harder to see. One cannot point to any specific non-offender. How do you identify people who are in prison but would not have offended had they been released? It's a profoundly difficult counterfactual, unlike the case of Bob, where we can easily say that if Bob had been in prison, Mary would not have been victimized.

Difficult, but not impossible. We can identify, statistically, that certain pools of people are being detained too long or too often. It is possible to say, "Look, according to [hypothetical] Table 5, we can predict that 90 percent of those in Risk Group A would not have been rearrested within five years of release." We cannot say that any one detainee in particular wouldn't reoffend, but we can say that a certain bunch of people belong to a group that, on average, is quite unlikely to reoffend, and that, on average, it is needlessly costly to lock them up.

Of course, to any elected official, "This is Mary, victimized by Bob thanks to your policies," is far scarier than "Table 5 suggests you were too harsh and wasted taxpayer money." The salience and emotional impact of errors are asymmetric, and politically aware prosecutors (and judges, and parole officials) will respond accordingly. The false-positive problem also interacts with the budgetary free-riding problem in toxic ways. Judges and prosecutors are already inclined to over-punish to avoid the risk of a false negative blowing up a reelection campaign. That they don't have to pay the costs of sending the defendant to prison only strengthens this incentive.

Defect 2: The "Willie Horton Effect"

Voters care a lot about crime, but they do not pay much attention to criminal justice outcomes. They have a poor understanding of how criminal justice operates, and they have a surprisingly weak grasp of how crime rates move up or down.[19] A 2014 Gallup poll, for example, reported that between 2001 and 2014, the fraction of respondents saying that crime had risen since the previous year went up from 41 to 63 percent (peaking at 74 percent in 2009), despite the rate of violent crime falling almost every year during that time, for a total decline of about 30 percent.[20] When it comes to crime, Americans are, to use academic jargon, "low-information, high-salience" (LIHS) voters: they do not pay much attention to the routine, day-to-day facts, but instead vote based on one or two particularly shocking—and thus salient, but likely not representative—cases.

In his book *Courtroom 302*, Steve Borgia provides a good example of this reality.[21] In 1998, Chicago judge Daniel Locallo faced what was initially a straightforward retention election until he ran into an unexpected complication: he found himself presiding over an attempted-murder trial in which the defendant was the son of a politically powerful figure with strong ties to Chicago's Italian criminal underworld. As the case heated up—one witness disappeared, another turned up dead—Locallo suddenly found that the family of the defendant had launched a campaign to unseat him in his upcoming election.[22]

In many ways, Locallo's retention election became a referendum on how he handled one shocking (and also racially charged) case, with almost no reference to the hundreds, if not thousands, of other cases that should have defined his accomplishments (or lack thereof) over the six years since his previous election. (The voters ended up retaining him.) We've seen how the same problem plagues prosecutor elections. These elections are infrequently contested, but when they are, the debates focus on one or two high-profile successes or failures, or one or two particularly egregious scandals.[23] The more mundane cases are ignored, even though they matter so much more in the aggregate. Voters don't ask about them, and prosecutors don't really talk about them.

The problem posed by LIHS voters in criminal justice is so well-known—and feared—that it has a name: the "Willie Horton Effect." As governor of Massachusetts in the 1980s, Michael Dukakis had presided over a furlough program, one he didn't create but supported, that allowed select inmates to leave prison for brief periods in order to help them prepare to reenter society. It was considered a success, with over 99 percent of those furloughed returning to prison without incident.[24] No one knows that, however. In fact, the program likely would have operated in almost total obscurity, even within Massachusetts, had it not been for one of those less-than-one-percent-of-all-cases failing in a particularly shocking, salient way.

In 1986, William "Willie" Horton absconded from the program, and about a year later, he viciously assaulted a man and repeatedly raped the man's fiancé during a brutal home invasion in Maryland. When Dukakis ran for president in 1988 as the Democratic nominee, the campaign of his opponent, Republican vice president George H. W. Bush, released a powerful attack ad saturated with racist overtones (Horton was black, both his victims were white), using the Horton case to argue that Dukakis was soft on crime. All it took to discredit the program, as well as the politician who simply supported it, was one high-profile failure.

In hindsight, it's now clear that in this particular case, the ad had little effect on the campaign.[25] Politicians, however, absorbed the broader point: that in an LIHS world, no amount of success can top one spectacular failure. Why take that risk, especially if there is so little reward for the successes, as evidenced by the fact that Americans continue to think that crime is rising despite sustained declines.

Defect 3: Geography

Another defect in the politics of punishment, one we have seen time and again in this book, is the complicated interaction of race, geography, and punishment.[26] In general, people are pulled in two directions: they want to see those who offend punished to ensure their own safety, but they don't want to see their friends, neighbors, and family members suffer the costs of avoidable or unjust punishment. One partial explanation, then, for why prison populations remained stable prior to the 1960s is that those who lived in high-crime urban neighborhoods—Irish, Italians, and other white immigrant communities—also tended to have political control over them, or at least over the local police and prosecutors. Those in charge of enforcement felt both the costs of unprevented crime and the costs of unnecessary punishment. In the postwar era, however, the Irish, Italians, and other whites began moving to the suburbs, while blacks—who were excluded from the suburbs—continued moving to northern cities as part of the tail end of the Great Migration. These shifting demographics, however, were not reflected in the criminal justice system, which continued to be dominated by whites.[27] Those who exerted power in the criminal justice system were no longer bearing the brunt of the costs associated with either crime or enforcement. At first, the new suburbanites were indifferent to urban crime, and enforcement actually declined even as crime rose in the 1960s. The urban riots of the 1960s and 1970s, however, galvanized suburban voters. And because those suburban voters didn't feel the costs of enforcement, they overreacted, at times strongly.

This situation persists today. The suburbs remain disproportionately white, continue to face substantially lower crime rates than cities, and still exert undue influence on who is elected to prosecute disproportionately urban crime. The result, predictably, is overly aggressive prosecutorial behavior. Although we have little data on how prosecutors make their decisions, it's reasonable to assume that when they are deciding whether to file charges, they will put more weight on the benefits of safety (as desired by white suburbanites) than on the costs of wrongful convictions or excessive punishment (which is more of a concern for black urbanites—who obviously value and campaign for safety, but who are also more aware of the costs of enforcement).[28]

Defect 4: Prisoners of the Census

As we touched on earlier, the US Census faces the tricky issue of deciding where to count prisoners as residing: the area where the prison is located, or the areas where the prisoners lived before they were locked up. A lot turns on this decision, since counting prisoners as "residing" where the prison is located effectively transfers thousands of people from more urban areas to less urban ones. In New York State in 2011, for example, 48 percent of the state's prisoners came from New York City alone (which was home to 42 percent of the state's population that year), and 65 percent came from New York City and the counties containing Buffalo, Rochester, Yonkers, and Syracuse (the state's next four largest cities). Yet only seven of the state's fifty-seven prisons are in those counties, and some of those seven are relatively small minimum-security institutions.[29] This pattern is repeated nationwide. Yet in all but four states (California, Delaware, Maryland, and New York), prisoners are counted as residents of the counties in which they are incarcerated.

This policy results in greater political power for nonurban politicians, and thus for more conservative parties. Outside of Maine and Vermont, people in prison cannot vote, so counting them as residing in the areas where they are imprisoned creates a rightward ideological shift, since a majority of prisoners are black or Hispanic, and blacks and Hispanics tend to vote for Democrats.[30] Counting prisoners as residing in more rural, whiter, and thus more conservative counties while denying them the vote effectively bolsters conservative representation at the expense of liberal representation. In some cases, this Census system is essential for Republican political survival. Before 2010, Republicans in New York State fiercely resisted efforts to count inmates as residing in their former counties because they knew it could lead to redistricting that would hurt their narrow edge in the state senate. Tellingly, New York adopted such a law in 2010—which, was one of only two recent years that the Democrats controlled both chambers of the legislature and the governor's mansion.[31]

Similar issues arise in other states. One study, for example, pointed out that several nonurban state senate districts in Pennsylvania had enough people to satisfy the federal requirements for proportional representation only as a result of counting their prisoners—prisoners who disproportionately came from that state's cities.[32] Sometimes, the results almost defy credibility, especially in small towns. Perhaps the most remarkable is that of Ward 2 in Anamosa, Iowa. Most wards held about 1,400 people. Ward 2 had only 58—and a prison. One of its councilmen won his seat with a total of *two* write-in votes.[33]

This effect does have limits. In New York, each state assembly district contains almost 130,000 people and each state senate district more than 300,000.[34] The largest prison in New York, the Clinton Correctional Facility, has a capacity of just under 3,000—or about 2 percent of an assembly district population and 1 percent of a senate district population. New York, though, is a fairly population-dense, low-incarceration state. In a higher incarceration, less densely populated state, such as Texas, a large prison can make up as much as 12 percent of a district's population.[35]

The Census problem is one of the few criminal justice issues that we can solve pretty easily, at least in theory. All a state (or county for county representatives, or city for city council seats) needs to do is pass a law refusing to count inmates as residing in the districts where they are imprisoned. Of course, in practice this change will be difficult to accomplish, since one party, the Republicans, will fight it. It's unsurprising that the Democratic Party is consistently powerful in the four states that have changed their approach.

Representatives from districts with prisons would still have other incentives to fight reform—such as avoiding the loss of jobs—and the Census issue does not address this problem; even without the Census bump, local politicians still benefit from having a prison in their area. Even if the real economic benefit from a prison is slight, it is perceived as being significant, and those employed by prisons will still lobby hard against reform.

ALL FOUR DEFECTS—THE FALSE-POSITIVE PROBLEM, THE WILLIE Horton effect, the problem of geography, and the problem of the Census—have played important roles in creating the criminal justice challenges of today. They pushed the system to be excessively punitive as crime rose in the 1960s and 1970s, and their persistence to this day remains a serious barrier to reform. These defects continue to give political actors strong incentives to overreact to rising crime and weak incentives to change behavior in response to falling crime rates.

To be clear, these political problems alone did not cause mass incarceration; in fact, each long predates mass incarceration. When other attitudes changed, however, these four defects helped to fuel the systematic overreaction that took place across the United States. So correcting these defects will be essential to creating durable reforms that can survive the pressure to overrespond to unavoidable crime increases in the future. Reform bills must pay more attention to the routine politics of punishment.

THE DEMAND FOR PUNISHMENT

These four political defects alone could only exacerbate, not cause, the nationwide overreaction that led to mass incarceration. Hence, it is essential to ask what else occurred that changed the political incentives of the police, the prosecutors, the legislators, and others involved in the criminal justice system. The immediately obvious answer is "crime," which, as we've seen, soared between 1960 and 1991. The story of how crime caused this overreaction, however, is not as obvious as it may seem.

Most Standard Story accounts of the politics of punishment downplay, almost to the point of ignoring, the rising rate of crime in those decades. They view the reaction against crime as an elite-led, top-down affair rather than an organic, populist, bottom-up response to a pressing social crisis. Rather than looking to crime, these arguments point to a host of other social upheavals at the time—the civil rights movement, feminism, the oil crisis of the 1970s, and so on—and claim that the government used crime policy as a way to navigate these broader political and cultural shocks. The "New Jim Crow" hypothesis, for example, claims that crime control was used as a way to roll back the gains won by the civil rights movement.[36] The "end of modernity" theory argues that the challenges and unrest of the 1960s and 1970s gutted the public's faith in the "modern state," at least in the United States and the United Kingdom. People lost faith in the government's ability to provide for them through an effective and efficient welfare state, and the government tried to justify itself by saying it could "protect them from" threats—like crime.[37]

There's much to be said for these theories.[38] The rise of Donald Trump in the 2016 presidential campaign, for example, certainly bolsters the "end of modernity" claim. Some studies have found that in times of substantial social disruption, a significant fraction of voters are drawn to authoritarian leaders like Trump—those politicians whose views are "simple, powerful, and punitive."[39] And there's no doubt that criminal justice policy was used at times to push back against minorities. Blackness and criminality have been closely linked since the end of the Civil War, so an attack on "crime" would easily be understood by many as a critique of black Americans and their push for social inclusion.[40] As Nixon adviser John Ehrlichman chillingly explained in 1994, looking back on the early 1970s, "We knew we couldn't make it illegal to be either against the war or black, but by getting the public to associate the hippies with marijuana and blacks with heroin, and then criminalizing both heavily, we could disrupt those communities."[41]

Standard Story theories on the politics of punishment therefore posit that rising incarceration rates have been part of a somewhat cynical effort by those at the top levels of government to manipulate voters. One prominent study suggested that instead of being responses to the public's fear of crime, government anticrime efforts are what cause the public to fear crime in the first place.[42] And rising incarceration is not caused by rising crime, according to this argument, but is instead the result of purely political *choices*. To bolster this argument, Standard Story accounts often look to Western European countries and Canada, many of which saw substantial increases in crime during the 1970s and 1980s but without similar increases in incarceration. Many of them also saw crime drop in the 1990s, still without large prison populations. All of which supposedly provides evidence that mass incarceration was not driven by rising crime rates but instead was just a policy choice.[43]

Not surprisingly, there are several critical flaws with this account. The first is that the political reaction to crime was much more bottom-up than many think. The study most widely cited for showing that government programs were driving fear of crime more than they were responding to it used a fairly delicate measure of this relationship, namely the correlation between crime policies and whether voters ranked crime as their "number one" concern at the time.[44] It's easy to imagine this measure of fear being more responsive to policies than to underlying crime rates. Voters may have always held crime in the top two or three spots on the list of things that scared them, but a new, well-publicized anticrime campaign could push that fear from second or third to first.

A new study, however, weaves together richer measures of the public's fear of crime, looking beyond just those cases where crime was the "number-one" issue, and it tells a very different story: the public's fear of crime, and thus its punitiveness, moved roughly in sync with crime rates.[45] Punitive attitudes grew stronger over the course of the increase in crime. They also continued to grow for a few years after crime began to decline—but that's understandable, since crime statistics come with a lag, and so it wasn't clear in 1991 or 1992 whether crime had really begun to drop. Several prominent criminologists at the time were also vocally warning—incorrectly—that a wave of "superpredators" was right around the corner, which also kept fear of crime high.[46] Yet by the mid-1990s, people's fear of crime had started to decline; as a general rule, public punitiveness has tracked crime, and prison growth in turn has tracked punitive attitudes.

As crime grew over the 1970s and 1980s, then, people adopted harsher and harsher attitudes toward crime, and prison growth increased accordingly. As crime dropped, people became increasingly less concerned about crime, and prison growth slowed. To be clear: over the 1990s, as people's fear of crime declined, prison populations didn't *fall*, but they did grow at ever slower rates, as we saw in Figure 4.1. Crime leads to fear leads to tough penal policies: it's far more a bottom-up story than a top-down one where penal policies lead to fear.[47]

The second flaw in the "incarceration is just policy" claim is that it glosses over institutional differences between the United States and Europe. In a tautological sense, the number of people a country sends to prison is always a policy choice, since policymakers have complete control over it. If politicians wanted to abolish prison, they could do so tomorrow, although they would face serious political costs. Those costs are important. Simply comparing the relationship between crime and prison in the United States to that in other countries ignores the fact that the political system in the United States is structured in a way that makes it harder for politicians to respond to rising crime in a nonpunitive manner.

Our politicians may be more sensitive than European policymakers are to citizens' fears about crime in part because they are often more directly accountable to the public than many European policymakers are. Moreover, our durable history of racism may make rising crime seem more frightening to white voters than it is to Europeans, or at least it may ensure greater rewards (or fewer risks) for politicians who crack down on poor minority communities.[48] The decentralized, disaggregated nature of punishment in the United States also makes it harder for any legislature or governor to quickly or unilaterally slow down prison growth.[49] And don't forget the four defects described above.

Furthermore, the rough similarity between US and European crime rates breaks down in one key area: a crime victim in the United States is significantly more likely to end up dead than one in Canada or Europe, particularly as the result of gun violence.[50] The probability of being killed in the United States is still quite low—likely lower than what the average voter thinks, thanks to media sensationalism—but comparatively it is still quite high. The fear that any crime could result in death plays an outsized role in our politics of crime. As a result, we demand much tougher punishments in the United States not just for crimes like murder, but for other crimes where murder *could* happen, such as robbery and burglary. This fear of lethal violence explains why New York and Mississippi both treat burglary of a residence—even of an empty house, and even if the burglar is unarmed—as a violent crime, since the risk of serious harm permeates our stereotype of what a burglary looks like and makes the crime feel much more inherently violent.[51] In other words, American politicians did not simply "choose" to respond to rising crime more harshly. Or at least framing it that way blinds us to factors like electoral accountability and fears of deadly violence that constrain the choices available to them.

The third problem with the top-down, "just a policy" perspective is that it ignores the real scope of the growth of crime, and especially how it interacted with punishment early on. Between 1960 and 1991, official violent crime rates rose by almost 400 percent, and property crime rates by almost 200 percent. Even if crime rates were higher in 1960 than the official statistics suggest, we still saw a tremendous increase in crime over those thirty years—and it's less than the official increase only because things were already *worse* at the start of the upswing in offending. It's hard to believe that such an upheaval would have no effect on people's fears and the policies they would demand.

Recall, however, that as crime started to rise significantly, punishment in the United States, including incarceration, actually declined. Think back to Figure 3 in the introduction, which plotted the incarceration rate not as "per 100,000 people," but as "per 1,000 property crimes" and "per 1,000 violent crimes." When measured that way, the incarceration rate *decreased* over the 1960s and was flat throughout the entire 1970s, even as crime steadily rose. As William Stuntz pointed out, that sort of disconnect between crime and enforcement was sure to produce a popular backlash, which it did.[52]

The full implications of this political story for our situation today are unclear. Pessimistically, it appears to reinforce the idea that prison reform is tolerable only as long as crime rates stay low. Politicians react to crime because they are democratically compelled to do so, and the electorate's views on the need to be punitive seem to track crime rates. There is, however, an optimistic take, too: if people's attitudes about the need to be punitive change—or if we are able to change them—then politicians do not appear to be as likely as the Standard Story suggests to try to rile up punitiveness for their own purposes.

SAFETY FIRST?

Perhaps surprisingly, even liberal reform groups tend to employ rhetoric that reinforces the problematic politics of crime control. Like everyone else, they consistently, if implicitly, define safety as the most important value. Pew frequently releases reports showing how many states have seen both prison populations and crime decline.[53] The Brennan Center for Justice's proposed Reverse Mass Incarceration Act makes clear that states would not qualify for federal grants unless they both reduced prison populations and avoided increases in their crime rates (or at least avoided large increases).[54]

While it is essential to appreciate just how much we've gained from the twenty-five-year crime drop, these approaches have an unexpectedly old-school, 1980s-style tough-on-crime feel to them that is unfortunate. This "safety-first" approach is actually bad social science. We've seen that punishment imposes substantial costs not only on offenders but also on their families and their communities and a safety-first approach puts far too little weight on these costs. Why doesn't Pew compare trends in decarceration with, say, children who no longer have a parent in prison, instead of the crime rate? Why doesn't Brennan insist that federal funding only go to states whose decarceration policies lead to better employment opportunities for those released from prison, or better opportunities and outcomes for the state's children?

I'm not naïve. I understand the politics. Groups working closely with legislators probably cannot ask them to put their name on the "Releasing Violent Offenders Regardless of the Impact on Crime Act." Furthermore, policies that acknowledge the costs of punishment as well as the costs of crime require us to ask those with more power to give up some of their benefits in order to reduce the costs being imposed on other people, people from whom they are often separated by geography, class, and race.

Reformers also face a demographic challenge. Although the country has never been safer for those under the age of about forty or forty-five, for the Baby Boomers (those born between 1946 and 1964), violent crime in 2014 was still twice as high as it (officially) was in 1960, and property crime 50 percent higher. And the Boomers are a major political force: 22

percent of all voters in 2012 were over the age of sixty-five, and 61 percent were over forty-five. Right now the Boomers seem fairly quiescent when it comes to criminal justice reform—likely because they are much more focused on what the 2008 fiscal crisis means for their retirements—but it probably would not take much of an increase in crime—perhaps even just the *perception* of an increase in crime—for them to start caring again. This is an ever-present risk, as highlighted starkly by Newt Gingrich's claim during the 2016 campaign that even if crime rates are relatively stable, as long as people *think* they are rising politicians should pander to, and thus reinforce, those beliefs.[55]

This is where scholars, the media, and advocacy groups (especially those less involved with pushing specific bills through state legislatures) need to play a bigger role. Reformers need to raise these tougher issues and ask these seemingly "impossible" questions about the costs and benefits of crime control. To the extent that reformers resign themselves to focusing on just what is feasible now, they will never achieve what may be feasible tomorrow.

Those who continue to insist that safety must come first keep us locked in a dangerously tough-on-crime mindset, just in a (temporary) time of low crime. They reinforce, instead of challenge, the problematic attitudes that encourage immediate, punitive responses to any potential crime-rate increase. Fortunately, there appears to be at least some movement in a new direction. An increasing number of scholars and journalists are starting to point out that decarceration will require us to talk about punishing violent crimes less severely, and that that may mean talking frankly about trading off the costs of safety and enforcement.[56]

WHY POLITICIANS MAY WANT TO BE SOFTER ON CRIME

Furthermore, there is a rather surprising reason to be optimistic that some politicians, if given the space, may already want to be less tough on crime than they have appeared in the past. Consider the following two rough summaries of some recent empirical findings.

One: It is true that more conservative states tend to be harsher on crime, and that conservatives have become tougher on crime over the years. Yet when the Republican Party is in the majority, a legislature's penal policies depend to a large extent on how vulnerable the majority is. The more vulnerable the majority, the more punitive the laws.[57]

Two: State legislatures seem more likely to adopt sentencing commissions to rein in prison growth when prison populations are high and the majority party's control is weakening.[58]

These two studies at first seem contradictory, but they actually tell an interesting, complementary story. If being tough on crime were a core conservative policy, then we would expect state legislatures to be harsher when there was a large, stable Republican majority than when the Republican majority was slight. The stronger the majority, the freer the conservatives would be to indulge in their policy preferences. What we see, however, is the opposite: that legislatures grow tougher on crime out of electoral necessity more than innate desire. At the same time, the very moment when legislators feel the need to use crime as a political tool—when their majority control is weakening—appears to be the moment when they are most likely to try to take the issue off the table for everyone, by establishing quasi-independent sentencing commissions.

Taken together, these results paint legislators as somewhat grudging warriors against crime. They seem more likely to crack down on crime out of political necessity than real desire, and as the issue becomes more and more politically unavoidable, they look for ways to delegate it away. Legislators try to avoid being tough on crime more than we would expect, and certainly more than the Standard Story suggests.

As always, results that come from just two studies should be viewed as tentative at best. Nonetheless, they certainly complicate the conventional "never hurts to be tough on crime" narrative, and they suggest that politicians may be open to passing laws that restrain their own ability to be punitive in the future. Which makes reformers' silence on structural political and institutional issues all the more unfortunate.

THE GAMBLE

Whether they know it or not, reformers today are gambling. They are relying on the system that gave us large-scale incarceration to unravel it, without trying to change how that system really works. If it overreacted before, it can certainly overreact again. Congress's back-and-forth actions on mandatory minimums for drug offenses—abolished in 1970, restored in the 1980s, then simultaneously targeted for abolition and expansion in 2016—provide a clear warning about how easily changes can be reversed.

Explanations of prison growth have focused so much on broad social upheavals that they have largely overlooked the role played by (less exciting but no less important) institutional failings. These social changes certainly made the problem worse, but prison populations likely would have trended steeply upward without them just because of the institutional failings. The political system is inherently (if unintentionally) designed to overreact to changes in crime. Decentralized responsibility leaves no one in control; low-information, high-salience voters reward severity and punish the inevitable errors of "smarter" policies; and the costs of enforcement aren't borne by those with the most control over them. As a result, criminal justice systems across the nation overreact asymmetrically. They crack down hard when crime is going up, but they do not relax nearly so easily when it starts to go down.

We should conclude this exploration of the politics of punishment, then, by thinking a bit about how to address some of these structural defects. Two broad solutions immediately suggest themselves: less direct democratic accountability, and more localism. Many of the core defects described in this chapter arise from political actors confronting a low-information electorate. One approach, then, would be to replace elected prosecutors with appointed ones. We already see a push for this with judges. It's easy to see how prosecutors, who, like judges, are called upon to "do justice," could benefit from the lack of immediate accountability that comes with appointment. Both the false-positive and "Willie Horton" challenges are tied to problematic accountability. (Of course, a prosecutor appointed by a county executive may exhibit many of the same biases as one elected by county voters, a point I'll turn to shortly.)

We obviously cannot replace elected legislators with appointed ones, but we could still help insulate them from immediate voter demands. Many states already have sentencing commissions that are designed, in part, to do just this by requiring new crime and sentencing bills to work their way through a separate bureaucracy. By slowing down the legislative process, sentencing commissions could (imperfectly) shield the criminal code from aggressive demands arising from the "crime of the week."

On the other hand, localism—by which I mean having cities and suburbs separately choose prosecutors, and perhaps even judges—would help ensure that prosecutors (and judges) were selected by people who directly experience both the gains from enforcement and its costs. We have repeatedly seen the problems that arise when those in the suburbs have control over urban crime policy. City prosecutors and city judges may be more sensitive to the various tradeoffs that come with severe policies toward crime. The goal would be for the officials themselves to be socially and culturally closer to both the offenders and the victims of crime, so that the process would lead to more nuanced and just outcomes.

Localism, though, is not without its risks. Smaller jurisdictions can restrict the pool of qualified prosecutors and judges, a problem that has bedeviled some of New York's smaller, more local courts; in the end, localism may work best in large cities where the pool of applicants is large.[59] Too much localism also increases the coordination costs of dealing with crimes that cross jurisdictional lines, and it raises the risk that officials will try to displace crime one jurisdiction over rather than eliminate it— that they will focus less on trying to thwart crimes and more on trying to encourage offenders to move one jurisdiction over. That said, increasing localism still may be more efficient than restricting democratic accountability. Given the choice between having the county executive appoint prosecutors or having the city (not the county) elect them, I would probably choose the second option. Many of the problems with criminal justice come from an indifference to the costs, and that indifference is bred by distance.

So far, however, we have seen no real movement on any of these fronts. To its great peril, the reform movement has not yet begun to address the political defects that brought about mass incarceration in the first place.

CHAPTER SEVEN

THE THIRD RAIL: VIOLENT OFFENSES

T HE EMPHASIS CURRENT REFORM EFFORTS PLACE ON REDUCING punishments for people convicted of low-level, nonviolent crimes is understandable, but it should be clear by now that the impact will be limited. Any significant reduction in the US prison population is going to require states and counties to rethink how they punish people convicted of violent crimes, where "rethink" means "think about how to punish less."

A simple example makes this clear. Assume that in 2013 we released half of all people convicted of property and public-order crimes, 100 percent of those in for drug possession, and 75 percent of those in for drug trafficking. Our prison population would have dropped from 1.3 million to 950,000. That's no minor decline, but this sort of politically ambitious approach only gets us back to where we were in about 1994, and 950,000 prisoners is still more than three times the prison population we had when the boom began. Or consider that there are almost as many people in prison today *just* for murder and manslaughter as the *total* state prison population in 1974: about 188,000 for murder or manslaughter today, versus a total of 196,000 prisoners overall in 1974. If we are serious about wanting to scale back incarceration, we need to start cutting back on locking up people for violent crimes.

Not surprisingly, almost all politicians steer clear of this topic. Reformers are more open to the idea in theory, but they almost always emphasize the need to focus on the "low-hanging fruit" of nonviolent offenders first. Build coalitions around those successes, they say, then see what is possible next.[1] There is certainly a lot of validity to this idea. We can't go from soaring prisons one day to emptying them of the most serious offenders the next. Progress is incremental, and a reform movement that races ahead of itself could end up foundering as a result.

At the same time, for all the talk of "low-hanging fruit," there doesn't appear to be anyone building ladders to pick the fruit higher up the tree. Prison reform has been on the political radar since about 2000, and it has been taken seriously since about 2008; that's somewhere between nine and seventeen years. Yet reform efforts are still aimed entirely at this "low-hanging fruit," and there seems to be no effort to move the discussion on to tougher issues.

In fact, the situation is arguably worse that this makes it sound. It isn't just that reform bills focus only on those convicted of nonviolent crimes, but that, as we've seen, reform options, such as drug diversion, often explicitly exclude those convicted of violence. Even more troubling, many states generate the political support for lessening property and drug crime sentences in part by toughening those for violent crimes. To belabor the metaphor, far from building taller ladders, we seem to be burning the wood we need to build them. If the goal is real, substantial reform, this approach is untenable. The sheer volume of violent offenders in prison acts as a barrier to deep cuts built solely on nonviolent offenders.

Maybe deep reforms really aren't the goal. Maybe the goal is merely to release prisoners who really don't scare us, but otherwise leave things untouched. That, however, doesn't seem to match the rhetoric of transformative change coming from both the Left and the Right. Furthermore, even if the goal is only the modest one of releasing those who "don't scare us," we should still be less punitive toward many of those who are serving time for violent crimes. Our current approach to punishing those convicted of violence is almost entirely blind to mountains of sophisticated research about violent behavior. The harsh sentences we impose on people convicted of violent crimes are not buying us the security we think they are: they incapacitate people longer than necessary and provide little deterrence in exchange. It's a situation that begs for real reform.

THE MATH OF VIOLENT OFFENSES

Recall Michelle Alexander's claim that "the uncomfortable reality is that arrests and convictions for drug offenses—not violent crime—have propelled mass incarceration." As this comment reminds us, the Standard Story doesn't just argue that drug-related admissions are important, but that they are the most important force driving prison growth.

This assumption, however, is incorrect. As we saw in Table 1.1, 52 percent of the growth in state prisons came from people serving time for violent offenses. The importance of locking people up for violence has only grown in recent years, as Table 1.2 showed. Thirty-six percent of prison growth in the 1980s came from incarcerating more people for violent crimes (although some of the additional prisoners serving time for drug offenses were likely imprisoned as part of an effort to rein in violence). From 1990 to 2009, however, about 60 percent of all additional inmates had been convicted of a violent offense. In short, the incarceration of people for violent crimes has always been at the center of contemporary prison growth.

And not just violent crimes, but generally, fairly serious violent crimes. Almost one-fourth of all people in prison for a violent crime are serving time for murder or manslaughter; these prisoners make up about one in eight inmates overall. Another one-fourth of all people convicted of violent crime are in for robbery, with 95 percent of those having been convicted of armed robbery. That's 300,000 people, or nearly one in four prisoners, serving time for killing someone or for armed robbery.[2] Another 10 percent of all prisoners are in prison for aggravated assault, which usually requires serious bodily injury, the risk of death, or a dangerous weapon.

Moreover, the official number of people in prison for violent crimes represents the *minimum* number of people incarcerated for acts of violence.

A person who is factually guilty of a violent act but pleads guilty to a nonviolent offense does not appear in the official statistics as someone in prison for a violent crime. Then there is the fact that gun offenses, such as possession of a loaded firearm by a convicted felon, count as "public-order" offenses, which are ranked lower than even property or drug crimes. A drug dealer caught with a loaded pistol thus appears as a nonviolent drug offender, even though the gun possession points to the potential for violence.

Another way to show the importance of violent crimes to prison growth is to look at how much bed-space those convicted of violence use. Consider the following example, which relies on data on about 300,000 admissions (slightly under half the national total) from seventeen states in 2003.[3] Those 300,000 people spent a total of 184.4 million person-days in prison between 2003 and the end of 2013. Those convicted of index violent crimes (murder/manslaughter, forcible sexual assault, aggravated assault, and robbery) made up about 20 percent of the admissions, but they used up 40 percent of the bed-days, or 69.9 million days. Add in those convicted of any violent crime, and the share of admissions rises to 30 percent; of bed-days, to 51 percent. Violent offenders take up a majority of all prison beds, even if they do not represent a majority of all admissions. This is, of course, because they serve longer sentences. But that doesn't necessarily mean *long* sentences. Those 69.9 million bed-days translate into an average of 3.2 years.[4] That's definitely longer than the 1.7 years for the overall average (looking at 184.4 million days), but likely less than one would expect for index violent crimes.

The experiences of these 300,000 prisoners also illuminates the extent to which almost all inmates serving long sentences are in for violent crimes, contrary to the Standard Story. Of those admitted to prison in 2003, only 3 percent had not yet been released or paroled by the end of 2013—that in and of itself should be surprising, given all the "everyone serves such long terms" rhetoric—and almost all of the people in that 3 percent were serving time for serious violent crimes. Fully 65 percent of this 3 percent had been convicted of an index violent crime, with 25 percent of the 3 percent in for murder or manslaughter. In total, 83 percent of these inmates had been convicted of an index or non-index violent crime. Almost any way you cut it, the majority of those in prison, and a large majority of those serving long terms, have been convicted of violence.

All of this raises an obvious question: if most people serving long sentences are people convicted of serious violent crimes, where does the widely held belief that our prisons are full of people serving long sentences for nonviolent offenses come from? I have two related hypotheses. The first is that there has been an overemphasis on the federal system and its pathologies. Even though the federal government holds only about 12 percent of the nation's prisoners, its criminal justice system receives almost all of the national media and scholarly attention. Problematically, federal criminal justice outcomes look much different from those in the states. While people with drug convictions make up about 16 percent of state prisoners, they make up approximately 49 percent of federal prisoners. The federal system is also distinctly more punitive in general, and especially so when it comes to drugs. This focus on federal policy leads people to overestimate how many people are in prison for drugs and how long they spend in prison.

The second hypothesis is a variant of the "man bites dog" problem. The media never reports when a dog bites a man—or when a bank robber with a gun gets five years, or a murderer ten or fifteen. They want to cover the rare, surprising cases where the man bites the dog: the shockingly short or long sentences, not the regular ones. So we see dozens of articles about the "affluenza" teen who was sentenced to probation after killing four people in a drunk driving accident; the judge apparently bought the defense attorney's argument that the kid was too rich and spoiled to understand the difference between right and wrong.[5] Or we see the extensive coverage of a first-time drug dealer convicted of selling only a small amount but given life without parole.[6] The reality, however, is much different, and these cases make the news *because* they are the exceptions, not the rules.

I understand why politicians shy away from reforms aimed at violent crimes. The political risks of being lenient are too great. Whatever sort of political cover the fiscal crisis has provided—"I want to be tough on crime, but financial realities are forcing me to make cuts"—likely does not extend to being generous toward those convicted of violence. None of that, of course, changes the math.

Yet there is a deeper problem here. It's quite likely that being less harsh toward people who commit violent crimes might actually make us *safer*. Or at least it would have no impact on safety while freeing up resources to be better used elsewhere and reducing the social costs of punishment as well. The two strongest policy arguments for punishing violent crimes harshly simply lack strong empirical support, and in fact are often contradicted by the evidence.

TWO FAILINGS

There are two primary policy justifications for punishing people for long periods: long sentences are needed to incapacitate those who pose an ongoing threat to public safety, and long sentences deter people from committing crimes, such as acts of violence, in the first place. (There are, of course, also moral arguments for severity, but I won't address those here.[7]) Both arguments, despite their intuitive appeal, falter upon close examination. These sorts of long sentences are not just unnecessary, but in many cases they are counterproductive. Shorter terms would be cheaper, impose fewer collateral costs, and keep us safer.[8]

Both arguments in favor of long sentences are based on dangerously simplistic views of human behavior. The incapacitation argument takes too static a view of violence, seeing the person as inherently violent, rather than as someone who engaged in violence at a particular time. The deterrence argument, meanwhile, significantly overstates the extent to which people—particularly young people, who are more likely to engage in violence than older people—view ever longer sentences as ever greater punishments. Once we realize the implications of these errors, long sentences for those convicted of violence become generally hard to defend, except perhaps for purely retributivist reasons.

Let's start with the flaws in how we incapacitate violent offenders. Even that sentence, which seems so banal, is actually quite misleading. "Violent offenders." We use this term a lot, but we shouldn't. Of course, there are people who merit the term: persistently violent people who consistently engage in dangerous, violent actions. For almost all people who commit violent crimes, however, violence is not a defining trait but a transitory state that they age out of. They are not violent people; they are simply going through a violent phase. Locking them up and throwing away the key ignores the fact that someone who acts violently when he's eighteen years old may very well be substantially calmer by the time he's thirty-five.

Offending patterns vary predictably over the course of people's lives.[9] Generally speaking, people age into and out of the risk of engaging in criminal or antisocial behavior; individuals who commit crimes usually fall into one of five or six fairly broad patterns, which criminologists describe with terms like "high rate adult peaked" or "low rate desister."[10] The differences across the groups, however, are more quantitative than qualitative. People differ in terms of when they peak (in their teens, twenties, or thirties) and how many criminal acts they are committing at that peak, but their behaviors all tend to follow a bell curve. Most people who end up committing crimes commit few offenses when young, and the ones they do commit are relatively nonviolent; criminality and violence rise in the late teen years through the twenties or thirties; and thereafter, both criminality and violence subside.[11] Of course, not everyone follows this general pattern—recall that the average age of prisoners in the United States is rising, in no small part because an older cohort is not aging out of crime as fast as expected—but most people do.

There are many reasons we should expect offending, including violent offending, to follow this sort of "life course" pattern. Some of them are biological. The bell-shaped curve of offending tracks various hormone levels, like that of testosterone, or the body's declining ability to absorb dopamine over time.[12] Juvenile brains are also less well developed than adult brains, which leads kids to be more vulnerable to peer pressure and to act more impulsively.[13] And if nothing else, a fifty-year-old is less likely to get in a fight than a twenty-year-old simply because he knows he is more likely to lose.

Some of the pathways out of crime are also social. Sociologists Robert Sampson and John Laub have shown that marriage and employment appear to help people desist from crime.[14] One reason is self-perception. Someone with a spouse thinks of himself as a "husband," and someone with a job starts to think of himself as an "employee." People's behavior then adjusts to reflect the social conceptions of how they should act in these roles.[15] Another reason is an "incapacitation" effect, to use the term somewhat awkwardly. Time spent with a partner or at a job is time not spent hanging out with friends and potentially getting into trouble. (An interesting variant of this effect is that the Friday night of the release of a major new violent movie produces a noticeable decline in violent crime.[16] A large number of aggressive young men spend a chunk of that Friday night in a movie theater rather than in a bar, and less mayhem ensues.)

In short, a person's level of aggression fluctuates over time, and in ways implying that long sentences frequently over-incapacitate. We don't need to lock up most violent twenty-year-olds for thirty years to keep ourselves safe, since most of them would naturally desist from offending much sooner than that. Perhaps our goal, then, should be to target longer sentences at those twenty-year-olds who are on a persistent-offender path and lock them up for a long time, while imposing much shorter sentences on the twenty-year-old "low rate desisters" who will naturally stop engaging in antisocial behavior shortly. Criminologists and prison officials have long sought to develop these sorts of "selective incapacitation" models.

Whatever their theoretical appeal, however, these models fail in practice. For all the "big data" advances in predicting human behavior, we still cannot really predict in advance who will end up on which paths. Sampson and Laub, for example, had lifetime offending data on five hundred high-risk Boston men as they aged from seven to seventy. They attempted to predict each person's path using only the data available when that person was young. No matter how hard they tried, their models basically failed.[17] We just don't know what trajectory someone will be on until he is well along it.

This failure points to a stinging irony in one of the most popular types of sentencing laws, namely enhancements for recidivists such as three-strike laws. On the one hand, such laws seem consistent with our inability to predict future pathways. We don't know whether someone will be a high-rate offender until we have a lot of data on his or her offending patterns, so we hold off throwing the book at someone until we are sure. On the other hand, by the time we gather this information, the person is much more likely to be on the verge of aging out of his peak offending years, and in fact may already be on the declining side of the bell curve.

In California, for example, the average age of someone at the time he is convicted for a third strike—and thus facing at least twenty-five years in prison—is forty-three.[18] Recall that Proposition 36, adopted in 2012, modified California's three-strike law and authorized the early release of many of those who had been sentenced under the old version. Those released early under Prop 36 have a much lower recidivism rate, about one-tenth the state average, in no small part because they are simply older.[19]

Thus the irony. We don't have enough information to impose a harsh sentence on someone until he gets close to aging out of crime.

Long prison sentences can also be self-defeating. Stints in prison hurt a person's employment options, and the stigma of incarceration—combined with the inability to find employment—keeps former inmates from finding partners or spouses.[20] Incarcerating people when they are young may prevent crime in the short run, but it also undermines some of the social pathways to desistance in the longer run once they are released.

If long sentences fail to incapacitate efficiently, then can we at least justify them because of their ability to deter? The answer is almost certainly no. The evidence on the deterrent impact of severe punishment is pretty well settled: the certainty of punishment matters far more than the severity. Economists have long argued that certainty and severity can be easily traded off. A one-year sentence imposed every other time someone commits a crime, the argument goes, should deter just as much as a five-year sentence imposed on one out of every ten offenses.[21] The mathematical perfection of these claims, however, has foundered on the rocks of empirical reality.

Empirically, it is hard to separate out the deterrent impact of longer sentences from their incapacitation effect, so the number of studies isolating the deterrent impact of longer prison terms is few. One review of the few methodologically sound studies, however, found little to no evidence that long sentences have any real deterrent effect.[22] Moreover, whatever deterrent effect they do have is certainly subject to diminishing returns: it is quite unlikely that a thirty- or fifty-year sentence deters much more than something substantially less.[23] What really deters is the certainty of being caught. Policing deters. The punishment that follows an arrest, much less so.

There are at least two major reasons why the harshness of the sentence doesn't deter that much. First, one of the most well-documented risk factors for criminal behavior is impulsivity.[24] Those who engage in antisocial or criminal behavior are also more likely to smoke, to have unsafe sex, to use risky drugs, and so on. Actions like these are evidence of someone being very present-minded—which means they will put less weight on criminal sentences that will be imposed or experienced well into the future. Second, the state punishment is just one sanction someone faces when arrested. People also experience social stigma, ostracism, job loss, and more. Importantly, none of these other costs require a conviction, and they can all start at the moment of arrest. After all, a person's family, friends, and employer are not required to presume innocence; that applies only to the court system. Even those who put more weight on the future may fear apprehension, and all the social penalties it brings, more than the final state punishment.

Yet our policies get this completely backward. As we've seen, for most crimes clearance rates—the fraction of crimes that result in an arrest, which is a decent proxy for apprehension risk—have either held steady or declined since the 1960s, and for most offenses they are fairly low. By 2014, the clearance rate for murder was just under two-thirds, and that for aggravated assault a bit above 50 percent, while clearance rates for all other index violent and index property crimes were below 50 percent, often substantially, with the lowest being burglary (14 percent) and auto theft (13 percent).[25] But although the risk of apprehension remained low, legislators kept passing tougher and tougher sentencing laws: mandatory minimums, sentencing enhancements, truth-in-sentencing laws, strike laws, and so on. Much attention has been given to severity, very little to certainty. Like I said, backward.

This was not a mistake, or the product of ignorance. The problem will not be fixed simply by showing legislators an empirical study explaining the "right way" to approach crime. This misallocation is the predictable result of structural failures we've already looked at, ones that continue to receive too little attention—in this case, that cities pay for policing while states pay for prison. Since states lack any real power to keep local police and prosecutors from sending people to prison, cities and counties have an incentive to free-ride off the state.

Unfortunately, punishment debates seem to remain fixated on using longer sentences to deter crime. Senator Tom Cotton (R-AR), for example, recently argued that the United States suffers from an *underincarceration* problem, claiming that we needed to make sure punishments are severe to compensate for our low clearance rates.[26] Although he is correct about our clearance rates, it's unfortunate that Cotton argued for more imprisonment, not more funding for police.

There is some evidence that the importance of certainty is getting more attention. In 2004, Judge Steven Alm in Oahu started a program called Hawaii's Opportunity Probation with Enforcement—HOPE—which was designed to help people with addiction problems stay sober while on probation. Rather than relying on infrequent (usually monthly) drug testing combined with the threat of (eventual) revocation back to prison, HOPE focuses on certainty and speed. At the start of their term, probationers have to check in every morning to see if they have a drug test that day, knowing they will be tested at least once a week, although the frequency can drop with continued success. Unlike with traditional probation, HOPE's sanctions are immediate. If the probationer tests positive, he or she is immediately detained pending a hearing, and usually sentenced at the hearing to a short jail term for the violation, although he or she remains enrolled in HOPE during the process. The sanction is certain and immediate, but not severe.

In a randomized trial comparing HOPE to conventional probation practices, HOPE came out significantly ahead.[27] Prior to the experiment, those enrolled in HOPE abused drugs more than the control group; three months in, use by those in HOPE had dropped by about 83 percent, while use by those in the control group had risen by 50 percent.[28] Those in HOPE also experienced fewer revocations (9 percent vs. 31 percent), and spent fewer subsequent days in prison (111 vs. 303), although both groups spent about the same number of days in jail (around 20). HOPE has been sufficiently successful that it has now been introduced around the country under the name "Swift, Certain, and Fair" (since the "H" in HOPE limits the acronym's portability).

There are obvious limits to the HOPE model. It can only be used to prevent reoffending by those who are already under supervision, not as a general deterrent. Moreover, it only works for crimes that are easily, objectively detectable. The evidence of drug use lingers in a person's bloodstream for some time after the offense. But what could we do to make people "call in" to prevent robbery or assault? There may be some ways to approximate this—electronic monitoring, in theory, would at least allow us to objectively see where people went, although we wouldn't know what they were doing—but these methods are limited. Yet while the specifics of HOPE may restrict its application to certain problematic behaviors, its success further demonstrates the importance of the certainty of punishment and that policymakers may be increasingly aware of it.

HOW TO CUT TIME SERVED FOR VIOLENT OFFENSES

Throughout this book, I've shown that rising admissions, not time served, has been at the heart of prison growth. But that should not be taken to mean that sentence lengths are irrelevant, particularly when it comes to violent crimes. As I pointed out before, the impact of any one admission on total prison population will be greater the longer that person spends in prison. And while the median time spent in prison by someone convicted of a violent crime, at slightly more than three years, is not that long, it is still longer than the time spent by those convicted of nonviolent crimes, and it has crept up a bit over the past few decades. Furthermore, almost all the people serving really long sentences—the ones whose reduced sentences would have the biggest impact—have been convicted of serious violent offenses. Cutting time served for these prisoners, however, is among the riskiest of reforms.

Which isn't to say that we should despair: there are ways to reduce time served by people convicted of violence, just few that seem to come up in reform bills. For example, it may be politically impossible to cut the statutory maximum for most violent crimes, but there are ways we can limit how often people receive the longest sanctions. One option, of course, is to adopt plea bargain guidelines that restrict when prosecutors can impose particularly harsh sentences. If those guidelines are too challenging to implement, states should also consider sentencing guidelines, a more "mainstream" type of proposal with a longer history of at least modest success in reining in prison growth.[29]

Sentencing guidelines have been effective in no small part because they are less transparent than legislative acts (an argument that applies to plea guidelines too). Newspaper accounts at the time of a high-profile arrest or conviction will generally report the statutory maximum more than the likely guideline sentence: "He faces up to 25 years in prison," not, "As a second-time offender without any apparent additional aggravating factors, his guideline range is probably six to nine years." Guidelines allow legislators to limit the sentences for run-of-the-mill violent crimes in a less obvious, and thus politically safer, way. Moreover, we may not want to lower official maximums, because there may be cases where the current maximum sentence is politically (or even morally) necessary. We may be better off in a system where the default for aggravated assault is set to ten years, but the maximum remains twenty-five, rather than one where we lower that maximum to ten years only to have a particularly horrific assault result in demands to raise the maximum—for all aggravated assaults—back to twenty-five.

States adopted guidelines at a fairly rapid clip in the 1980s and early 1990s. By the 2000s, about twenty-four states and the federal government were using some sort of sentencing guidelines.[30] A majority of them fit into the category of what were called "presumptive" or "determinate" guidelines, which meant the trial judge had to impose a sentence in the guideline's recommended range unless he or she found specific aggravating or mitigating factors; failure to follow the guidelines, by being either too severe or too lenient, was grounds for appeal by either party. Over the course of the 1990s and 2000s, the US Supreme Court threw several wrenches into presumptive guideline systems, but states generally have been able to work around these complications, and today eight states (out of originally thirteen) still use them.[31]

At one level, it may seem somewhat ironic that I'm proposing guidelines here. A major criticism of sentencing guidelines is that they have made prosecutors more powerful.[32] Prosecutors can often choose which of many different offenses to charge, each with a different default guideline range, and by choosing the right charges and the right prior criminal histories prosecutors can effectively force judges to sentence in very narrow ranges of the prosecutors' own choosing—yet another reason for adopting charging guidelines. I just spent an entire chapter pointing out the risks posed by giving prosecutors too much power, and now I appear to be suggesting that we give them even more power in the name of *less* severity for *violent* crimes.

This is not, however, as confusing or contradictory as it initially appears. It comes down to design. If most default guideline ranges are shorter than the average sentences imposed for those crimes before the guidelines are adopted, then prosecutors will still be able to pigeonhole judges, but only for sentences that are consistently shorter than they were able to secure before. To the extent that guidelines have helped prosecutors become more severe, that is simply a problem with how the guidelines are written, not with the idea of guidelines per se.[33]

Another option for cutting time spent in prison by people convicted of violence would be to expand the use of parole. After years of limiting and restricting it, states have started to rely on parole more extensively. Such reforms are in fact perhaps the most widely adopted type of prison reform to date. In almost all cases, however, these changes have been limited to people convicted of nonviolent crimes. There are exceptions, however, like Mississippi's 2014 reform law—these are quite rare, but they show that expanding back-end opportunities is possible even for people convicted of violent crimes.

One development that has encouraged states to expand back-end reforms is the growing use of quantitative risk-assessment tools in the parole process; in mid-2016, the White House announced a plan to try to expand the use of such tools in criminal justice more generally.[34] An extensive literature in psychology and other social sciences has established that well-designed, quantitative risk-assessment tools generally make better predictions about future outcomes than people do, and this appears to be true when it comes to assessing future violence as well.[35] Although social scientists have found it hard to predict the lifetime offending history of people when they are young, risk-assessment tools are more successful because they make fairly short-run predictions, such as the risk of rearrest or readmission to prison within five years or so. It is much easier to make this sort of narrow prediction.

These tools, however, are not without controversy. Perhaps the biggest concern is that the factors these models use may be correlated with race and gender in deeply problematic ways, and there are legitimate concerns that using them may increase the severity of sanctions faced by poor and (especially) minority defendants. However, most critics of risk-assessment models simply point out that they can lead to worse outcomes for minority defendants than for otherwise identical white defendants, which isn't really the right point to make.[36] The question we have to ask isn't, "Are these models biased?" but rather, "Are these models *more* biased than the humans who currently have to make the decision?" and, "Even if they are more biased, is it easier to fix the bias in the model or in the person?" Framed comparatively, the appeal of these models becomes stronger, although plenty of valid concerns remain.[37]

That these models likely outperform people is notable, because the models' political advantages are significant. The risk for a parole board member, as for any politician, is that dreaded false negative: the parolee who recidivates in a salient way while on parole. No one wants to be the person who signed off on the release. As the former chairperson of the New York State Parole Board said, "It's not like it's written down anywhere, but every board member knows, if you let someone out and it's going to draw media attention, you're not going to be re-appointed."[38] A model, however, is indifferent to politics. It spits out a number, and that number determines if someone is granted parole. Obviously, if the model produces enough salient false negatives who vividly recidivate, people might demand a new model or no model at all. But changing or abolishing the model is often a legislative fix, which is much harder to accomplish than simply firing the responsible parole board member, who is generally an at-will employee of the state government. In a way, the risk-assessment tool is another means of lessening problematic political accountability in criminal justice.

THE "LOW-LEVEL VIOLENT CRIME"

If cutting time served for serious violent crimes is difficult, perhaps it is worth thinking about whether there is low-hanging fruit even within the category of "violent offenses." When we hear the term "violent crime," what immediately comes to mind is surely something like murder or rape. But what about breaking into an empty home while unarmed? After all, that's classified as violent crime in New York and Mississippi.[39] So perhaps one way to cut the number of people in prison for violent crimes is by focusing on "low-level violent crimes."

So far, when talking about types of crimes, we've mostly focused on the FBI's index violent crimes: murder/manslaughter, forcible sexual assault, robbery, and aggravated assault. All other violent crimes are defined as non-index offenses, including acts like involuntary (that is, negligent) manslaughter, simple assault, kidnapping, non-forcible sexual assault, and other forms of sexual abuse and lewd behavior (including with children), blackmail and extortion, hit-and-run driving, child abuse, and other forms of endangerment.[40] Given that these non-index crimes are often less severe than index offenses, they may provide more possibilities for diversion or sentence cutting. Table 7.1 uses the same NCRP data cited above to estimate the number of bed-days used by people convicted of various non-index violent crimes.[41]

Recall that those convicted of index violent crimes and admitted in 2003 spent a total of about 69.9 million days in prison before their first (if any) release. For non-index violent crimes, usage runs to about 23.7 million bed-days over those eleven years. That comes to 25 percent of the 93.6 million total bed-days used by those admitted for both index and non-index violent crimes, and about 12.5 percent of the 184.4 million bed-days used by all offenders. Two facts stand out here. First, people convicted of non-index violent crimes make up a minority of those serving time for violence—there is not really all that much "low-hanging

Table 7.1 Total Bed-Days Used per Violent Crime, 2003–2013

Offense	Bed-Days	Percent of Total Bed-Days
Kidnapping	1.6 million	7
Statutory Rape	1.5 million	6
Sex Abuse	7.1 million	30
Lewd Acts with a Child	4.9 million	21
Forced Sodomy	0.8 million	3
Simple Assault	3.2 million	14
Aggravated Assault of a Peace Officer	1.2 million	5
Blackmail/Extortion	1.5 million	6
Hit & Run with Injury	0.2 million	1
Child Abuse	0.8 million	3
Other Violent Crime	1.0 million	4

Source: Data from US Department of Justice, Bureau of Justice Statistics, "Data Collection: National Corrections Reporting Program," www.bjs.gov/index.cfm?ty=dcdetail&iid=268.

fruit" among violent crimes. Second, approximately 60 percent of those serving time for non-index violent crimes are in for some sort of sex offense. Given current attitudes toward sex offenders—which boil down to unrelenting harshness, even in this time of reform—it is unlikely that these really count as "low-hanging fruit" to begin with.

So it should be clear that real reform will be impossible if we continue to avoid talking about how to change the way we punish serious violent crimes. There is, however, reason to be optimistic that we can make these changes, and it comes from a surprising source. Between 2010 and 2013 (the last year for which we have data), the number of people in prison for violent crimes fell from 725,000 to 705,000—a decline almost equal to the 29,000 fewer people incarcerated for drug crimes during that time. In fact, between 2012 and 2013, overall state prison populations rose by about 10,000, but the number of people in state prisons for violent crimes fell by almost 3,000. That the number of people in prison for violent crimes fell by about the same absolute number as those in for drug crimes is startling, given that drug crimes were the primary focus of reform efforts, and violent offenses were either ignored or subjected to harsher sanctions. There's no explanation for how this happened that I've seen; in fact, no one really seems to have commented on this development at all. It suggests, however, that there is hope, and that cutting the number of people in prison for violent offenses more systematically is not an impossible goal.

By now, I hope the inadequacies of the Standard Story are clear, as well as the need to focus on prosecutors, political institutions, and violent crimes. I thus want to conclude by looking at the really hard question: What would a reform program look like that tackles these three issues?

CHAPTER EIGHT

QUO VADIS?

BEING A CRITIC IS EASY. PROPOSING POLICIES TO REPLACE those you've criticized is harder.

Although the Standard Story is widely accepted, its flaws are fairly easy to illuminate; demonstrating the importance to prison growth of prosecutors, of misaligned political incentives, and of locking people up for violent crimes is a relatively straightforward task as well. Much of what I've argued so far has relied on facts hiding in plain sight. That said, it is critically important to shed light on the Standard Story's flaws, given how much it impedes significant decarceration; I hope the arguments I've made here will, on their own, help to change how we approach penal reform.

And yet there is still the matter of what sort of reforms these findings suggest are needed. Whenever I present my results, the first question I always get is, "Okay, so what should we be doing differently then?" It's a fair question, and it's also a profoundly difficult one. Identifying solutions would be challenging enough even if we assumed that reasonable and efficient policies would be easy to implement. Determining how to proceed becomes far more daunting when we realize just how hard it is to adopt such policies, given how the costs and benefits of enforcement are divided along geographic, social, economic, and—perhaps most importantly—racial lines.

Nonetheless, it is possible to identify a set of more efficient reforms. This chapter does not offer a comprehensive, A-to-Z reform plan; nor does it give an account of many of the changes already underway (like scaling back punishments for drugs, establishing drug courts, and improving post-release employment opportunities). Nor will I touch on many of the non-prison-oriented reforms that have already been launched, such as reining in asset forfeiture laws, improving policing (better training, body cameras), amending bail procedures and improving pretrial detention policies more generally, and so on. All of these are important measures, and some may even reduce prison growth (like improved policing and bail reform). Here, however, we will just look more closely at reforms that target the three central causes of prison growth that I have described in this book: unregulated prosecutorial power, structural political failures, and the punishment of people convicted of violent crimes.

There have been steps taken to address these issues, but they have been halting and piecemeal at best, and many problems have been almost completely ignored. This sort of uncoordinated reform effort will not work. The defects in American criminal justice all interact with each other, as do law, policy, and cultural attitudes more broadly. A prosecutor who feels politically compelled to use his discretion to throw the book at someone suspected of committing a violent crime reinforces the impression among the public that violent crimes are particularly threatening, which leads to more prosecutorial aggressiveness in the future. Fixing only one piece of the criminal justice system at a time might produce very little in return. That decarceration has been so slow so far should not surprise us.

We need to think bigger and aim higher. What follows, then, are some thoughts on where to go from here. A common reaction to many of these ideas will certainly be, "That sounds great, but it's politically impossible." In many cases, that may be absolutely correct—today. But not necessarily tomorrow. The politics of the current moment always look more durable than they really are. Andrew Sullivan was considered crazy for proposing same-sex marriage in 1989, as were those who came before him; barely twenty-five years later, it's a constitutional right.[1] Not every social issue "cascades" so quickly and convincingly, but given the bipartisan frustration with the criminal justice system, there's at least reason to be cautiously optimistic that something similar could happen with penal reform as well.[2]

It will not be easy. Reform will require prodigious and sustained effort, at both the grassroots and political elite levels. But the current visibility and influence of groups interested in prison reform, ranging from Black Lives Matter and Cut50 on the Left to Right on Crime and the Charles Koch Foundation on the Right, show that the national discussion can shift, and is shifting.

TWO SMALL STEPS FORWARD

As we've seen, focusing on nonviolent offenses and time served won't produce the returns reformers hope for. And yet that doesn't mean these sorts of reforms are a bad idea. A lot of people in prison for low-level, nonviolent crimes—perhaps many, if not most—would be less likely to recidivate, and more likely to go on to better outcomes, if their issues were dealt with outside of the prison, or even outside of the criminal justice system altogether. Releasing them is good policy. These reforms, however, need to be implemented in a way that does not undermine more challenging reforms in the future. If the "easy" reforms are poorly framed, or if they cost too much political capital, they may hurt the overall reform effort in the end. And right now, it's quite possible that current reforms are doing just that.[3]

Perhaps the easiest correction would simply be to change the rhetoric surrounding low-level reform efforts. Many of these reforms purchase leniency for nonviolent offenses by imposing tougher sanctions for violent offenses. There are two clear costs to this approach. First, it reinforces the idea that the only proper response to a violent offense is prison, and second, it will make it harder for states to implement reforms aimed at violent crimes in the future.

In the current framing, any future efforts to scale back incarcerating people convicted of violence will seem to run contrary to the earlier goal: these were the very types of inmates we were trying to make room for. If reforms aimed at low-level, nonviolent crimes were justified by simply saying they would scale back expensive prison populations, without making any reference to freeing up space for those convicted of violent crimes, then future proposals aimed at violent offenses would seem to flow *from* the earlier reforms, not *against* them. Language matters. It sets the parameters of the debate.

Another quick reform would be to stop requiring fiscal impact statements—an increasingly common practice—and instead demand broader cost-benefit analyses. Effective alternatives to incarceration are often more expensive than prisons in terms of dollar expenditures by state and county governments.[4] One unfortunate appeal of prison is its budgetary advantage: warehousing people is cheap, especially when we look at the marginal (as opposed to average) cost—it's a fairly inexpensive way to keep people from committing crimes against the general public, at least in the short run. More comprehensive cost-benefit analyses would highlight the deeper social costs of incarceration that make it so inefficient, and would make the broader net gains of less punitive alternatives much clearer.

Changing the rhetoric of reform and broadening cost-benefit analyses will help, but these shifts alone will not fix the problems we face. For that, we'll need deeper reforms.

REGULATING THE PROSECUTOR

Prosecutors have been and remain the engines driving mass incarceration. Acting with wide discretion and little oversight, they are largely responsible for the staggering rise in admissions since the early 1990s. Any attempts to fight mass incarceration, then, must involve thinking anew about the prosecutor's incentives. Fortunately, even in the short run, there are numerous legislative options for reining in prosecutorial aggressiveness. These fixes will surely face serious political opposition, but it's unclear how much reforms can really accomplish if they continue to overlook or ignore the prosecutor.

Funding the Other Side

Perhaps the most effective way to regulate prosecutors would be to adequately fund public defenders and other indigent counsel. Prosecutorial discretion is unavoidable, and as the people who represent about 80 percent of all defendants facing prison or jail time, indigent counsel are those best able to police that discretion. As the current crisis in indigent defense makes clear, we can't trust the states and counties to fund indigent defense well, especially with the current emphasis on budget cutting. Even in flusher times, though, indigent defense was politically unpopular, and funding indigent defense is one area where the federal government can actually make a significant contribution. As we saw before, a small federal grant program of about $4 billion per year would double the resources available to indigent defense. The federal government could also take a more comparative than absolute approach, providing grants that tie indigent defense budgets to prosecutorial budgets. The government could offer, say, to provide some sort of subsidy to ensure that indigent defense budgets were at least 80 percent of prosecutor budgets, or perhaps fund indigent defense above prosecutor levels to account for the police subsidy that prosecutors receive.

The idea of federalizing indigent defense funding has come up before, although it has usually gone nowhere.[5] Part of the problem is the blithe dismissal many people offer when the idea is raised: "Well, don't do the crime if you can't afford a lawyer." This not only misstates the fact that the government must presume a defendant is innocent, but overlooks the fact that some number of defendants likely *are* innocent. A deeper problem is the recurring interaction of race, class, and social and physical distance, a challenge that arises again and again in every area of reform. Funding indigent defense calls on wealthier, whiter, more suburban areas to fund criminal defense for poorer defendants who are more likely to be members of minority groups. The benefits of better representation will not go to the politically powerful, or to people to whom those in power can easily relate, but instead to members of politically weaker groups toward whom those in power feel less empathy.[6]

That said, this proposal should appeal to both parties. For Democrats, it simultaneously addresses issues of economic and racial inequality, and it is an effective and important policy that national-level leaders can actually implement. Promisingly, the 2016 Democratic Party Platform stated that the Democrats would "assist states in providing a system of public defense that is adequately resourced and which meets American Bar Association standards."[7] For Republicans, funding public defense could be framed as an example of pushing back against the power of the state. Criminal law is the government at its most powerful, and indigent defense is about protecting the weakest from that power—something that should appeal to a party that often expresses concern about the risks that powerful government actors pose to citizens' liberty. Of course, in practice, Republicans may be less concerned about this issue, given that nearly 60 percent of those in prison are black or Hispanic, both groups that today generally lean Democratic.[8] Furthermore, given the current emphasis on austerity, Republican legislators may prefer to focus on ways of cutting government power that do not require separate, countervailing government programs. Nonetheless, there should be bipartisan ways to frame increased indigent defense funding.

Money Talks

Another reform that states could consider is expanding the use of incentive grants that encourage prosecutors to focus on more serious offenses. Historically, these grants have largely been used to do just the opposite, to encourage prosecutors to focus on *less* important crimes that state leaders think get too little attention. In one perhaps extreme example from 1995, the governor of California, Pete Wilson, funded a grant to encourage local DAs to go after statutory rape cases more aggressively, in hopes that doing so would reduce welfare expenditures by discouraging teenage motherhood.[9] There is nothing about these grants, however, that requires them to be used like this.

Recall one of the more appalling facts in Jill Leovy's *Ghettoside*. While the clearance rate (the fraction of crimes that result in arrest) for murder in Los Angeles County was about 50 percent, in poorer, more minority areas like South Central LA and Watts it was under to 40 percent. Serious crimes are often seriously under-addressed. And while clearance rates are the responsibility of the police, not the prosecutors, the police do not ignore what prosecutors do. If prosecutors consistently declined to handle drug cases because a state grant diverted their attention to more serious violent cases, police would likely shift their resources from drugs to homicide. Greater police emphasis on murder cases may result in more people facing convictions for serious violent crimes in the short run (and thus increase the prison population), but in the longer run it may help push down murder rates, and thus the number of long murder sentences.

Again, the political challenges are clear. Suburban and rural voices are overrepresented in state and county electorates alike; even within cities, wealthier, more gentrified areas likely wield outsized power, although perhaps less excessively so. So state grants aimed at reducing violence may not be as popular as efforts aimed at fighting drug trafficking (or even reining in welfare expenditures). Urban drug trafficking is a crime that suburbanites and wealthier urbanites fear can spread to their communities; murder seems more contained.

Peering Inside the Black Box

It's clearly essential that prosecutors provide more data. Right now, these offices are generally black boxes, and any sort of insight would be helpful. We should, however, be thoughtful about what data we gather. The numbers we choose to collect are important, because they will shape how the offices allocate resources. If the state requires prosecutors to report the fraction of *filed cases* that result in convictions, prosecutors will target easier cases and drop harder ones, even if the harder ones are serious crimes like murder.[10] Conversely, if we measure the fraction of *arrests* that result in convictions, prosecutors will focus on pleading out cases, even ones that perhaps should be dismissed, and they may offer weak pleas just to avoid the risk of acquittal.

We need to think carefully about what "just" outcomes looks like, and then how to measure whatever these are. As Adam Foss, a former Boston prosecutor, argued in a powerful TED talk, even prosecutors themselves don't have a good idea of what "justice" really entails, so they tend to focus on securing convictions.[11] Justice, however, is more than convictions; it's more than recidivism or crime rates, too, although those are the other metrics that could be useful as well.

The National District Attorneys Association (NDAA), in conjunction with the American Prosecutors Research Institute, has designed a model set of metrics, and it demonstrates how wide-ranging prosecutorial goals are.[12] The metrics ultimately include thirty-five specific measures, divided up across three major goals ("to promote fair, impartial, and expeditious pursuit of justice," "to ensure safer communities," and "to promote integrity in the prosecution profession and coordination in the criminal justice system"), which are in turn divided into nine sub-goals. The metrics range from things that are easily assessed (decline in felony crimes) to those that are not ("community attitudes about crime and safety"). Overall, the complexity of the NDAA proposal may make it hard to adopt—smaller jurisdictions lack the infrastructure for such detailed data-gathering, and the more subjective items may be hard for even biger agencies to gather—but this complexity also highlights the fact that our current approach so far for assessing prosecutorial outcomes has been too crude. We need more data on prosecutors, and we need to make sure we gather the right data. What we count, and how we count it, will strongly shape what prosecutors do.

Funding indigent defense and gathering data are reforms we can adopt fairly quickly. Let's turn now to options that may take more time to implement, but that may also have bigger returns once we do.

Some Sort of Guidance

Besides funding indigent defense, the most important reform states could adopt would be to follow in New Jersey's footsteps and implement plea bargaining guidelines. If properly designed, such guidelines would restrict the threats prosecutors could exert during the plea process. In fact, guidelines could take on an explicitly decarcerative role, especially if they are expanded—as they should be—to cover charging decisions as well. Instead of leaving the decision about whether to file a charge or dismiss the case, or whether to file a misdemeanor or felony charge, or whether to file a charge that carries a mandatory minimum or not, to the discretion of the prosecutor, the guidelines could, say, instruct the prosecutor to dismiss all charges against a certain type of defendant in the presence of certain mitigating factors, or state that a mandatory minimum cannot be filed against a defendant with no prior criminal record unless certain aggravating factors exist. Not only could such guidelines help manage prison growth, but they would also assist line prosecutors in making tough calls about recidivism risk and other policy issues they may have little training to address.[13] And while New Jersey's experience reveals that these sorts of guidelines can increase severity and disparities rather than reducing them, it also demonstrates that these problems can be fixed by recalibrating the guidelines: they are not inherent to guidelines themselves.

Some people have told me that only states with appointed district attorneys, like New Jersey, could adopt charging and plea guidelines. I disagree. As long as judges enforce the guidelines, even elected prosecutors will have to follow them. The catch is that in states with directly elected county district attorneys, guidelines will have to come from the state legislature, not from the state attorney general. In states with elected district attorneys, the attorney general has very limited legal authority over local prosecutors, so courts would likely view AG-written guidelines as nonbinding. The legislature, however, *does* have the authority to pass these sorts of rules, so just as courts tend to obey and enforce legislatively written sentencing guidelines, they should also enforce legislatively enacted prosecutorial guidelines. The one clear cost to legislative adoption, however, is that it will require more time and political capital, perhaps limiting the number of states willing to undertake the effort.[14]

This is a critically important reform. Prosecutors are called on to make more discretionary choices than anyone else in the criminal justice system—police choose whether to arrest and judges what sentence to impose, but prosecutors choose whether to charge and to what degree, they generally control whether someone is diverted to a drug court or other alternative treatment option, they determine whether a defendant faces the risk of prison or jail, and so on. Yet they alone face no guidance or restrictions on how they wield this power. Even well-intentioned prosecutors are likely to (inadvertently) make serious mistakes without some form of assistance and the risk of malicious abuse is absolutely clear. Our one tool for regulating prosecutors—electing the person at the top—is just too blunt a tool to control these sorts of important day-to-day decisions.

Almost all stages of the criminal justice system now operate under some sort of guideline or actuarial regime. The lone exception is the prosecutor. Although prosecutors need room to exercise discretion, their job is not so uniquely different from the other parts of the criminal justice system that they alone cannot do it if they are subjected to some sort of guidance.

New Tools

It's worth thinking a bit more about what charging guidelines should look like. In particular, states should develop risk and needs assessment tools, which wouldn't just assess the risks a defendant poses in the future, but also provide guidance about the sorts of treatment options—perhaps even noncriminal ones—that could work best.[15] Prosecutors think about these issues every day, but they have to make decisions about them fairly quickly, without any real training, and without any real guidance, certainly without any sort of formal tool. If we don't trust parole boards to decide who should be released without a risk tool, why do we trust prosecutors to make multiple similar calls without something similar?

Such tools would look different from current parole tools, and they would take some time to develop. A front-end tool would have to address far more complex questions than those currently confronted in the parole process. A parole tool considers two basic choices (release or detain), and is concerned with primarily one risk (recidivism). A front-end tool for prosecutors would need to consider a wider array of options (dismiss, divert, probation, jail, felony, registration, and more), each with different short- and long-run impacts on recidivism and other outcomes. A front-end tool would also need to take into account a greater range of possible goals besides just preventing recidivism; after all, in theory, a prosecutor is called upon to "do justice," not just "minimize crime."

A second-year prosecutor, just a few years out of law school, is handed a case involving a drug-addicted twenty-year-old arrested for the first time and accused of stealing a laptop to sell for drug money. Does the prosecutor charge this as a felony or a misdemeanor? Does he require the defendant to plead guilty but divert him to a drug court for treatment? Should he decline to charge at all as long as the defendant enters drug treatment outside the criminal justice system? The array of choices available to a prosecutor at the start of a case is dizzying in its complexity, and there are so many ways—both in terms of excess severity and leniency—for the prosecutor to get it wrong.

At first blush, this complexity makes the idea of a front-end tool seem implausible, but in fact it makes the need for such a tool all the clearer. Right now we are calling on young, inexperienced line prosecutors to make these decisions with little psychological and social science training and little time to process all the information. Whatever the flaws and challenges involved in these decisions, should we trust overworked, inexperienced people—however well-meaning—more than a (well-designed) front-end tool?

Moral Hazards

Legislators also need to target the moral-hazard problem of allowing county-elected prosecutors to send prisoners to state-funded prisons. Charging and plea guidelines could take this concern into account, but there are several other options that they have available to them.

The most comprehensive so far has been California's Realignment program, which requires people convicted of certain generally nonviolent felonies to serve their sentences in county jails rather than state prisons, even if these are years long. California enacted this under court-ordered duress, but Indiana has now voluntarily adopted a similar policy for its lowest felony class, suggesting that the idea is politically viable in less extreme situations than that faced by California with its overcrowding crisis. The big challenge with Realignment is that it is hard to extend it to cover people convicted of serious violent crimes, who continue to make up the bulk of state prison populations. The concern is clear: we don't necessarily want to force a poorer, higher-crime county to make tough choices about whether to trade off safety for, say, better schools—choices that richer counties wouldn't have to consider. A state-funded prison system may entail some desirable cross-subsidization, and realignment across the board—every county on its own for all crimes—eliminates that.[16]

A related concern is that forcing counties to internalize the costs of punishment may encourage them to adopt tactics that focus more on displacing crime to adjoining counties rather than actually reducing it. This already happens sometimes at the state level—at least one state adopted a sex-offender residency restriction law with the goal of basically trying to force everyone convicted of a sex offense out of the state—so there's no reason to assume it won't happen with counties as well.[17] Furthermore, few county jails are ready to handle a major increase in incarceration. In California, the solution was to provide temporary grants to counties to expand jail capacity. Unfortunately, in a cautionary tale all states should consider, the state eventually made the subsidies permanent, which undermined the cost-internalization goals of Realignment.

Realignment, of course, isn't the only way to make counties internalize the costs of incarceration. One recent paper proposed establishing a "cap-and-trade" market for prison beds.[18] Under such a plan, each county would be assigned a certain number of prison beds per year, and if they wanted to go over their limit they would need to buy the beds from other counties. These markets would function just like the cap-and-trade systems that have been successfully used in the environmental context. States could also use this system to gradually decarcerate by removing beds from the market over time. Such a centralized approach to bed management would provide a useful check on the unfettered ability prosecutors currently have to send people to prison. Decarceration could also arise if private advocacy groups bought up beds and took them out of circulation, like some environmental groups do with carbon pollution permits.[19]

Zones of Influence

The problem with prosecutor elections isn't just that too few people vote, or that voters vote based on limited information and in response to salient but idiosyncratic events. It is also that the "wrong" people have too much say. Powerful suburban voters may want prosecutors to go after crimes that are less pressing to the residents of high-crime neighborhoods (like drugs instead of murders), and they may not punish prosecutors for the collateral costs that aggressive enforcement may impose on those neighborhoods, since these suburbanites have little social or cultural interaction with those who do pay these costs.

One solution would be to rezone many prosecutors' offices, splitting the more urban counties into urban and suburban districts. Instead of a single Cook County State's Attorney in Illinois, there would be one for Chicago and one for the Cook County suburbs. Likewise, Detroit would have a prosecutor, as would the suburbs in the rest of Wayne County. We already see arrangements like this today in a few cities. Baltimore has its own state's attorney, and St. Louis its own district attorney, since both cities do not belong to any surrounding county. The district attorneys' offices in New York City likewise don't contain ring suburbs, although in that case it is because each borough is its own county. We could even go smaller. Chicago, among other places, has tried this model, establishing "community offices" to help prosecutors identify and focus on local concerns, and evidence suggests that this approach may be effective in reducing crime.[20]

The benefits of such localism are clear. Those who are most affected by a prosecutor's choices, for good or ill, would have a much bigger say in who held the job. Prosecutors in urban areas would likely focus more on the crimes that mattered most to the higher-crime areas, and they would be more sensitive to the costs these enforcement decisions imposed. The solution isn't perfect, since even within cities crime is densely concentrated, so the safer, more gentrified areas—which will likely still be wealthier and whiter—may act somewhat like mini-suburbs, and it's not like urban minorities speak with one voice when it comes to addressing crime either.[21] Those in high-crime areas would nonetheless have a larger voice, even if others remained larger still. Moreover, the more powerful constituencies in cities are generally more liberal than those in the suburbs, so their voting patterns may track those in higher-enforcement areas more than those in the suburbs.

Localism isn't without its risks. As with realignment approaches, we may be concerned that some prosecutors would just try to push crime over the border rather than eliminating it. And while most crime tends to be fairly localized, offending doesn't always respect political borders, so more localism will lead to more coordination costs. That said, the probable gains from better political oversight and control suggest that the idea of rezoning deserves more attention than it has received so far.

Expanding the Political Check

One more way to regulate prosecutors would be for the groups that get out the vote for prosecutors' elections to visibly monitor the prosecutors they subsequently vote in. Voting out a prosecutor in the wake of a major scandal may not change outcomes all that much if the new prosecutor assumes that he or she will be more or less ignored as long as there are no scandals.

In Chicago, for example, many of the activists who mobilized the vote in 2015 to oust Anita Alvarez, the incumbent prosecutor, were motivated more by their dislike of Alvarez than their support for her challenger, Kim Foxx. In fact, the night of Foxx's primary victory over Alvarez, activists made it clear they intended to hold Foxx accountable as well.[22] If these groups effectively keep pressure on Foxx, even in the absence of any attention-grabbing scandal, then they may show that the electoral check can force prosecutors to think more carefully about both the costs and the benefits of enforcement over the course of their terms. Furthermore, the more-local voters will likely be higher-information voters and thus less vulnerable to the false-positive and "Willie Horton" problems. Closer to both the costs of crime and the costs of enforcement, they would be more aware of the gains from the smarter programs and thus more tolerant of—and less panicked by—the inevitable mistakes.

POLITICAL DEFECTS

The ultimate solution to the political defects is significant cultural change: a move away from insisting that the costs of crime consistently trump any costs associated with enforcement, and away from an assumption that all crimes require a punitive response. There are, however, steps we can take even today to fix the worst excesses of the system. We should try to adopt these now, while crime rates remain low and the desire for reform is high.

We see, however, almost no action on this front. This failure to prepare for the political dangers of a future rise in crime is a major oversight. Maybe crime won't go back up; perhaps the decline of lead in car exhaust and paint, the rise of a cashless society that makes robbery and burglary less appealing, and medical improvements that turn potential murders into aggravated assaults are among the factors that herald a permanent change in crime rates. But there is no guarantee that current lows will hold indefinitely. The risk of rising crime remains, and it is better to prepare for it now.

One point I have made repeatedly is that political accountability isn't just an imperfect check on criminal justice actors, but a systematically flawed one. Voters put more weight on the costs of leniency than the costs of harshness, they focus too much on rare and shocking cases, and those who exert the most political power tend to be those who bear the fewest costs of failed policies. There are two broad ways to address these defects: change how prosecutors and other enforcers are chosen, and change who chooses them.

Appointing Prosecutors and Judges

One obvious way to shield those in charge of the criminal justice system from a low-information, high-salience electorate is to use appointments instead of elections. This is how the federal system operates: judges are appointed to jobs with lifetime tenure, and prosecutors are appointed by the president and confirmed by the Senate. Politics obviously still matter, even for appointed officials, but appointment provides them a bit more space to avoid having to respond as strongly to the latest shocking (and exceptional) crime.

There is already a movement, motivated by far more than just criminal justice issues, to replace elected judges with appointed ones. This is not a new concern; this effort goes back as far as 1931.[23] But the call for eliminating elections has been growing stronger lately, with criminal justice reformers increasingly pushing the issue.[24]

Events in Northern California in 2016 show the concerns that judicial elections raise. Aaron Persky, a judge in Santa Clara, sentenced a Stanford University student to six months in jail and three years on probation after he was convicted of attempting to rape an incapacitated woman outside a campus party. Outrage over the apparent leniency of the sentence sparked a well-orchestrated campaign to recall the judge. Even though the sentence imposed by Persky seemed quite light—the default sentence recommendation for the crime was a minimum of two years in prison—the campaign against him could have significant collateral costs.

The recall effort does not appear to be built around a claim that Persky is systematically too lenient in rape cases, or that he systematically favors defendants coming from privileged backgrounds.[25] Instead, the campaign appears to be based on the idea that a single sentence can be low enough to merit a recall. If the campaign is successful (it is still ongoing at the time of this writing), the implications will be clear: judges will not be able to guess which sentence will catch the public's eye for being too lenient, and so they will default to more punitiveness across the board to minimize the risk of the "one bad outcome."

If voters focused on overarching themes during elections—how does this judge sentence in general, or how do judges as a whole handle certain categories of offenses or defendants or victims—then making judges directly accountable could be useful. The Persky case, however, is a stark reminder that these elections inevitably turn on highly salient, though not necessarily representative, cases—and as a result, they will make judges more punitive in all the cases they decide.

Despite the current interest in judicial selection methods, however, no state has really changed its approach since the 1980s. On top of this, outside of a few think-tank arguments, the idea of using the criminal reform movement as a lever to help push for judicial appointment more generally does not seem to come up.

When it comes to prosecutors, however, there is almost no move toward appointment whatsoever. Despite concerns about the incentives of locally elected prosecutors, no reform bill has sought to change how prosecutors are chosen, and the issue does not appear to come up in reform discussions. In some cases, prosecutorial elections are enshrined in state constitutions, which means that reform would require amendments, but those are not too hard to ratify at the state level.

Arguing for appointed prosecutors may seem to contradict my earlier proposal on strengthening the electoral check. That idea, however, rested on a few assumptions: *if* enough of the electorate keeps its attention on the prosecutor throughout the term, and *if* that electorate effectively represents the people who most directly receive the benefits and bear the costs of enforcement, then elections may work. But if we think those conditions may not hold, then it may make more sense to appoint the prosecutor.

My sense—and I have no data to support this, only instinct—is that the geography of prosecutors is a bigger problem than the ill-informed electorate. In other words, if forced to choose between prosecutors elected by city electorates or prosecutors appointed by county officials, I would lean towards elected-by-city-voters. After all, the appointing county official likely suffers from many of the similar biases as the county electorate as a whole. The city voters, still relatively uninformed, are at least closer to the costs and benefits. Localism isn't without risks, but my sense is that those risks are the lesser evils.

Winning Elections, Carefully

As long as we are going to continue to elect criminal justice officials, however, we should at least think carefully about who we are electing. Take events in Chicago and Columbus, Ohio, in March 2016. In both cities, incumbent prosecutors lost primary challenges. For all their similarities, however—both campaigns involved urban prosecutors who had covered up or otherwise refused to pursue shocking, high-profile police killings—there was a critical difference between these two elections: the challengers' attitudes toward criminal justice reform. In Chicago, Kim Foxx was a former prosecutor who had grown disenchanted with the tough-on-crime policies of the incumbent, Anita Alvarez, and she had the backing of reform-minded political insiders, including the president of the Cook County Board of Commissioners and Cook County's powerful sheriff. In Cleveland, by contrast, challenger Michael O'Malley had been an assistant to the prior district attorney, whom the incumbent, Timothy McGinty, had replaced four years earlier—with

McGinty then running as the reform-minded challenger.[26] There was little, if any, evidence during the campaign that O'Malley had strong reformist leanings.

In short, Foxx seems like a reformer, while O'Malley seems more like a replacement—someone who will at best maintain the status quo. Both cases proved that a motivated electorate can unseat an unpopular incumbent. Both cases, however, may also prove to show in the years to come that it matters who the challenger is: the way criminal justice is administered is more likely to change in Chicago than in Cleveland. The electoral check is a blunt tool, and it does not control much of what a prosecutor will do. It is important that the person voted into the office has values that align with the electorate's—that the prosecutor can be trusted to do what the public wants even without constant monitoring.

This means that in the long run, reform groups will have to focus not just on getting out the vote, but on grooming people to run in these races. In many places, this may take time. It requires identifying people with the desired political views as well as the personality and temperament to run for elected office; it also requires helping them to develop the political and institutional contacts that it takes to win campaigns, especially in the larger counties where their impact will be the greatest. Ensuring that there are qualified, reform-minded candidates waiting to challenge a needlessly harsh incumbent when the latter becomes vulnerable is an essential, if long-run, project.

A Peculiar Omission

One major problem with relying on legislative reforms to end mass incarceration—besides the fact that much of the problematic discretion held by prosecutors and others cannot be fully legislatively contained—is that any victory can be easily undone in the future, as we saw with Congress and drug mandatories. And unlike with prosecutors and judges, we obviously can't replace legislators with appointed officials. Yet we can restrict the impact of problematic political pressure even on them—for example, by using sentencing commissions.

Establishing a commission removes (some) direct criminal justice policymaking from the hands of legislators, who are immediately accountable to voters and thus prone to overreact (even to just one or two shocking events), and transfers it to a small group of appointed individuals. The commissions that exist today vary in exact design, but in general they bring together a wide range of stakeholders—prosecutors, judges, legislators, defense attorneys, academics, even former inmates and victims in some cases—and they are given some control over how sentencing laws are written and implemented. Commissions are often tasked with gathering data and reporting on how the criminal justice system in fact functions; and they can slow down the decision-making process so that final decisions will be reached after the anger over a shocking crime has died down.

Today, at least twenty-one states, plus the District of Columbia and the federal government, have sentencing commissions, and there is some evidence (although little that is rigorous) that these commissions can be effective in resisting the political pressure to continuously expand prison populations.[27] Now, to be fair, not all commissions succeed. Louisiana has a commission as well as the highest incarceration rate in the country, and the federal system has also seen rapid growth. Conversely, some states, like New York and New Jersey, have experienced substantial declines without commissions.[28] The effectiveness of commissions turns heavily on how exactly they are designed.[29] For example, as one scholar (and federal sentencing commissioner) has pointed out, complete independence might not be a good thing—commissions need to be tied into the politics of the legislature enough that they can act like an effective interest group. With enough political influence, though, commissions can help counter tough-on-crime voices.

Also, how a commission's proposals go into effect matters as well. In some states, the legislature has to affirm the commission's proposals; in others, a proposal becomes law unless the legislature explicitly rejects it within some number of days. The latter approach is likely to produce a more rational set of laws, especially when it comes to scaling back punishments, since it is much less risky for politicians to fail to reject reforms than to explicitly support them.

In short, a well-designed commission could at least reduce some of the problematic political pressure legislatures face while giving experts a bigger voice in policymaking. Unlike some of the other ideas we have considered, sentencing commissions actually have a (somewhat) successful history—which makes it all the more peculiar, and disappointing, that they are currently overlooked.

How to Close More Prisons

I've talked extensively by now about the challenge posed by Census gerrymandering, so I won't belabor it here. In the short run, there likely won't be much progress along these lines. As we saw, prison gerrymandering generally favors the Republican Party, and the Republican Party is much more powerful than the Democratic Party at the state level. Census reform likely requires the Democratic Party to control both houses of the legislature and the governor's mansion, and in 2016 it had this sort of "trifecta" in just seven states (compared to twenty-three for the Republican Party).[30] When Republican control inevitably slips sometime in the future, however, states could work to end this sort of gerrymandering, which may make it easier to close prisons by shifting political power away from districts with correctional institutions.

Even without the Census issue, however, closing prisons is hard. New York, for example, is a state without Census gerrymandering, yet it has struggled to close facilities despite a significant decline in prison populations.[31] If states cannot close prisons as prison populations fall, then most of the hoped-for savings will not materialize. Closing prisons and cutting guard jobs, however, is not easy, both because of the guard unions, which often wield significant power, and because legislators in districts where there are prisons want to retain the (perceived) economic benefits they provide.

The problem is similar to one Congress faced at the end of the Cold War: How could it close military bases, when members of the House and Senate whose bases faced closure would fight hard to block any change? The solution Congress came up with was the Base Realignment and Closure (BRAC) process. Under BRAC, the Pentagon submits a list of proposed base closings to a commission, which can then add or delete bases; the resulting list is submitted to the president, who can approve or reject it in its entirety. If he approves it, then closures go into effect unless Congress rejects the list—again, only in its entirety—within a set period of time. The appeal of this process is that it eliminated a lot of the pork-barrel politics that would have otherwise occurred. Members of Congress could no longer argue, "But if you just keep *my* base open, how much will that cost?" It also eliminated logrolling ("You vote for my base, and I'll vote for yours"), given the all-or-nothing nature of the voting process. Moreover, the BRAC committee was subject to almost no oversight or review, which made it easier for its members to push through closures. BRAC is generally viewed as a success.[32]

The same approach could work for prison closures. The challenge, really, is getting such a commission approved in the first place. In New York, efforts to set up a commission just to *study* prison closures ended in defeat; tellingly, the committee chairman who killed the proposal came from Elmira, home to one of New York's larger prisons.[33] Recent efforts to implement a new BRAC round for military bases have similarly been thwarted by certain members of Congress whose districts have bases that are obviously prime targets for closure.[34]

This proposal would likely work best in states where prisons are concentrated in only a few counties—or perhaps in states where almost every district has a prison (so that most state representatives might face the same risk, and thus the same gain, from the program). Regardless, it seems that trusting legislatures to close prisons as prison populations shrink is akin to hoping Congress on its own would close military bases. Political scientists have long known that when the costs of a bill are concentrated and the benefits diffuse, proposals generally fail. BRAC should give reformers hope.

Going Private

Another way to cut the number of people in prison may be to rely *more* on private prisons. Given that private prisons are generally viewed as having helped cause mass incarceration, and as trying to thwart current reforms, this proposal might seem preposterously contrarian. Yet for all the criticism such institutions receive, there is a way that they could be used to fix one of the core political failures in the criminal justice system. As we saw earlier, the real problem with private prisons is inadequate contracts.

With better contracts, private prisons could actually be used as a tool of rehabilitation and decarceration.

At the heart of this argument is the "false-positive" problem, and the asymmetric costs of being too lenient versus too harsh. As we've seen before, excessive leniency has a much greater political cost than excessive harshness. A too-lenient sentence results in an identifiable victim, and an identifiable political actor (prosecutor, judge, parole board member) who could have prevented the crime through tougher choices. These costs are particularly high when it comes to people convicted of violent crimes—who, of course, make up a majority of those in prison. Excessive harshness, however, has a much more diffuse political cost, because it is impossible to identify specific inmates who would not have recidivated had they been released early; the best we can do is point to low-risk groups, most of whom likely would not reoffend.

Yet while excessive harshness does not have much political cost, it could have a much bigger economic cost if we structure contracts appropriately. Imagine that instead of paying private prisons based on the number of prisoners they held each day, we paid them based on how those prisoners performed upon release—that is, we would incentivize the output rather than the input. Medicine has been moving in this direction, attempting to replace a fee-for-service model that pays based on inputs (tests, scans, surgeries) with a value-based reimbursement system that rewards outputs (quality of the care provided, quality of the patient's life post-treatment). The movement is still in its infancy and faces numerous challenges—such as figuring out how to define and measure quality—but a few scholars have started to ask if similar incentives could be adopted in criminal justice.[35]

Under our current private prison contracts, program failure is actually rewarded: if a former prisoner returns, the private prison profits again. (So too in medicine, where a fee-for-service program can actually reward multiple imperfect surgeries more than one surgery done correctly the first time.) Rewarding private prisons based on outputs could encourage them to adopt—or even develop—effective rehabilitation and treatment programs. A contract that pays based on post-release behavior imposes a direct economic cost for each prisoner who is held too long. Every day an inmate needlessly sits in prison, the private prison company is throwing money away. It is now in the prison's interest to get the inmate out quickly, but with proper treatment.

There are myriad challenges with such an approach. What exactly is the right definition of "success" or "failure"? How long should we track each released prisoner for purposes of paying the institution? To what extent should we punish prisons by withholding funds for cases that don't succeed, as opposed to rewarding them for those that do? Moreover, even private prison officials will likely be somewhat risk-averse when it comes to releasing inmates. Even if all their releases make sense from a cost-benefit and risk-assessment perspective, too many high-profile failures—even if they happen purely by chance and are "justifiable" in the abstract—could lead to the loss of the contract. All these issues, however, are manageable with the right contracts. Even if there are imperfections to the system in the end, contracts offering better incentives could make private prison officials much more sensitive to the costs of harshness and thus less likely to over-detain in general.

Along these lines, it also makes sense to think about how to design better incentives for public-sector prisons. As it stands now, public prisons are basically fee-for-service institutions as well. Prisons remain open, and thus guards retain their jobs, so long as enough prisoners pass through. Moreover, given that most prisons are located far away from prisoners' homes, the costs of poor programming and the resulting recidivism are generally borne by distant communities, not by the warden and the local politicians. It may not be possible to design incentive contracts for public-sector employees and institutions that are exactly the same as those used for private contractors, but it is surely the case that promotions, funding, and other incentives should also be structured to reward outcomes.

Sunset Provisions

Thinking small, states could simply require that all new criminal and sentencing laws come with "sunset" provisions: unless the legislature explicitly reauthorizes the law in some number of years (five, ten, fifteen), the law automatically expires at the end of the period. Sunset provisions concede that during a time of rising crime or moral panic, it may simply be impossible to prevent the legislature from passing new, tough sentencing laws. The goal, then, is to make it easier to repeal these laws when the threat or panic has passed.

As we just saw with commissions, it is much easier not to reauthorize a law than it is to actively repeal it. If nothing else, no one is on the hook for sponsoring "softer" legislation. In fact, sunset provisions arguably seem win-win. If crime has fallen, legislators can point to their fiscal responsibility without having to take the step of actually repealing a sentencing law. If crime is still high at the sunset moment, however, legislators can reaffirm their toughness by reauthorizing the law—which would have remained valid in the absence of a sunset provision anyway.

A Wider View

One political issue that could be addressed fairly quickly is the often incoherent way that responsibility is fractured across various bureaucracies. A promising approach would be to expand the reach of the Justice Reinvestment Initiative, which so far thirty-one states have used in some capacity to divert money from prisons to effective alternatives to incarceration.[36] The JRI works by getting states to adopt non-incarcerative programs that have been proven to improve public safety and then reallocating the correctional savings to these projects.

JRI is appealing because it provides a way to transfer funds across various bureaucracies and levels of government (that is, state to county or county to city), thus reducing some of the costs created by the way the system currently spreads responsibility around. However, most JRI programs, if not all, focus on moving money from state criminal justice programs to more local criminal justice programs. The criminal justice system, however, is not the only means of managing and reducing crime. Primary education, public mental health treatment, job training and placement programs: all of these can help divert or deter people from engaging in crime, but none fall within the "criminal justice system" that is the focus of JRI.

Politicians often talk about the need to spend money on schools and mental health instead of prisons, but they never say how to accomplish this. JRI is an option, but it is not how the programs seem to be currently designed. If our goal is not just to reduce prison populations, but also to scale back our punitive approach to crime more generally—to view it, perhaps, more as a public health problem than anything else—then we need to embrace a wider view of where JRI funds can end up.

Hearts and Minds

More important than any legislative reform effort will be attempting to change people's attitudes toward crime. In many ways, this is perhaps the most important—and also the most challenging—project that reformers can undertake. Ronald Reagan famously said at a press conference in 1986 that the "nine most terrifying words in the English language are: I'm from the Government, and I'm here to help."[37] I disagree. The nine most terrifying words an elected official can say are, "My most important job is keeping the public safe."

Although it may be stated in slightly different ways, it's a bipartisan standby. Liberal New York City mayor Bill de Blasio invoked this trope when Tyrone Howard—who was free after a drug arrest owing to a diversion program—shot and killed New York police officer Randolph Holder.[38] Senator Tom Cotton, a staunch conservative from Arkansas, echoed this line several months later when he tried to block federal sentencing reform that would have led to the early release of several thousand people convicted of nonviolent crimes.[39] The attitude is bipartisan because it resonates with so much of the electorate. Nearly 60 percent of the US population today was at least fifteen years old in 1991, when crime peaked.[40] About 12 percent of the total population was at least fifteen in 1960, and thus lived through both the rise in crime and its (not completely offsetting) decline.

A public that has a less fearful attitude toward crime, that is willing to accept that safety is not the only goal, or not even necessarily the primary one, is a public that would be more likely to demand less aggressive and less punitive approaches to crime than what we now have. There is some cause for optimism. Younger Americans may not be that much better informed than older Americans about trends in crime, but they do appear to hold less-tough attitudes: they are more likely to favor targeting the root causes of crime than to emphasize deterrence, and to oppose the death penalty.[41] Both of these positions reflect less punitive attitudes, attitudes that are likely the product of the generally lower (and declining) crime rates younger Americans experienced growing up.

As always, however, race exerts its pernicious effects here. Take the gun control debate, a rare crime-control issue where people are often willing to say that some other value—here, the importance of Second Amendment rights—is more valuable than safety.[42] The history of gun control laws tells a concerning story. In 1967, as governor of California, Ronald Reagan signed the Mulford Act, which banned the open carry of loaded guns; the law was a response to the Black Panthers exercising their right to carry weapons.[43] "Safety," in other words, became paramount when those with the guns were black, not white. We should expect a similar response when it comes to crime as well. When those perceived as posing the threat are black, and when the costs of enforcement fall disproportionately on black Americans, "safety" will consistently receive undue emphasis.

Obviously, effecting "cultural change" is a very difficult task. Attitudes change slowly. In the short run, though, we can at least focus on making sure reform efforts don't unintentionally strengthen tough-on-crime attitudes, and that they reinforce the rehabilitation-oriented attitudes of younger voters. It is a change in attitude, more than anything else, that will prevent legislatures from bringing back tough laws they earlier repealed. Commissions, sunset provisions, impact statements: these can slow such reversals, but they cannot stop them. The best protection is to have legislators and prosecutors who simply do not respond in that way—because the electorate does not want them to.[44]

Which isn't to say that we should stop focusing on the laws. The relationship between attitudes and laws is complex. People's attitudes set limits on what legislators can do, but laws often shape how people think about issues and how to respond to them. It is vital to attack mass incarceration on both fronts.

VIOLENT CRIMES

When I say that safety should not automatically be our paramount concern in every instance, what I am saying, in essence, is that our attitude toward violent crime needs to change if we hope to end mass incarceration. The math may be inarguable, but the politics certainly are not. Indeed, this is a profoundly difficult issue to address politically, which explains some of the silence on the part of reformers on the matter.

As we saw near the beginning of this chapter, at the very least we should change the rhetoric we use when pushing for reforms aimed at nonviolent crimes in order to avoid making reforms aimed at violent crimes harder to adopt in the future. Better private prison contracts may also help us better account for the costs of being too harsh toward those convicted of violence. But now let's consider a few direct solutions.

Pilot Programs

In the short term states might consider developing pilot programs offering alternatives for those convicted of violent crimes. In general, reforms aimed at drug offenders have been more successful than those aimed at perpetrators of violent crimes, partly because people do not fear drug offenders as much as they fear people convicted of violence, but also partly because we simply have more validated alternatives for drug problems than for violence. We thus need to experiment more aggressively with testing programs (both inside and outside of prisons) that may work to reduce violence. This is another area where the federal government may actually be able to make a real difference. A few years ago the Brennan Center for Justice suggested that the US Department of Justice reorient its Edward Byrne Memorial Justice Assistance Grant program to provide "success-oriented funding"—that is, that it spend money on programs that clearly reduce both crime and incarceration rates.[45] Such grants could be used to fund pilot programs seeking to develop a better set of options for people convicted of violent offending. Local officials may be wary of funding such programs themselves, but they would perhaps accept federal money for these projects, and it could be an effective use of what is still, in the end, a fairly small amount of money.[46]

"Social-impact bonds" represent another, related option. Social-impact bonds involve the private sector funding a particular public-sector program. If the program fails to meet certain predetermined benchmarks, the funders receive nothing, but taxpayers have spent nothing as well. If it succeeds, the funders receive a payout tied to the gains from the program (ideally, both fiscal and social). The private actors funding these bonds may be more immune than legislators to the risks posed by a low-information, high-salience electorate. In a government-funded pilot program, one bad outcome could mean a legislator's loss in the next election. Private entities (for example, Goldman Sachs, which funded the first criminal justice social-impact bond in the United States, a rehabilitation program at Rikers Island jail in New York City) may be better able to weather the costs of failure.[47]

A Gradual Approach

One of the main reasons we should treat people convicted of violent crimes less harshly—besides basic human decency—is that it is simply good policy. Long sentences generally over-incapacitate while producing little to no additional deterrence in exchange. The data are clear on this lose-lose relationship, even if the public is not convinced. And it will be difficult to convince people that alternative approaches to managing people convicted of violence may be improvements.

So states could take steps to introduce reforms gradually—for example, by scaling back sentences for those convicted of violent crimes in stages. A state could experiment with, say, granting early release to a large cohort of inmates convicted of violent crimes who are over the age of forty, or who have served at least fifteen years in prison. The following year it could push back a little more, releasing a cohort of those who are over thirty-nine, or who have served at least fourteen years in prison. With each release, the state could track recidivism rates to keep an eye on the public safety implications. Such an approach would take longer to carry out than some sort of mass commutation or dramatic truncation of the official sanction. Yet it has several advantages. For example, it is simply more politically palatable than a bigger change; it can also be stopped before the political cost becomes too great, especially if there are design problems and the approach needs to be reevaluated.

A gradual approach may also allow states to lock in some incremental reforms that a single, big, all-or-nothing change could compromise. If crime spiked in the wake of some sort of mass commutation or other large-scale release, even if just by coincidence, lenient policies in general could become politically radioactive. With a gradual approach, politicians could hit the pause button on the program if crime started to rise, while still defending the earlier steps of the process. Furthermore, the more incremental the reform, the less severe, and thus the less salient, any bad result would be.

This sort of reform need not even explicitly refer to violent crimes. It could be framed as a graduated release program for "older inmates or those who have already served long sentences." As long as it doesn't explicitly *exclude* those convicted of violence, as so many of these reform laws do, its impact would fall disproportionately on those convicted of violent crimes. Subsequent analyses could then (hopefully) show that releasing these offenders did not hurt public safety.

A Phase, Not a State

Another appeal of the gradual approach is that it can be used to educate the public about what is perhaps the biggest and most important misperception of violence: that it is not a state, but a phase. Our rhetoric does not reflect this reality. We call people "violent offenders" instead of saying that they committed violent crimes. An attitude shift is essential, but it's very difficult to achieve. Proposing some sort of "let's just educate the public" campaign is the worst sort of useless idealism.

As we saw earlier, California's Proposition 36 provides an interesting lesson. Prop 36, adopted in 2012, reformed California's notoriously harsh three-strikes law and allowed many in prison for a third strike to petition for early release. Three years later, the *New York Times* reported on the remarkably low recidivism rates of over 2,000 third-strikers released early under Prop 36.[48] The article stressed that these parolees were older, and that older inmates tend to commit fewer crimes.

Direct education will likely fail—that's the whole problem with a low-information, high-salience electorate: that it doesn't really pay attention to non-salient outcomes. But if other programs succeed and win mainstream attention, a shift in attitudes and views could indeed occur. By showing the transitory nature of violent behavior, and by showing that the abstract charts and tables of criminology journals translate into released people not acting like they did when they were younger, graduated release programs could subtly shift the public's attitude about the permanence of violence. And that, perhaps, is the most fundamental change that we need.

CONCLUSION

I T'S HARD TO OVERSTATE THE SCOPE OF MASS INCARCERATION today. There are over 1.5 million people behind bars in state and federal prisons, and easily tens of millions who have passed through prison at some point in their lives. State and local governments spend over $200 billion per year on criminal justice, and about $50 billion just on locking people up in prisons; much of that money could be far better spent elsewhere. And neither that $50 billion nor that $200 billion takes into account the costs that incarceration imposes on individuals and communities, from lost income to disease to strained or broken families to children growing up with a missing parent.

After four decades of steady growth, the United States' sprawling prison system is finally facing concerted, bipartisan opposition. Prison populations dropped—slightly—in 2010 for the first time in nearly forty years, and states continue to push reform laws through their legislatures, often to great political fanfare.

I don't have that many drums, but I like to beat the few that I do have a lot. So I'm sure that by this point my main points are clear: Most of the reform efforts today are looking in the wrong places. The "Standard

Story" issues that concern reformers—drugs and other nonviolent crimes, long sentences, private prisons—are not irrelevant, but forces that are much more important to mass incarceration receive far less attention.

We need to restrict prison growth on the front end (admissions) even more than on the back end (parole), which means we need to regulate prosecutors more directly. We need to worry less about private-sector actors and admit that mass incarceration is almost entirely the product of the public sector, politicians and public-sector unions alike. Similarly, we need to accept that mass incarceration is a state and local problem, not a federal one, and that almost all the solutions must come from state and county governments. We need to correct the faulty incentives shaping enforcers' behavior, and we need to better insulate the criminal justice system from political passions. Finally, we certainly need to stop sending so many people convicted of nonviolent crimes to prison—but real, significant decarceration will require us to ask very tough questions about how to manage those convicted of violent crimes as well.

I don't want to seem churlish. It would have been impossible to immediately jump from the tough-on-crime, prison-for-all-offenses attitude that dominated the 1980s to the 2000s to punishing those convicted of murder and serious violent crimes less. The movement against mass incarceration had no option but to start where it did, focusing on drugs and other nonviolent crimes. That movement is nearly a decade old now, however, and it is important to pause and acknowledge that the gains have not been great. For all the energy and time and money poured into the process, for all the bridge building and collaboration across party lines, total prison populations outside of California are down by less than 2 percent since 2010 (and by barely 4 percent when we include California).

Given the rate of growth during the 1980s and 1990s, simply halting expansion is a victory; achieving any sort of decline is something truly worth celebrating. Yet in 2015, people quickly started to get nervous about rising crime, despite only small increases in only some cities, suggesting that the reform movement does not have the luxury of time. Its gains remain tentative and vulnerable. The standard justification for the current focus on drug and nonviolent crimes, on longer sentences, and on private prisons, is that we should go after the "low-hanging fruit" first, then move on to the harder-to-reach goals. Fair enough. But the time to start making that move is now.

The challenges are immense. Prosecutors are politically powerful, structural political reforms are difficult to enact, and addressing violent crimes poses significant political risk. At a deeper level, the pervasive racial geography of crime and punishment always imposes a serious barrier to reform. The costs and benefits of enforcement are borne disproportionately by poorer, more minority-based communities where the residents have relatively weaker political voices. As a result, the wealthier, whiter voters best able to implement reforms are also those who are least sensitive to the costs of our current approaches.

Still, there are a host of strategies we should be pursuing. Some appear straightforward enough, like changing how we talk about people who are in prison ("people convicted of violent crimes," not "violent offenders"). Some have been used before to some success and could, I hope, be resurrected, like sentencing commissions. Some may be harder to implement but could yield bigger returns, like prison closing commissions, well-designed incentivized prison contracts, better-funded public defenders, or prosecutorial guidelines. Finally, some require us to change our own and our fellow citizens' attitudes about how to balance the costs of crime and the costs of punishment—a profoundly difficult, but immensely important, task.

I find myself cautiously optimistic about the future of prison reform. Progress so far has been slow, but then it hasn't focused on the biggest drivers of prison growth. Prison reform remains one of the few truly bipartisan issues in our politically fractured time, which suggests that there is a genuine chance of turning attention to prosecutors, public incentives, and violent crimes.

There are still many ways that reform efforts can fail. Too ambitious a plan could produce a backlash that undermines current successes. By contrast, an overly cautious approach that limits itself to just what seems politically viable now will almost certainly dwindle away.

Simply stopping the rise in incarceration has been a huge accomplishment. If the goal is real decarceration, however, it is time to shift focus to the much broader, much more confounding issues that keep us locked in to our current predicament.

ACKNOWLEDGMENTS

First and foremost, I have to thank my wife, Molly, without whose constant love and support—and especially her unflagging patience—this book never could have been written. And our children, who were more understanding of all the times I couldn't play with them than I could have asked.

This book is the culmination of years of research on the causes of prison growth, so I also want to thank all my colleagues at Fordham and other schools across the country, as well as the administration at Fordham Law. I've received innumerable helpful comments over the years at workshops and conferences, and the law school has fully supported my work the entire time. I'd like to especially thank my reference librarian, Larry Abraham, who has been helping me with this project for years now; the entire library staff has always been there when I needed them. I'd also like to thank the army of research assistants who have helped me with the various papers that laid the foundation for this book.

Thanks, too, to Beau Kilmer at RAND, Ryan King at the Urban Institute, and Peter Enns at Cornell for insightful comments on various chapters of the book. I'd also like to thank Bret Bucklen, Scott Henson, Paul Levande, David Menschel, John Roman, and many others on "criminal justice Twitter" for many helpful debates and disagreements over the issues I've raised here; without doubt some of the most productive comments came up over the course of the long-running, 140-character conversations I've had with reformers and criminologists over the past several years.

Finally, I'd like to thank my incredible and tireless editor, Dan Gerstle, who did a fantastic job at every stage of this process. I also want to thank everyone else at Basic Books who helped put this together: Sandra Beris, Nicole Caputo, Betsy DeJesu, Carrie Majer, and Kathy Streckfus.

NOTES

INTRODUCTION: AMERICAN EXCEPTIONALISM

1. Technically, Seychelles now has a higher rate than the United States, which puts America in second place. But Seychelles is a small nation with fewer than 90,000 people, and only 735 people in prison. It seems unfair to compare it to the United States, where New York City alone has over 8 million people, and its local jail, Rikers Island, has a daily population of about 10,000. Seychelles would drop back to second place if it just released fewer than one hundred prisoners. World incarceration rates are from "Highest to Lowest—Prison Population Total," Institute for Criminal Policy Research, accessed July 6, 2016, www.prisonstudies.org/highest-to-lowest/prison-population-total. Note that this list does not include data from Eritrea, Somalia, and North Korea, and it relies on countries' own reports about prison populations. See Roy Walmsley, "World Prison Population List," 11th ed., Institute for Criminal Policy Research, February 2, 2016, accessed August 24, 2016, www.prisonstudies.org/sites/default/files/resources/downloads /world_prison_population_list_11th_edition.pdf.

2. Alfred Blumstein and Suomyo Moitra, "An Analysis of the Time Series of the Imprisonment Rate in the States of the United States: A Further Test of the Stability of Punishment Hypothesis," *Journal of Criminal Law and Criminology* 70 (1979): 376.

3. A quick definition: "Prisons," in the United States, hold people who have been convicted of "felonies," crimes that, in general, carry sentences of at least one year behind bars. Prisons are run and funded by the state. "Jails" hold people awaiting trial who have

either been denied bail or have yet to make bail, as well as those convicted of "misdemeanors," which are less serious crimes that generally carry sentences of less than one year behind bars. Jails are funded by the counties. The exceptions to this division are the states of Alaska, Connecticut, Delaware, Hawaii, Rhode Island, and Vermont, where the state governments run both prisons and jails. Much of the rest of the world does not separate out jails and prisons in this way, and as we'll see, this split between state and county responsibility can create some serious problems.

4. How can these numbers be so different? The annual numbers for prisons and jails—1.5 million for prisons, 700,000 for jails—come from counts of all people in the institutions on December 31 of that year. So someone in prison at the start of 2014 but released before December 31, 2014, doesn't appear in the 2014 prison count. Most prison terms are for at least a year, so a one-day count doesn't miss that many people. But jails are used for pretrial detention and for misdemeanor sentences, which in most states are for less than one year. So many people may be in jail for just a few days until their friends and families can pull together bail money. As a result, a single count on December 31 will miss a very large fraction of those who enter and leave jails over the course of the year.

5. The caveat: It's risky to compare crime statistics across long periods of time. Data gathering has improved, and how the FBI processes the data has changed as well. It's possible that crime rates were higher than officially reported in 1960, which, if true, would mean that the rise in crime has been less dramatic than we think—but only because things were worse in the 1960s than is evidenced in the records.

6. Marie Gottschalk, *Caught: The Prison State and the Lockdown of American Politics* (Princeton, NJ: Princeton University Press, 2015).

7. See, for example, Joycelyn Pollock, Steven Glassner, and Andrea Krajewski, "Examining the Conservative Shift from Harsh Justice," *Laws* 4 (2015): 107–124.

8. Unless I say otherwise, all data on prison populations and crime rates come from the US Department of Justice, Bureau of Justice Statistics, "Data Analysis Tools," available at www.bjs.gov/index.cfm?ty=data.

9. "Budget Deficit Slips as Public Priority," Pew Research Center, accessed July 6, 2016, www.people-press.org/2016/01/22/budget-deficit-slips-as-public-priority.

10. Eric L. Sevigny and Jonathan P. Caulkins, "Kingpins or Mules: An Analysis of Drug Offenders Incarcerated in Federal and State Prisons," *Criminology & Public Policy* 3 (2004): 401–434.

11. Eric Schlosser, "The Prison-Industrial Complex," *The Atlantic*, December 1998, accessed July 6, 2016, www.theatlantic.com/magazine/archive/1998/12/the-prison-industrial-complex/304669.

12. A recent study provides some sharp clarity on the debate over whether the racial disparity in punishment is due directly to race, or due more to class combined with the fact that blacks are disproportionately poor. Looking at the risk of incarceration by income decile, the paper shows that blacks in every income class—except for the top 10 percent—are more likely to end up in prison than even the *poorest* (bottom 10 percent) of whites. Both race and class, and the interaction between the two, matter, but race in-

arguably exerts a powerful independent force. Max Ehrenfreund, "Poor White Kids Are Less Likely to Go to Prison Than Rich Black Kids," *Washington Post*, March 23, 2016, accessed July 6, 2016, https://www.washingtonpost.com/news/wonk/wp/2016/03/23/poor-white-kids-are-less-likely-to-go-to-prison-than-rich-black-kids.

13. One leading legal academic, David Garland, attempted to define mass incarceration as prison populations that are above historical and comparative norms, and that in effect become the incarceration of entire groups instead of individuals. The second part may do some real work—the incarceration rate for black men without high school degrees can be as high as one in three—but the first part provides little guidance about when "high" becomes "mass." David Garland, "Introduction: The Meaning of Mass Imprisonment," *Punishment & Society* 3 (2001): 5–7.

14. James Jacobs is one of the few people to point out that no one ever seems to assemble any data to *establish* that incarceration rates are too high, but instead just generally assert it as a self-evident truth—which it isn't. James B. Jacobs, "Facts, Values, and Prison Policies," *Punishment & Society* 3 (2001): 183–188.

15. See Cut50, "What We Do," accessed July 6, 2016, www.cut50.org/mission.

16. Rucker Johnson and Steven Raphael, "How Much Crime Reduction Does the Marginal Prisoner Buy?" *Journal of Law & Economics* 55 (2012): 275–310. Many commentators cite a recent study by the Brennan Center for Justice, an advocacy group based at New York University, as showing that not only has the effectiveness of prison declined, but that it has hit zero. Oliver Roeder, Lauren-Brooke Eisen, and Julia Bowling, "What Caused the Crime Decline?," February 12, 2015, accessed July 6, 2016, https://www.brennancenter.org/publication/what-caused-crime-decline. Given some significant methodological flaws in that report, it likely underestimates the impact of incarceration, both in the past and today. See, e.g., John Pfaff, "One Last Post on Omitted Variables: CompStat, Politics, and Immigration," Prawfsblawg, March 17, 2015, accessed August 24, 2016, http://prawfsblawg.blogs.com/prawfsblawg/2015/03/one-last-post-on-omitted-variables-compstat-politics-and-immigration.html. Its qualitative claim, however, that prison is less effective today than it was before, is supported by Johnson and Raphael's findings.

17. Francis T. Cullen, Cheryl Lero Jonson, and Daniel S. Nagin, "Prisons Do Not Reduce Recidivism: The High Cost of Ignoring Science," *The Prison Journal* 91 (2011): 48S–65S.

18. Steven D. Levitt, "Understanding Why Crime Fell in the 1990s: Four Factors That Explain the Decline and Six Factors That Do Not," *Journal of Economic Perspectives* 18 (2004): 163–190.

19. As we will see in Chapter 4, correctional spending runs to about 6 or 7 percent of states' more limited "discretionary" budget.

20. I am assuming here, at some risk, that statistics from the 1960s and 2010s are comparable, which is likely untrue, as mentioned in note 5 above.

21. "Most States Cut Imprisonment and Crime," Pew Charitable Trusts, November 10, 2014, accessed July 6, 2016, www.pewtrusts.org/en/multimedia/data-visualizations/2014/imprisonment-and-crime.

22. I discuss this topic in more detail in John F. Pfaff, "Federal Sentencing in the States: Some Thoughts on Federal Grants and State Imprisonment," *Hastings Law Journal* 66 (2015): 1567–1600.

23. While the national and state incarceration *rates* peaked in 2008, national and state prison *populations* peaked in 2009: prison populations grew between 2008 and 2009, but the US population grew faster.

24. The twenty-five states that decarcerated shed 77,000 prisoners, while the states that grew added 21,000, for a net decline of 56,000. California's 35,000-prisoner reduction is 62 percent of the 56,000 net decline, and 45 percent of the gross 77,000 decline in the shrinking states.

25. "New York Prison Population," *Democrat & Chronicle*, accessed July 6, 2016, http://rochester.nydatabases.com/database/new-york-prison-population. To be fair, those twelve counties include the five counties of New York City, all of which saw steep declines, and which contain about half the state's population.

26. Philadelphia may be relinquishing its title as the county most inclined to impose life-without-parole sentences on children. In the wake of two US Supreme Court decisions (*Miller v. Alabama*, 567 US __ [2012] and *Montgomery v. Louisiana*, 577 US __ [2016]) that called many of these earlier juvenile life-without-parole (JLWOP) sentences into question, the district attorney in Philadelphia, Seth Williams, decided in June 2016 to seek life-with-parole sentences for all those who had been sentenced to JLWOP. Editorial Board, "When a Life Sentence Starts at 15," *New York Times*, June 8, 2016, accessed July 6, 2016, www.nytimes.com/2016/06/08/opinion/when-a-life-sentence-starts-at-15.html.

27. Jo Craven McGinty, "How Many Americans Have a Police Record? Probably More Than You Think," *Wall Street Journal*, August 7, 2015, accessed July 6, 2015, www.wsj.com/articles/how-many-americans-have-a-police-record-probably-more-than-you-think-1438939802.

28. For a good discussion of just how many blind spots exist in criminal justice data, see Tom Meagher, "13 Important Questions About Criminal Justice We Can't Answer, and the Government Can't Either," The Marshall Project, May 15, 2016, accessed July 6, 2016, https://www.themarshallproject.org/2016/05/15/13-important-questions-about-criminal-justice-we-can-t-answer.

29. The different counts come from Tables 29, 30, and 32 of *Crime in the United States: 2014*. Filling in these gaps is trickier than it might seem at first. If agencies just randomly forget to report in some months (perhaps a small force has only one part-time stats person, and he happened to be sick a lot one June), then it's easy to just average out the missing months. But it's quite possible that police departments are strategically choosing which months not to report—although it is hard to know why. Perhaps the more obvious claim would be that they are omitting months when crime was particularly high, and the police departments don't want to look bad. That's certainly plausible. But there's a more cynical possibility as well. Perhaps they are omitting months when crime rates are particularly *low*, because the police departments don't want to risk losing

outside funding to fight crime. The FBI has techniques for filling the gaps, but there's no settled way to handle this problem, and disputes can sometimes arise. See Michael D. Maltz and Joseph Targonski, "A Note on the Use of County-Level UCR Data," *Journal of Quantitative Criminology* 18 (2002): 297–318.

30. Other datasets face similar extrapolation challenges. For example, the BJS reported that in 2013, 53 percent of state prisoners were in prison for violent crimes, 19 percent for property crimes, and 16 percent for drug crimes. E. Ann Carson, "Prisoners in 2014," US Department of Justice, Bureau of Justice Statistics, accessed July 6, 2016, www.bjs.gov/content/pub/pdf/p14.pdf. This seems like it would be a fairly easy calculation to make, but in a footnote, the BJS notes that these numbers come from a specific study—and only if you're familiar with the study do you know that it tends to oversample northern, more industrial, more liberal states, and thus may not paint a completely accurate picture of national trends.

31. The BJS recently announced plans to start trying to gather data on police-involved killings. See Jon Swaine, "Police Will Be Required to Report Officer-Involved Deaths Under New US System," *The Guardian*, August 8, 2016, accessed August 24, 2016, www.theguardian.com/us-news/2016/aug/08/police-officer-related -deaths-department-of-justice.

32. The Bureau of Justice Statistics, the statistics-gathering arm of the federal Department of Justice and the source of almost all the data I use here, does a fantastic job. An *amazing* job, once you realize the constraints under which it operates. One way that Congress has sought to rein in a $3.5 trillion budget has been to cut the BJS's budget between 2009 and 2015 by $4 million, from $45 million to $41 million (although at the start of the 2010s, the budget did rise somewhat to help improve one specific dataset). That $4 million is 0.0001 percent of that $3.5 trillion. To the extent we are flying blind here, it is almost entirely by choice. See US Department of Justice, "FY 2010 Budget Request at a Glance," accessed July 6, 2016, https://www.justice.gov/sites/default /files/jmd/legacy/2014/07/28/ojp-bud-summary.pdf; and "US Department of Justice FY 2016 Budget Request," accessed July 6, 2016, https://www.justice.gov/sites/default /files/jmd/pages/attachments/2015/02/02/7._state_and_local_fact_sheet.pdf.

CHAPTER ONE: THE WAR ON DRUGS

1. Michelle Alexander, *The New Jim Crow* (New York: The New Press, 2012), 6.

2. John F. Pfaff, "For True Penal Reform, Focus on the Violent Offenders," *Washington Post*, July 26, 2015, accessed July 6, 2016, https://www.washingtonpost.com/opinions /for-true-penal-reform-focus-on-the-violent-offenders/2015/07/26/1340ad4c-3208 –11e5–97ae-30a30cca95d7_story.html. Note that Obama managed to merge together two major errors of the Standard Story: drug offenses and long sentences. To his credit, in a later interview with the Marshall Project he acknowledged that the incarceration of people for violent crimes has been a much bigger factor in pushing up prison populations than locking up people convicted of drug crimes. "Transcript

of White House Discussion on Criminal Justice Reform," The Marshall Project, October 22, 2015, accessed July 6, 2016, https://www.themarshallproject.org/documents /2480829-transcript-of-white-house-discussion#.wkdj23pQy.

3. Andrew Glass, "Reagan Declares 'War on Drugs,' October 14, 1982," *Politico*, October 14, 2010, accessed July 6, 2016, www.politico.com/story/2010/10/reagan -declares-war-on-drugs-october-14-1982-043552.

4. Taking into account the federal system, which focuses much more on drugs, raises the number of people in prison on drug charges by 2013 from about 200,000 to 300,000, and the percentage of prisoners locked up for drug offenses by around four or five points (so from 16 percent to 20 percent in 2013).

5. Of course, that means that arrests for possession rose by over 300,000 during that time. Although this was only 10 percent of all arrests in 2012, this volume of possession arrests is surely an important misallocation of resources.

6. See, for example, Dan Werb, Greg Rowell, Gordon Guyatt, Thomas Kerr, Julio Montaner, and Evan Wood, "Effect of Drug Law Enforcement on Drug Market Violence: A Systematic Review," *International Journal of Drug Policy* 22 (2011): 87–94. The *net* effect of the war on drugs, however, is slightly trickier to ferret out, as we'll see shortly. Perhaps the killing that happened in a fight over drug territory would have happened in the absence of prohibition, too, only for a different reason. Furthermore, prohibition may prevent some crimes if the threat of punishment causes some people to abstain from drugs and thus to avoid drug-related criminal conduct.

7. John F. Pfaff, "The War on Drugs and Prison Growth: Limited Importance, Limited Legislative Options," *Harvard Journal on Legislation* 52 (2015): 173–220; John F. Pfaff, "The Micro and Macro Causes of Prison Growth," *Georgia State University Law Review* 28 (2012): 1237–1272; John F. Pfaff, "Escaping from the Standard Story," *Federal Sentencing Reporter* 26 (2014): 265–270; Leon Neyfakh, "Why Are So Many Americans in Prison? A Provocative New Theory," *Slate*, February 6, 2015, accessed July 6, 2016, www.slate.com/articles/news_and_politics/crime/2015/02/mass _incarceration_a_provocative_new_theory_for_why_so_many_americans_are.html.

8. Leon Neyfakh, "'A Profound, Glaring Injustice': Sen. Cory Booker on Mass Incarceration—and the Hard Choices We'll Need to Make If We Want to End It," *Slate*, August 21, 2015, accessed July 6, 2016, www.slate.com/articles/news_and_politics /crime/2015/08/cory_booker_interview_the_new_jersey_senator_on_how_to_end _mass_incarceration.html; Leon Neyfakh, "Cory Booker and Newt Gingrich Want to Redefine What Is Considered a 'Violent' Crime," *Slate*, March 26, 2015, accessed July 6, 2016, www.slate.com/blogs/the_slatest/2015/03/26/bipartisan_summit_on_criminal _justice_reform_cory_booker_wants_to_redefine.html.

9. "South Carolina's Public Safety Reform," Pew Center on the States, June 2010, accessed July 6, 2016, www.pewtrusts.org/~/media/assets/2010/06/10/pspp_south _carolina_brief.pdf.

10. Michael Dresser, "Hogan Signs Bill to Overhaul Maryland Criminal Justice System," *Baltimore Sun*, May 19, 2016, accessed July 6, 2016, www.baltimoresun.com /news/maryland/politics/bs-md-justice-reinvestment-20160518-story.html.

11. "Report of the Georgia Council on Criminal Justice Reform," State of Georgia, February 2015, accessed July 6, 2016, www.gjp.org/wp-content/uploads/2014–2015-CJRC-Report.pdf.

12. See, for example, Eloise Dunlap, Bruce D. Johnson, Joseph A. Kotarba, and Jennifer L. Fackler, "Macro-Level Social Forces and Micro-Level Consequences: Poverty, Alternate Occupations, and Drug Dealing," *Journal of Ethnicity in Substance Abuse* 9 (2010): 115–127.

13. Legalization and decriminalization are often used interchangeably, but they should not be. Legalization would result in a regime like that for tobacco or alcohol, while under decriminalization, transportation and distribution would still remain illegal, but the possession of consumption-level amounts would no longer be punished. The impact of legalization would surely be greater than that of decriminalization. Private firms, for example, would enter the market under legalization, but not under decriminalization, leading to very different impacts on price. Likewise, under legalization, disputes could be resolved by the legal system, whereas decriminalization would force people to still resort to more informal—that is, more violent—solutions.

14. It's true that the price of drugs like cocaine and heroin have fallen over much of the time that the war on drugs has been taking place. But this is because the international producers have professionalized their shipping networks. One study estimates that the price of drugs was about 15 percent higher than it otherwise would have been but for interdiction. Mark A. R. Kleiman, Jonathon P. Caulkins, and Angela Hawken, *Drugs and Drug Policy: What Everyone Needs to Know* (New York: Oxford University Press, 2011).

15. Decriminalization would have a lesser impact on price. The risk that dealers face would technically remain the same, so prices would have to remain higher to reflect that. Yet the amount of risk may fall—police may enforce drug laws less, and fewer buyers would turn on dealers to cut plea deals—possibly leading to some decline in price, albeit one less than the drop that legalization would produce. Moreover, the riskiness of buying drugs would decrease for users, which would likely lead to an increase in demand, even if prices didn't decline.

16. Kleiman et al., *Drugs and Drug Policy*.

17. Devah Pager, *Marked: Race, Crime, and Finding Work in an Era of Mass Incarceration* (Chicago: University of Chicago Press, 2007).

18. Jill Leovy, *Ghettoside: A True Story of Murder in America* (New York: Random House, 2015), 48. For LA-wide clearance, see "Crime Clearance Rates," Los Angeles Almanac, accessed July 6, 2016, www.laalmanac.com/crime/cr05.htm. Note that this means the white rate was even further above the average of 50 percent.

19. Justin Glawe, "The War on Drugs Could Be Making Our Communities More Dangerous," *Vice*, November 8, 2015, accessed July 6, 2016, www.vice.com/read/the-war-on-drugs-could-be-making-our-communities-more-dangerous-456. Given that violent and property crime have generally been on the decline since 1991, even though arrests for drugs (at least for possession) have risen over the 2000s and 2010s, it's not clear that the existence of drug units has led to an increase in crime, although perhaps crime would have fallen faster still but for the existence of drug units.

20. See Sudhir Venkatesh, *Off the Books: The Underground Economy of the Urban Poor* (Cambridge, MA: Harvard University Press, 2009). This work shows that focusing on how to improve second chances ignores the fact that, even absent criminal records, many poor people lack "first chances" to start with, a point that Marie Gottschalk echoes in *Caught*. Note, too, the structural barriers to stable employment poor urban minorities often face. Without the war on drugs, fewer inner-city residents would have prior felony records due to drug crimes, which would eliminate some of the stigma that makes second chances so hard.

21. Brendan O'Flaherty and Rajiv Sethi, "Homicide in Black and White" (working paper, 2010), accessed July 6, 2016, www.columbia.edu/~rs328/Homicide.pdf.

22. Alexia Cooper and Erica L. Smith, "Homicide Trends in the United States, 1980–2008," US Department of Justice, Bureau of Justice Statistics, November 2011, accessed July 6, 2016, www.bjs.gov/content/pub/pdf/htus8008.pdf.

23. It overstates the impact because some of these people would have ended up in prison regardless, and it understates the impact because it excludes those non-drug offenders who would not have been in prison in a world without prohibition.

24. Richard Nixon, "Special Message to the Congress on Drug Abuse Prevention and Control," June 17, 1971, accessed July 6, 2016, archived at American Presidency Project, www.presidency.ucsb.edu/ws/?pid=3048.

25. Jacob Sullum, "Was Nixon a Drug Warrior or Reformer," *Reason Hit & Run Blog*, June 14, 2011, accessed July 6, 2016, http://reason.com/blog/2011/06/14/was-nixon-a-drug-warrior-or-a.

26. Molly M. Gill, "Correcting Course: Lessons from the 1970 Repeal of Mandatory Minimums," Families Against Mandatory Minimums, July 2013, accessed July 6, 2016, http://famm.org/wp-content/uploads/2013/07/Correcting-Course-Final-version.pdf.

27. The challenge is that it is really hard to disentangle cause and effect: Did Nixonian rhetoric toughen attitudes, or was Nixon a savvy enough politician that he realized attitudes were hardening as crime and drug use rose, and therefore adapted his rhetoric accordingly? This is a perennially unaddressed problem in "this politician's rhetoric caused some policy" stories. Emily Dufton, "The War on Drugs: How President Nixon Tied Addiction to Crime," *The Atlantic*, March 26, 2012, accessed July 6, 2016, www.theatlantic.com/health/archive/2012/03/the-war-on-drugs-how-president-nixon-tied-addiction-to-crime/254319.

28. Glass, "Reagan Declares 'War on Drugs.'"

29. Margaret Wener Cahalan, "Historical Corrections Statistics in the United States, 1850–1984," US Department of Justice, Bureau of Justice Statistics, December 1986, accessed July 6, 2016, www.bjs.gov/content/pub/pdf/hcsus5084.pdf. In fact, somewhat ironically, 1983 and 1984 were among the *slowest* growing years of that era.

30. James Austin and Michael P. Jacobson, "How New York City Reduced Mass Incarceration: A Model for Change?" Brennan Center for Justice, January 2013, accessed July 6, 2016, www.brennancenter.org/sites/default/files/publications/How_NYC_Reduced_Mass_Incarceration.pdf. Note that admissions for drug crimes started to de-

cline in 1992, while the total number serving time for drugs peaked in 1995 and started to decline in 1997; this suggests that people in New York prisons for drug offenses in the early 1990s were spending three to four years in prison: not long, but longer than drug sentences tend to be. While I'm arguing that the importance of the RDLs is overstated, that doesn't mean they are irrelevant.

31. Brennan doesn't break down the non–New York City counties; it would be interesting to see if other urban counties, such as Erie (Buffalo) and Onondaga (Syracuse), also saw declines. If so, that would imply that drug crime admissions from rural counties grew even more steeply.

32. Stephanie Clifford and Joseph Goldstein, "Brooklyn Prosecutor Limits When He'll Target Marijuana," *New York Times*, July 8, 2014, accessed July 6, 2016, www.nytimes.com/2014/07/09/nyregion/brooklyn-district-attorney-to-stop-prosecuting-low-level-marijuana-cases.html.

33. For example, even as the federal government scaled back its enforcement of marijuana laws in states that had legalized marijuana's use, one federal prosecutor continued to aggressively file federal charges against California dispensaries. Carly Schwartz, "Justice Department Continues to Crack Down on Medical Marijuana in California," *Huffington Post*, February 3, 2015, accessed August 24, 2016, huffingtonpost.com/2015/02/03/harborside-melinda-haag-appeal_n_6608768.html.

34. The 1994 Violent Crime Control Act offered millions of dollars to states that adopted "truth-in-sentencing" (TIS) laws that restricted parole for people convicted of certain violent offenses. Yet most states said that the grants had little impact on their decision whether to adopt TIS laws (which some states had started implementing prior to 1994), with only four saying it really shaped their decisions. "Truth in Sentencing: Availability of Federal Grants Influenced Laws in Some States," United States General Accounting Office, Report to Congressional Requesters, February 1998, accessed July 6, 2016, www.gao.gov/archive/1998/gg98042.pdf. Conversely, the federal Sex Offender Registration and Notification Act threatened to cut some funding to states that did not adopt the federal government's harsh sex offender registration standards by 2011, but as of today only seventeen have met the new standards, with the rest opting to take the hit rather than change their laws. See "SORNA," Office of Sex Offender Sentencing, Monitoring, Apprehending, Registering, and Tracking, accessed July 6, 2016, http://www.smart.gov/sorna.htm; "Some States Refuse to Implement SORNA, Lose Federal Grants," *Prison Legal News*, September 19, 2014, accessed July 6, 2016, https://www.prisonlegalnews.org/news/2014/sep/19/some-states-refuse-implement-sorna-lose-federal-grants.

35. My focus in this book is primarily on the states, but I should highlight how much the federal government is an outlier here. Due to the limits the Constitution places on the sorts of crimes the federal government can prosecute, nearly *half* of all federal prisoners are in for drug crimes, compared to about 16 percent of state prisoners. "Offenses," Federal Bureau of Prisons, May 28, 2016, accessed July 6, 2016, https://www.bop.gov/about/statistics/statistics_inmate_offenses.jsp.

36. Most of this discussion comes from Pfaff, "War on Drugs and Prison Growth."

37. Eric L. Sevigny and Jonathan P. Caulkins, "Kingpins or Mules: An Analysis of Drug Offenders Incarcerated in Federal and State Prisons," *Criminology and Public Policy* 3 (2004): 401–434. Prior arrest rates were much higher than that, but arrests are ambiguous signals of guilt, and even more ambiguous signals of seriousness.

38. Simplifying greatly, it may be impossible to charge Sam with murder unless a few witnesses come forward, and these may be slow to materialize in high-crime neighborhoods with uneasy relationships with the police. Making the drug bust is far easier, and conviction may just require the testimony of the arresting officers.

39. Paul Guerino, Paige M. Harrison, and William J. Sabol, "Prisoners in 2010," US Department of Justice, Bureau of Justice Statistics, December 2011, accessed July 6, 2016, www.bjs.gov/content/pub/pdf/p10.pdf; E. Ann Carson, "Prisoners in 2013," US Department of Justice, Bureau of Justice Statistics, September 2014, accessed July 6, 2016, www.bjs.gov/content/pub/pdf/p13.pdf; E. Ann Carson, "Prisoners in 2014," US Department of Justice, Bureau of Justice Statistics, September 2015, accessed July 6, 2016, www.bjs.gov/content/pub/pdf/p14.pdf..

40. If we released every prisoner and jail inmate confined for drug charges, the combined (no-drug) prison and jail incarceration rate would drop from nearly 700 per 100,000 to about 557. In 2014, that would have been the fourth-highest rate in the world, although the countries ahead of us would have been the small nations of the Seychelles (735 prisoners in a population of 90,000), St. Kitts and Nevis (334 prisoners in a population of about 54,000), and Turkmenistan (30,568 prisoners in a population of 5.2 million). Turkmenistan is the only country of any real size here, though it still has fewer people than just New York City. The data on populations is available at "Highest to Lowest: Prison Population Rate," Institute for Criminal Policy Research, www.prisonstudies.org/highest-to-lowest/prison_population_rate?field_region_taxonomy_tid=All.

41. Sevigny and Caulkins, "Kingpins or Mules." There is only one newer survey, conducted in 2004, and it wasn't available to Sevigny and Caulkins, since their paper came out in 2004. The survey is supposed to be done every six or seven years, but the congressional cuts to the Bureau of Justice Statistics' already too-small budget has forced it to delay the next wave of the survey.

42. Pfaff, "War on Drugs and Prison Growth."

43. It's not an unreasonable definition. One of Alexander's key points—an important one that is rightly getting more attention these days—is that the costs and stigma of going to prison cling to prisoners long after they have been released, so being outside of prison does not exactly mean people are free from it.

44. Here's an example: Assume that a criminal justice system sends one thief to prison each year for a one-year term, and two drug dealers to prison for six-month terms each, with each drug-dealer's term starting as soon as the other one ends (so one dealer is locked up from January 1 to June 30, and the next from July 1 to December 31). On any given day, there are two people in prison, and half of them are there for drug crimes. But in any given *year*, three people go to prison, *two-thirds* of them for drug crimes. Because the drug offenders leave more rapidly, we will observe fewer of them on any one day that we look.

45. The data came from the National Corrections Reporting Program (NCRP), a

large inmate-level dataset maintained by the Bureau of Justice Statistics. The NCRP gathers data from more than fifteen states, but for various reasons only fifteen provided sufficiently reliable data for a sufficient number of years. These states are California, Colorado, Georgia, Iowa, Kentucky, Michigan, Missouri, New York, North Dakota, Oklahoma, Oregon, Pennsylvania, Tennessee, Utah, and West Virginia.

46. These results are fairly consistent with other national-level data that report the percentage of people admitted to prison each year for drug offenses: the national data show a decrease from 32 percent in 2000 to 25 percent in 2011; the aggregate percentages shown in the table, between 18 percent and 27 percent, seems fairly close to that. It's possible that the states in this dataset are slightly less aggressive against drugs than the rest of the country, but likely not by much.

47. Between 1980 and 1990, about 50 percent of all people in prison were released in any one year. In the early 1990s, that percentage dropped to about 40 percent. By the 2000s, it had moved upward to about 45 percent.

48. Lawrence F. Travis III and James Stacey, "A Half-Century of Parole Rules: Conditions on Parole in the United States, 2008," *Journal of Criminal Justice* 38 (2010): 604–608.

49. Note that "possession of drugs" might not be a separate crime when that drug is alcohol. Generally parolees are required to abstain not just from illegal drugs but from alcohol as well, so being in possession of alcohol may be grounds for a parole violation even if it isn't a stand-alone offense.

50. The exceptions here are clear. First, plenty of arrests don't turn into charges, but in some cases the arrest itself is enough to send someone back to prison for violating parole. Second, even if the parolee admitted in the survey that he had committed a new crime, that doesn't mean that the prosecutor necessarily could have proven that beyond a reasonable doubt.

51. How many unique people make up those 43.4 million arrests is simply something we lack data on, which is a deeply problematic empirical blind spot.

52. Sean Rosenmerkel, Matthew Durose, and Donald Farole, "Felony Sentences in State Courts, 2006—Statistical Tables," US Department of Justice, Bureau of Justice Statistics, December 2009, accessed July 6, 2016, www.bjs.gov/content/pub/pdf/fssc06st.pdf.

53. It's also possible that the police could track those with prior records more closely, or that they find it easier to arrest those with records because they are already under surveillance by probation or parole, or because they have fingerprints and DNA evidence on file. Arrests, however, have fallen along with crime from the 1990s through the 2010s, so it's hard to see how prior records could be increasing prison populations by increasing arrests.

54. Hannah Laqueur, "Uses and Abuses of Drug Decriminalization in Portugal," *Law & Social Inquiry* 40 (2015): 746–781; George Murkin, "Drug Decriminalisation in Portugal: Setting the Record Straight," Transform: Getting Drugs Under Control, June 11, 2014, accessed July 6, 2016, www.tdpf.org.uk/blog/drug-decriminalisation-portugal-setting-record-straight; Alex Stevens, "Portuguese Drug Policy Shows That Decriminalisation Can Work, But Only Alongside Improvements in Health and Social Policies,"

London School of Economics and Political Science, October 12, 2012, accessed July 6, 2016, http://blogs.lse.ac.uk/europpblog/2012/12/10/portuguese-drug-policy-alex-stevens.

55. Stevens, "Portuguese Drug Policy."

56. Kleiman et al., *Drugs and Drug Policy*.

57. German Lopez, "Portugal Decriminalized Drugs in 2001: Barely Anything Changed," *Vox*, June 19, 2015, accessed July 6, 2016, www.vox.com/2015/6/19/8812263 /portugal-drug-decriminalization.

58. Kleiman et al., *Drugs and Drug Policy*.

59. The war on drugs is not the only thing that shapes the price of illegal drugs. From the 1960s and 1970s through today, drug producers have developed increasingly sophisticated distribution networks, which have driven down the price of drugs. The war on drugs pushed back against that decline, not so powerfully that it caused prices to rise, but enough that it caused prices to drop at a slower rate, with perhaps a few isolated exceptions (like possibly causing a rise in cocaine prices around 2006: Beau Kilmer, "Uncle Sam's Cocaine Nosedive: A Brief Exploration of a Dozen Hypotheses," RAND Corporation, May 4, 2016, accessed July 6, 2016, www.rand.org/pubs/external_publications /EP66463.html). Kleiman et al., *Drugs and Drug Policy*.

60. Craig A. Gallet, "Can Price Get the Monkey Off Our Back? A Meta-Analysis of Illicit Drug Demand," *Health Economics* 23 (2014): 55–68; Dhaval Dave, "Illicit Drug Use Among Arrestees, Price and Policy," *Journal of Urban Economics*, 63 (2008): 694–714. Some data suggest that users' demand for drugs are fairly insensitive to price, so cheaper drugs means that users will just buy the same amount for less. Some users, however, will likely buy more drugs as prices fall, which would increase the risk that they may offend more to cover rising total costs.

61. What those crimes are will vary with the type of drug. See Office of National Drug Control Policy, "Improving the Measurement of Drug-Related Crime," 2013, accessed July 6, 2016, https://www.whitehouse.gov/sites/default/files/ondcp/policy-and -research/drug_crime_report_final.pdf.

62. Stevens, "Portuguese Drug Policy."

63. Kleiman et al., *Drugs and Drug Policy*, 23.

64. Between 1984 and 1993, the homicide rate for black men aged eighteen to twenty-four rose by over 17 percent, to about 200 per 100,000 in 1993, a level ten times higher than the homicide rate of 20 per 100,000 for white males in the same age group. In 1980, the black rate for males in that group was about five times higher than the white rate (100 per 100,000 vs. 17 per 100,000). So the rise during the crack epidemic doubled the gap: it was a major increase, but from an already-high baseline. Cooper and Smith, "Homicide Trends."

65. "Quick Facts: United States," US Department of Commerce, Census Bureau, http://quickfacts.census.gov/qfd/states/00000.html.

66. Carson, "Prisoners in 2014," Appendix Table 4. Neither set of numbers adds up to 100 percent, due to other ethnic groups.

67. For the second claim, see, for example, Alexander, *New Jim Crow*; Katherine

Beckett, Kris Nyrop, Lori Pfingst, and Melissa Bowen, "Drug Use, Drug Possession Arrests, and the Question of Race: Lessons from Seattle," *Social Problems* 52 (2005): 419–441.

68. The inmate data is from Carson, "Prisoners in 2014." Population data is from "Quick Facts."

69. See, for example, the literature review in Ojmarrh Mitchell and Michael S. Caudy, "Race Differences in Drug Offending and Drug Distribution Arrests," *Crime & Delinquency* (2015), accessed July 6, 2016, doi: 10.1177/0011128714568427.

70. See, for example, Alexander, *New Jim Crow*, 6 n.10–11, who cites several studies to support the claim that whites and blacks use and sell drugs at the same rate. Almost all her studies, however, look only at use. The only study that discusses sales is a survey of juveniles, and it appears to only ask if the respondents "ever sold drugs," without accounting for how much was sold or how frequently the person sold drugs—clearly a critical factor when thinking about the risks of various punishments. Furthermore, while the study does show that whites under the age of eighteen were more likely to admit to selling drugs than similarly aged black respondents (17 percent to 13 percent), the results seem to imply—although the report itself is somewhat unclear on this point—that blacks aged eighteen and nineteen, an age more likely to result in incarceration, are more likely to sell than whites. See Howard N. Snyder and Melissa Sickman, "Juvenile Offenders and Victims: 2006 National Report," US Department of Justice, Office of Juvenile Justice and Delinquency Prevention, 2006, 70–71.

71. See Leah J. Floyd, Pierre K. Alexandre, Sarra L. Hedden, April L. Lawson, and William W. Latimer, "Adolescent Drug Dealing and Race/Ethnicity: A Population-Based Study of the Differential Impact of Substance Use on Involvement in Drug Trade," *American Journal of Drug and Alcohol Abuse* 36 (2010): 87–91, for some sources on the link between use and sale for adolescents. Joshua Bowers, however, points out that New York State felony drug courts are full of dealer-defendants who are *not* addicted to drugs because dealers are generally not users. Joshua Bowers, "Contraindicated Drug Courts," *UCLA Law Review* 55 (2008): 783.

72. Mitchell and Caudy, "Race Differences in Drug Offending." There are also some studies suggesting that police concentrate their drug enforcement efforts in minority communities that actually have lower drug-selling rates than other, nearby white neighborhoods, but the challenge of trying to estimate actual levels of sale has led to a fair amount of disagreement about how big the effect is. See, for example, Robin S. Engel, Michael R. Smith, and Francis T. Cullen, "Race, Place, and Drug Enforcement: Reconsidering the Impact of Citizen Complaints and Crime Rates on Drug Arrests," *Criminology & Public Policy* 11 (2012): 603–635.

73. Ta-Nehisi Coates, "The Black Family in the Age of Mass Incarceration," *The Atlantic*, October 2015; Venkatesh, *Off the Books*.

74. Steven D. Levitt and Sudhir Alladi Venkatesh, "An Economic Analysis of a Drug Selling Gang's Finances," *Quarterly Journal of Economics* 115 (2000): 755–789.

75. Gottschalk, *Caught*.

CHAPTER TWO: A BRIEF HISTORY OF TIME (SERVED)

1. Nick Gillespie, "Life Without Parole for a First-Time, Non-Violent Drug Offender," *Reason Hit & Run Blog*, September 1, 2015, accessed July 6, 2016, http://reason.com/blog/2015/09/01/life-without-parole-for-a-first-time-non. Jones's sentence was eventually commuted by President Obama. Jacob Sullum, "Obama Frees Sharanda Jones and 94 Other Prisoners Serving Draconian Sentences," *Reason Hit & Run Blog*, December 21, 2015, accessed July 6, 2016, http://reason.com/blog/2015/12/21/obama-frees-sharanda-jones-and-94-other.

2. Adam Banner, "Ariel Castro's 1000 Year Sentence Isn't the Longest on Record," *Huffington Post*, November 14, 2013, accessed July 6, 2016, www.huffingtonpost.com/adam-banner/castro-technically-still-_b_3922691.html.

3. Franklin E. Zimring, "Imprisonment Rates and the New Politics of Criminal Punishment," *Punishment & Society* 3 (2001): 161–166.

4. "Remarks by the President at the NAACP Conference," July 14, 2015, accessed July 6, 2016, online at White House Press Office, https://www.whitehouse.gov/the-press-office/2015/07/14/remarks-president-naacp-conference.

5. Traditionally, governor-appointed parole boards had tremendous discretion to decide when to release an inmate. They were subject to almost no oversight, and many, if not most, prisoners were released well before reaching their official maximum sentence. States that "abolished" parole eliminated this sort of *discretionary* release, but they preserved other forms of early release. Prisoners could still be released early, usually for good behavior, but on a much more fixed schedule. Even in states that abolished parole, leaders accepted that *some* sort of shot at early release was a necessary carrot to maintain discipline in prison.

6. Michael Tonry, "Explanations of American Punishment Policies: A National History," *Punishment & Society* 11 (2009): 377–394.

7. James Whitman, for example, has argued that Americans have historically held harsher views than Europeans on how to address lawbreaking. James Q. Whitman, *Harsh Justice: Criminal Punishment and the Widening Divide Between America and Europe* (Oxford: Oxford University Press, 2005).

8. "Behind bars" alone highlights differences between punishment in the United States and (some) European countries. The cell in which Breivik will spend the rest of his life does not have actual bars on it. Karl Ritter, "What Happens to Norway Mass Killer Anders Behring Breivik Now?" *National Post*, August 24, 2012, accessed July 6, 2016, http://news.nationalpost.com/news/what-happens-to-norway-mass-killer-anders-behring-breivik-now.

9. Under California's strike law, Ewing would not be eligible for parole until he had served twenty-five years in prison, and Andrade until he had served fifty (since both of his terms were consecutive). Unlike other prisoners, those sentenced under the strike law do not earn any time off for good behavior or any other reason.

10. *Ewing v. California*, 538 US 11 (2003); *Lockyer v. Andrade*, 538 US 63 (2003).

11. Justice Kennedy Commission, "Report to the ABA House of Delegates," Amer-

ican Bar Association, August 2004, accessed July 6, 2016, www.americanbar.org/content /dam/aba/publishing/criminal_justice_section_newsletter/crimjust_kennedy_Justice KennedyCommissionReportsFinal.authcheckdam.pdf.

12. William J. Stuntz, "Plea Bargaining and Criminal Law's Disappearing Shadow," *Harvard Law Review* 117 (2004): 2548–2569.

13. William J. Stuntz, *The Collapse of American Criminal Justice* (Cambridge, MA: Belknap Press of Harvard University Press, 2011).

14. To be clear, if prisoners spent less time in prison, then the impact of rising admissions would have been less too: ten more people serving one-year sentences will result in less prison growth than those same extra ten people serving two years. So while prison growth was due primarily to increases in admissions, the impact of those admissions did depend somewhat on time served. It's just that the amount of time served did not change much.

15. John F. Pfaff, "The Myths and Realities of Correctional Severity: Evidence from the National Corrections Reporting Program on Sentencing Practices," *American Law & Economics Review* 13 (2011): 491–531.

16. These results come from the National Corrections Reporting Program, a large but imperfect dataset gathered by the BJS. The sample here draws on data from eleven states that provided reliable data in both 2000 and 2010; these states held about 22 percent of all inmates in both of those years. If I include California, the share of prisoners would rise to over one-third; the relative trends would remain the same, but the values would generally drop by around half, because of abnormally short prison sentences in California. Note that southern states are somewhat under-sampled here; if southern states tend to be more punitive, these numbers could be lower than the national average. The trend, however, may still be correct, as long as southern states didn't grow relatively more punitive over the 2000s.

17. John F. Pfaff, "The Durability of Prison Populations," *University of Chicago Legal Forum* 2010 (2010): 73–115.

18. The five states with most of the LWOP prisoners are California, Florida, Michigan, Pennsylvania, and Louisiana, which are home to only about 39 percent of the nation's prisoners, so their use of LWOP is clearly disproportional to their overall use of incarceration.

19. Once again, limits in the data rear their ugly heads. The best dataset on time served only goes back to 2000. Using much cruder data, I've generated some results suggesting that time served may have been fairly stable all the way back to the early 1980s, but these findings should be viewed cautiously. See John F. Pfaff, "The Causes of Growth in Prison Admissions and Populations," Social Science Research Network, January 23, 2012, accessed July 6, 2016, http://papers.ssrn.com/sol3/papers.cfm?abstract_id=1990508.

20. Pfaff, "Myths and Realities."

21. "Time Served: The High Cost, Low Return of Longer Prison Terms," Pew Center on the States, June 2012, accessed July 6, 2016, www.pewtrusts.org/~/media/legacy /uploadedfiles/wwwpewtrustsorg/reports/sentencing_and_corrections/prisontimeserved pdf.pdf.

22. Times served in 1990 appear to be abnormally low, which means that estimating the change from 1990 to 2009 will yield bigger results than would estimating the change starting in 1989 or 1991. Given the dataset that Pew used to generate its results, 1990 is a very logical year to use as a starting date. That it also appears to have had relatively short times served is surely just a coincidence, but its impact on the estimates is no less because of that.

23. Derrick Neal and Armin Rick, "The Prison Boom & the Lack of Black Progress After Smith & Welch," University of Chicago, November 2013, accessed July 6, 2016, http://home.uchicago.edu/~arick/prs_boom_201309.pdf. It's worth adding, as a technical aside, that the methodology they use to try to show that longer sentences drove prison growth requires them to assume that the fraction of arrests that get prosecuted didn't change—an assumption that, as we will shortly see, is invalid. As a result, it is not immediately clear what exactly their results mean.

24. The mathy among you will recognize this as an example of Simpson's Paradox.

25. Sara Steen and Tara Opsal, "'Punishment on the Installment Plan': Individual-Level Predictors of Parole Revocation in Four States," *Prison Journal* 87 (2007): 344–366.

26. Given how many people are in prison, and how essential releases—and releases onto parole in particular—are to the system's ability to function, the Court's position that parole is merely an act of grace by the state seems somewhat naïve, but it remains the official position.

27. Travis and Stacey, "A Half-Century of Parole Rules." The rising number of conditions is a reversal of a decline in this number between surveys in 1956 and 1969.

28. In some cases, the parolee may be explicitly barred from public housing. In other cases, residents face zero-tolerance policies that threaten eviction if anyone in the apartment commits a crime in or near the unit, regardless of whether anyone else knows about it. Such risks make people unwilling to allow a parolee to live with them, even if it is a family-member.

29. State parole rules are often quite poorly and unclearly written, and counties within a given state will often disagree about what exactly triggers a violation. Fiona Doherty, "Obey All Laws and Be Good: Probation and the Meaning of Recidivism," *Georgetown Law Journal* 104 (2016): 291–354.

30. These bans are one indirect way in which the war on drugs exerts some power. That said, the law allowed individual states to opt out of the bans, and only a few states now maintain the full ban on people convicted of drug crimes. Eli Hager, "Six States Where Felons Can't Get Food Stamps," *Marshall Project*, February 4, 2016, accessed July 6, 2016, https://www.themarshallproject.org/2016/02/04/six-states-where-felons -can-t-get-food-stamps#.r5mmqiuaR.

31. In 2008, the legislature enacted a law that forbade categorical denials of licenses for many industries, including barbershops, solely because the applicant had a felony record. Clyde Haberman, "Ex-Inmate's Legacy: Victory over Bias and Catch-22 Bureaucracy," *New York Times*, August 28, 2008, accessed July 6, 2016, www.nytimes .com/2008/08/29/nyregion/29nyc.html.

32. "Florida Housing Sex Offenders Under a Bridge," CNN, April 6, 2007, accessed July 6, 2016, www.cnn.com/2007/LAW/04/05/bridge.sex.offenders.

33. Many job applications include a box that must be checked if the applicant has some sort of prior criminal record, in some cases for any sort of non-traffic ticket arrest (even if the case was dropped or dismissed). Eliminating this requirement has been a major goal of reform efforts recently, although some disturbing preliminary data suggest that banning the box may actually make things worse for many black job applicants, as employers appear to discriminate *more* against blacks when there is no official indication of prior criminal record (since they start to use race as a proxy for convictions). Jennifer L. Doleac, "'Ban the Box' Does More Harm Than Good," Brookings Institution, May 31, 2016, accessed July 6, 2016, www.brookings.edu/research /opinions/2016/05/31-ban-the-box-does-more-harm-than-good-doleac.

34. Of course, those being admitted to prison for the first time may have prior felony convictions that contributed to the most recent offense.

35. Ryan King, Bryce Peterson, Brian Elderbroom, and Elizabeth Pelletier, "Reducing Mass Incarceration Requires Far-Reaching Reforms," Urban Institute, n.d., http:// webapp.urban.org/reducing-mass-incarceration.

36. Obviously there is some variation across states here: national averages always flatten state- and county-level differences. A 25 percent cut in time served by people sentenced for violent crimes, for example, leads to an 11 percent drop in New Jersey's prison population but only a 5 percent drop in Kentucky's.

37. This is a product of *Washington v. Blakely*, 542 US 296 (2004), which made it harder for courts to employ presumptive sentencing guidelines or determinate sentencing laws. Almost all states with such policies responded by giving judges more discretion at sentencing. John F. Pfaff, "The Future of Appellate Sentencing Review: *Booker* in the States," *Marquette Law Review* 93 (2009): 683–714; John F. Pfaff, *Sentencing Law & Policy* (St. Paul: Foundation Press, 2016).

38. Stephanos Bibas, "Plea Bargaining Outside the Shadow of Trial," *Harvard Law Review* 117 (2004): 2463–2547.

39. These numbers come from an analysis I conducted on time served by over 300,000 people admitted to prison in 2003 in seventeen states; these people made up slightly under half the total number admitted nationwide. The data came from the National Corrections Reporting Program.

40. Patrick A. Langan and David J. Levin, "Recidivism of Prisoners Released in 1994," US Department of Justice, Bureau of Justice Statistics, June 2002, accessed July 6, 2016, www.bjs.gov/content/pub/pdf/rpr94.pdf; Matthew R. Durose, Alexia D. Cooper, and Howard N. Snyder, "Recidivism of Prisoners Released from 30 States in 2005: Patterns from 2005 to 2010," US Department of Justice, Bureau of Justice Statistics, April 2014, accessed July 6, 2016, www.bjs.gov/content/pub/pdf/rprts05p0510.pdf.

41. William Rhodes, Gerald Gaes, Jeremy Luallen, Ryan King, Tom Rich, and Michael Shively, "Following Incarceration, Most Released Offenders Never Return to Prison," *Crime & Delinquency* 62 (2016): 1003–1025; William Rhodes, "America's Prisons Are Not a Revolving Door: Most Released Offenders Never Return," London School of

Economics and Political Science, United States Centre, American Politics and Policy blog, October 17, 2014, accessed July 6, 2016, http://blogs.lse.ac.uk/usappblog/2014/10 /17/american-prisons-are-not-a-revolving-door-most-released-offenders-never -return.

42. This study looked at all people cycling in and out of prison, whether they were on parole or not at the time of reentry. This strategy allowed it to account for post-parole recidivism as well.

43. All these numbers are, however, just guestimates. We have no precise data on how many unique people have been to prison. This is yet another one of our unacceptable empirical blind spots.

44. Rafi Schwartz, "In 24 Tweets, This Law Professor Reveals Everything Wrong with the Way We Look at Prison Reform," *Fusion*, May 17, 2016, accessed August 24, 2016, http://fusion.net/story/303147/in-24-tweets-this-law-professor-reveals-everything -wrong-with-the-way-we-look-at-prison-reform. Recall that California was forced to severely cut back on prison populations as the result of a federal court order. It may seem that dropping California is akin to saying "things don't work when we exclude the successes," but that's not the case. As noted above, nearly two-thirds of the decline in prison populations in the United States has been in California alone. If we want to talk about decarceration in the United States more broadly, including California makes these efforts look much more successful than they are. Excluding four or five successful states would be concerning; excluding one dramatic outlier helps us see more clearly what is happening in the remaining forty-nine states.

45. State legislators are, of course, state officials. However, they are elected by—and thus responsive to—much smaller districts than, say, governors or attorneys general. In the case of urban representatives, the districts can be quite small.

46. John F. Pfaff, "The Micro and Macro Causes of Prison Growth," *Georgia State University Law Review* 28 (2012): 1237–1272; Pfaff, "Causes of Growth."

47. Put aside the fact that most empirical papers on prison growth make fundamental statistical errors (a point I discuss in depth in John F. Pfaff, "The Empirics of Prison Growth: A Critical Review and Path Forward," *Journal of Criminal Law and Criminology* 98 [2008]: 547–620). Assume that a perfectly good paper tells us that a 1 percent increase in a state's conservativeness leads to a 1.5 percent increase in the incarceration rate. What does this mean? Are conservative police more aggressive (even though crime tends to be concentrated in cities, and cities tend to be more liberal than the rest of the state)? Are prosecutors more conservative and thus tougher on crime? Or is it the judges—or maybe the governor-appointed parole boards? If I wanted to take that number and use it to figure out how to "reform" the system somehow, I would have no idea how to use it, because—again—criminal justice isn't a single system, and any factor is going to have a different impact in each bureaucracy.

48. These papers are: Alfred Blumstein and Allen J. Beck, "Population Growth in the US Prisons, 1980–1996," in *Prisons*, eds. Michael Tonry and Joan Petersilia (Chicago: University of Chicago Press, 1999); Alfred Blumstein and Allen J. Beck, "Reentry as a Transient State Between Liberty and Recommitment," in *Prisoner Reentry*

and Crime in America, eds. Jeremy Travis and Christy Visher (Cambridge: Cambridge University Press, 1999); Scott Boggess and John Bound, "Did Criminal Activity Increase During the 1980s? Comparisons from Data Sources," *Social Science Quarterly* 78 (1997): 725–739; and Patrick A. Langan, "America's Soaring Prison Population," *Science* 251 (1991): 1568–1573.

49. Jeremy Travis, Bruce Western, and Steve Redburn, eds., *The Growth of Incarceration in the United States* (Washington, DC: National Research Council, 2014), accessed July 6, 2016, www.nap.edu/catalog/18613/the-growth-of-incarceration-in -the-united-states-exploring-causes. The 2014 results were mostly updates of the results that Blumstein and Beck had produced in their 1999 and 2005 papers cited above that used the same decomposition. I discuss some of the flaws with the NRC study (and, by extension, the earlier studies) at "The Flawed NRC Report: The 'Prison Industrial Complex,' Part 1: Private Prisons," PrawfsBlawg, June 16, 2014, http:// prawfsblawg.blogs.com/prawfsblawg/2014/06/the-flawed-nrc-report-the-prison -industrial-complex-part-1-private-prisons.html (which contains links to other posts on the topic as well).

50. The limitation on states and years is driven entirely by the availability of data. The NCSC gathered data on felony filings before 1994, but it changed the way it gathered the data in 1994, making it hard to compare across years. Only thirty-four states provided reliable data—but these thirty-four are a fairly representative cross-section of US states.

51. Pfaff, "Causes of Growth." The dates used here, 1994–2008, reflect the data available when I wrote the paper.

52. I exclude marijuana offenses because marijuana crimes rarely result in prison time: only about 1 percent of the inmates in state prisons are serving time for a marijuana offense.

53. In January 2016, the FBI released its crime data for the first half of 2015, which showed a continued decline in property crime (of 4.2 percent), but a 1.7 percent increase in violent crime. "Preliminary 2015 Crime Stats Released," FBI, January 19, 2016, accessed July 6, 2016, https://www.fbi.gov/news/news_blog/preliminary-2015-crime-stats -released. Some commentators jumped on this rise to claim that sentencing reform and protests against the police nationwide in the wake of protests in Ferguson, Missouri, and Baltimore, Maryland, were pushing crime rates higher. But violent crime also rose by similar levels between 2005 and 2006 before declining again through 2014, so it is too early to say now if we are seeing an upward trend or an idiosyncratic bump. The full 2015 statistics, released as this book was going to press, ultimately reported a 3.9 percent increase in violent crime and a 3.4 percent decrease in property crime. See Federal Bureau of Investigation, "Crime in the United States: 2015," accessed October 11, 2016, http:// ucr.fbi.gov/crime-in-the-U.S./2015/crime-in-the-U.S.-2015.

54. Given all the advances in policing in recent years, this statement may seem somewhat surprising, but it's a long-standing result. Clearance rates have been flat since the 1970s, with the clearance rate for murder actually *declining*, from about 80 percent in the 1960s to about 60 percent today. See Pfaff, "Micro and Macro," Figure 5A.

55. "Public order" is the BJS's catch-all category for crimes that are not considered violent, property-related, or drug-related. It can include minor quality-of-life crimes like

public urination as well as more serious offenses like felony weapons charges (where the gun wasn't used) or drunk driving.

56. Given the noisiness and approximations that go into our arrest data, not to mention the fact that this is a sample of only thirty-four states, more weight should be put on the magnitude of the change than on the levels (that is, the doubling, not the one-third or two-thirds).

57. There is one dataset that gathers information on convictions, but it is the only dataset I've ever seen that comes with a warning against actually using it for empirical work. "State Court Processing Statistics Data Limitations," US Department of Justice, Bureau of Justice Statistics, March 2010, accessed July 6, 2016, www.bjs.gov/content /pub/pdf/scpsdl_da.pdf.

58. A 1987 study by the BJS reported that out of every one hundred felony arrests, fifty-seven cases were carried forward, fifty-six of which resulted in conviction. A 2006 follow-up reported that out of every one hundred felony arrests, sixty-nine were carried forward, sixty-eight of which resulted in conviction. Whatever else is changing, once the case moves forward, conviction rates appear to be stable—and quite high. Barbara Boland, Catherine H. Conly, Paul Mahanna, Lynn Warner, and Ronald Sones, "The Prosecution of Felony Arrests, 1987," US Department of Justice, Bureau of Justice Statistics, National Criminal Justice Reference Service, August 1990, accessed July 6, 2016, https://www.ncjrs.gov/pdffiles1/Digitization/124140NCJRS .pdf; Thomas H. Cohen and Tracey Kyckelhahn, "Felony Defendants in Large Urban Counties, 2006," US Department of Justice, Bureau of Justice Statistics, May 2010, accessed July 6, 2016, www.bjs.gov/content/pub/pdf/fdluc06.pdf.

59. Boland et al., "The Prosecution of Felony Arrests, 1987," reported that every one hundred felony arrests produced thirteen felony convictions and forty-three misdemeanor ones. The follow-up study by Cohen and Kyckelhahn, "Felony Defendants in Large Urban Counties, 2006," reported that every one hundred felony arrests produced twenty-four felony convictions and forty-four misdemeanor ones. This could mean that eleven arrests that would have been dropped before will now result in felonies. It could also mean that twelve cases that would have been dropped before are now charged as misdemeanors, and eleven cases that would have been misdemeanors before will now result in felony convictions. Note that while the probability of an arrest becoming a felony in these reports differs from what is stated in my paper, at around one-eighth in 1987 versus one-quarter in 2006, the trajectory remains the same, with the probabilities of an arrest turning into a felony conviction essentially doubling. The differences in percentages likely reflect things like different sample sizes and different ways of measuring arrests. Furthermore, the BJS results rely on the dataset mentioned above that comes with a warning to use it carefully.

60. The admission data are from Carson and Golinelli, "Prisoners in 2012: Trends in Admissions and Releases, 1991–2012," Table 4, US Department of Justice, Bureau of Justice Statistics, December 2013, accessed July 6, 2016, http://www.bjs.gov/content /pub/pdf/p12tar9112.pdf. The arrest data are from the BJS on-line data tool at www.bjs .gov/index.cfm?ty=datool&surl=/arrests/index.cfm#. While it is true that arrests in 1991

perhaps led to admissions in 1992 more than in 1991—convictions and admissions can take time—not much turns on the difference.

61. E. Ann Carson and William J. Sabol, "Aging of the State Prison Population, 1993–2013," US Department of Justice, Bureau of Justice Statistics, May 2016, accessed July 6, 2016, www.bjs.gov/content/pub/pdf/aspp9313.pdf.

62. Lauren C. Porter, Shawn D. Bushway, Hui-Shien Tsao, and Herbert L. Smith, "How the US Prison Boom Has Changed the Age Distribution of the Prison Population," *Criminology* 54 (2016): 30–55; Jeremy Luallen and Ryan Kling, "A Method for Analyzing Changing Prison Populations: Explaining the Growth of the Elderly in Prison," *Evaluation Review* 38 (2014): 459–486.

63. Porter et al., "Age Distribution."

64. See, for example, Jean Trounstine, "A Moral Imperative: Release Aging and Long-Term Prisoners," *Truthout*, February 10, 2015, accessed July 6, 2016, www.truth-out.org/news/item/29028-a-moral-imperative-release-aging-and-long-term-prisoners. Even well-respected research institutions like the Vera Institute of Justice tend to make this claim. See Tina Chiu, "It's About Time: Aging Prisoners, Increasing Costs, and Geriatric Release," Vera Institute of Justice, April 2010, accessed July 6, 2016, www.vera.org/sites/default/files/resources/downloads/Its-about-time-aging-prisoners-increasing-costs-and-geriatric-release.pdf.

65. Pfaff, "Durability."

66. W. David Ball, "Tough on Crime (on the State's Dime): How Violent Crime Does Not Drive California Counties' Incarceration Rates—And Why It Should," *Georgia State University Law Review* 28 (2012): 987–1084. The obvious question to ask is whether the rural county is choosing to be more punitive given its lower crime rate, or if it has a lower crime rate because it is more punitive. It's a tricky issue to resolve, but it seems likely that Ball is detecting a real effect here, that counties are choosing how punitive to be for reasons tied to underlying political values.

67. Josh Kron, "Red State, Blue City: How the Urban-Rural Divide Is Splitting America," *The Atlantic*, November 30, 2012, accessed July 6, 2016, www.theatlantic.com/politics/archive/2012/11/red-state-blue-city-how-the-urban-rural-divide-is-splitting-america/265686.

CHAPTER THREE: PRIVATE PRISONS, PUBLIC SPENDING

1. "A Bill, To Improve Federal Sentencing and Corrections Practices, and for Other Purposes," 114th Cong., 1st sess., Bernie Sanders's website, n.d., accessed July 6, 2016, www.sanders.senate.gov/download/justice-is-not-for-sale-act?inline=file; Elise Foley, "Hillary Clinton Says She'll End Private Prisons, Stop Taking Their Money," *Huffington Post*, October 23, 2015, accessed July 6, 2016, www.huffingtonpost.com/entry/hillary-clinton-private-prisons_us_562a3e3ee4b0ec0a389418ec. Congress could pass a law forbidding the federal prison system from using private prisons, but limited federal authority over the states would preclude it from telling the states what sorts of prisons to use. As for Clinton, at the time she returned the money, the $133,246 the private prison

groups had given her was only about 0.2 percent of the $55 million she had received by then. For perspective, as of early 2016, the largest donor to the Clinton campaign was Soros Fund Management, at over $7 million, and twenty groups (some, like the American Federation of Teachers, likely not fans of money going to prisons instead of schools) had given at least $1 million each. See "Top Contributors, Federal Election Data," Open Secrets, n.d., accessed July 6, 2016, https://www.opensecrets.org/pres16/contrib.php?id=N00000019&.

2. William J. Sabol, Heather C. West, and Matthew Cooper, "Prisoners in 2008," US Department of Justice, Bureau of Justice Statistics, December 2009, accessed July 6, 2016, www.bjs.gov/content/pub/pdf/p08.pdf.

3. Kevin Mathews, "For-Profit Prisons: Eight Statistics That Show the Problems," *Truthout*, December 27, 2013, accessed July 6, 2016, www.truth-out.org/news/item/20880-for-profit-prisons-eight-statistics-that-show-the-problems.

4. American Civil Liberties Union, "Banking on Bondage: Private Prisons and Mass Incarceration," November 2011, accessed July 6, 2016, https://www.aclu.org/files/assets/bankingonbondage_20111102.pdf.

5. The federal system held 31 percent, followed by Texas (11 percent overall, 16 percent of state private prisoners), Florida (9 percent overall, 13 percent of state private prisoners), Georgia (6 percent overall, 9 percent of state private prisoners), Oklahoma (5 percent overall, 8 percent of state private prisoners), and Arizona (5 percent overall, 7 percent of state private prisoners). Carson, "Prisoners in 2014," Table 9.

6. Gottschalk, *Caught*.

7. See, for example, the report released by the Office of the Inspector General for the Department of Justice on the lower quality of private federal prisons. Matt Zapotosky and Chico Harlan, "Justice Department Says It Will End Use of Private Prisons," *Washington Post*, August 18, 2016, accessed August 24, 2016, washingtonpost.com/news/post-nation/wp/2016/08/18/justice-department-says-it-will-end-use-of-private-prisons/?utm_term=.5170ff1b2534. Sasha Volokh, however, has pointed out that the empirical analysis of private prisons is fairly inconclusive. Sasha Volokh, "Are Private Prisons Better or Worse Than Public Prisons," *Washington Post*, February 25, 2014, accessed August 24, 2016, washingtonpost.com/news/volokh-conspiracy/wp/2014/02/25/are-private-prisons-better-or-worse-than-public-prisons/?utm_term=.79caac83bc0c; Sasha Volokh, "Don't End Federal Private Prisons," *Washington Post*, August 19, 2016, accessed August 24, 2016, washingtonpost.com/news/volokh-conspiracy/wp/2016/08/19/dont-end-federal-private-prisons/?utm_term=.a65f02b56cb2. Some of the uncertainty about the relative quality of prison conditions reflects the fact that private prisons are often exempt from various transparency laws. Gottschalk, *Caught*, 72. Also, we should expect inmates in public and private prisons alike to underreport acts of violence committed against them.

8. Christie Thompson, "Everything You Wanted to Know About Private Prisons . . . Is None of Your Damn Business," Marshall Project, December 18, 2014, accessed July 6, 2016, https://www.themarshallproject.org/2014/12/18/everything-you-ever-wanted-to-know-about-private-prisons#.8RVIB0kY8.

9. See Sally Q. Yates, "Phasing Out Our Use of Private Prisons," US Department of Justice, August 18, 2016, accessed August 24, 2016, www.justice.gov/opa/blog/phasing -out-our-use-private-prisons.

10. Florida Department of Corrections, "Quick Facts," accessed August 24, 2016, http://www.dc.state.fl.us/oth/Quickfacts.html.

11. For details on the Lake Erie facility, see Laura A. Bischoff, "Auditors Uncover Problems at Private Prisons in Ohio," *Dayton Daily News*, December 29, 2012, accessed July 6, 2016, www.daytondailynews.com/news/news/state-regional/auditors -uncover-problems-at-private-prisons-in-oh/nTgQ5. For Pelican Bay and Rikers Island, see James Ridgeway and Jean Casella, "America's Ten Worst Prisons," *Mother Jones*, May 1, 2013, accessed July 6, 2016, www.motherjones.com/politics/2013/05/10 -worst-prisons-america-part-1-adx.

12. When I say, "Stop talking about the privates and focus on the publics," some reformers reply, "Let's just fix it all!" It's a noble sentiment, but somewhat unrealistic. It's obviously impossible to quantify how much can be accomplished, but it is reasonable to assume that there are more things to fix than we have the collective political attention span to address. Triage is essential. And regardless of how much is possible, we can't fix everything at once, so we should order things by importance. That prioritizing knocks the privates down on the list.

13. For the connection between private prison groups and ALEC, see Cody Mason, "Too Good to Be True: Private Prisons in America," The Sentencing Project, January 2012, accessed July 6, 2016, http://sentencingproject.org/wp-content/uploads/2016/01/Too -Good-to-be-True-Private-Prisons-in-America. For ALEC's role in drafting criminal laws, see "ALEC and Criminal Justice," Center for Media and Democracy, n.d., accessed July 6, 2016, www.alecexposed.org/wiki/ALEC_%26_Criminal_Justice (which contains copies of the original ALEC model laws, which are seemingly no longer available elsewhere).

14. It is true that many fairly conservative states, including Georgia, South Carolina, and Texas, have been at the forefront of reform. But one reason they may have been able to implement reforms is that their incarceration rates were so high to start with. Georgia's and Texas's rates were above the national average in 2008 and remained so in 2014; South Carolina's was slightly above the national average in 2008 and slightly below it in 2014. All were above the average state incarceration rate in both 2008 and 2014.

15. Unless stated otherwise, all the data on political spending comes from Follow the Money, www.followthemoney.org.

16. Gottschalk, *Caught*.

17. Michael C. Bender, "Florida Vote Halts Largest Private-Jail Plan in Geo Setback," Bloomberg, February 15, 2012, accessed July 6, 2016, www.bloomberg. com/news/articles/2012-02-14/florida-senate-defeats-largest-u-s-private-prison -contract-in-21-19-vote.

18. Alex Friedmann, "Tennessee Prison Privatization Bill Fails to Pass," *Prison Legal News*, September 15, 1998, accessed July 6, 2016, https://www.prisonlegalnews.org /news/1998/sep/15/tennessee-prison-privatization-bill-fails-to-pass.

19. Ben Carrasco and Joan Petersilia, "Assessing the CCPOA's Political Influence and Its Impact on Efforts to Reform the California Corrections System," Stanford Criminal Justice Center Working Paper, California Sentencing & Corrections Policy Series, January 27, 2006, accessed July 6, 2016, http://law.stanford.edu/wp-content /uploads/sites/default/files/child-page/266901/doc/slspublic/BCarassco-wp4_06.pdf.

20. See Bret Bucklen's tweet of March 2, 2015, at https://twitter.com/kbucklen /status/572441442464993280.

21. Ken Stier, "NYS Prison Budget Climbs, Despite Fewer Inmates," *City Limits*, November 10, 2015, accessed July 6, 2016, http://citylimits.org/2015/11/10/nys -prison-budget-climbs-despite-fewer-inmates.

22. Jonathan Oosting, "Michigan to Close Kingsley Prison in Cost-Cutting Move," *Detroit News*, May 31, 2016, accessed August 24, 2016, www.detroitnews.com/story /news/politics/2016/05/31/michigan-close-kingsley-prison/85189746. As the article stated: "Layoffs are possible, according to Corrections spokesman Chris Gautz, but there are 'a lot of moving parts.' The department said it will work with employees and unions in an attempt to 'absorb' as many workers as possible by plugging them into other vacant jobs."

23. See, for example, Amy K. Glasmeier and Tracey Farrigan, "The Economic Impacts of the Prison Development Boom on Persistently Poor Rural Places," *International Regional Science Review* 30 (2007): 274–299; Gregory Hooks, Clayton Mosher, Thomas Rotolo, and Linda Lobao, "The Prison Industry: Carceral Expansion and Employment in US Counties, 1969–1994," *Social Science Quarterly* 85 (2004): 37–57.

24. A local prison is less central to the economy of a more urban district, and so that representative may be less likely to fight for it. This is troubling, though, since inmates come disproportionately from urban counties. So the closing of downstate (i.e., New York City–area) prisons in deference to upstate ones only makes it harder for downstate inmates now sent upstate to stay in touch with their families. Weakened social ties are well known to make reentry harder. See, for example, Jeremy Travis, Elizabeth Cincotta McBride, and Amy L. Solomon, "Families Left Behind: The Hidden Costs of Incarceration and Reentry," Urban Institute, June 2005, accessed July 6, 2016, www.urban.org /sites/default/files/alfresco/publication-pdfs/310882-Families-Left-Behind.PDF.

25. See Sarah Lawrence and Jeremy Travis, "The New Landscape of Imprisonment: Mapping America's Prison Expansion," Urban Institute, April 2004, accessed July 6, 2016, www.urban.org/sites/default/files/alfresco/publication-pdfs /410994-The-New-Landscape-of-Imprisonment.PDF, Fig. 8.

26. Texas provides an interesting variant to the rural economy story. Thanks to a booming oil economy, Texas has struggled to hire guards to staff prisons in rural areas. As a result, the prison-guard unions have actually come out in *favor* of decarceration, since it won't cost current guards any jobs (and may even lead to pay increases in the future) and will likely improve working conditions. The outcome is the opposite of what we usually see—the guard union is embracing, not resisting, reform—but for fundamentally similar reasons. See "Understaffing at Texas Prison Units Reaching Crisis Level,"

Grits for Breakfast, November 15, 2014, http://gritsforbreakfast.blogspot.com/2014/11 /understaffing-at-texas-prison-units.html.

27. See Prison Gerrymandering Project, Prison Policy Initiative, www.prisoners ofthecensus.org. The four exceptions are New York and Maryland, which changed their laws effective 2010, and California and Delaware, whose changes go into effect in 2020. In these four states, prisoners are treated as living at their last address before incarceration. In the remaining states, individual counties sometimes choose to avoid "prison gerrymandering" for county-level districts. See, for example, "Majority of Illinois' Counties & Cities with Large Prisons Reject Prison-Based Gerrymandering," Prison Policy Initiative, February 11, 2011, accessed July 6, 2016, www.prisoners ofthecensus.org/factsheets/il/10_IL_counties.pdf.

28. "The Census Bureau's Prison Miscount: It's About Political Power, Not Funding," Prison Policy Initiative, September 16, 2013, accessed July 6, 2016, www.prisoners ofthecensus.org/factsheets/ny/political_power_not_money.pdf.

29. John F. Pfaff, "The Complicated Economics of Prison Reform," review of *Cheap on Crime: Recession-Era Politics and the Transformation of American Punishment*, by Hadar Aviram, and *Caught: The Prison State and the Lockdown of American Politics*, by Marie Gottschalk. *Michigan Law Review* 114 (2016): 951–981.

30. David Segal, "Prison Vendors See Continued Signs of a Captive Market," *The New York Times*, August 29, 2015, accessed July 6, 2016, www.nytimes .com/2015/08/30/business/prison-vendors-see-continued-signs-of-a-captive-market .html; James Kilgore, "Five Corporations You've Never Heard of Are Making Millions from Mass Incarceration," *Truthout*, January 19, 2015, accessed July 6, 2016, www .truth-out.org/news/item/28501-five-corporations-you-ve-never-heard-of-making -millions-from-mass-incarceration.

31. These high collect-call fees—which the providers justified as necessary to properly monitor the calls—have come under sustained activist, and now governmental, attack. Timothy Williams, "High Cost of Inmates' Phone Calls May End," *New York Times*, September 30, 2015, accessed July 6, 2016, www.nytimes.com/2015/10/01/us /fcc-seeks-to-limit-and-lower-costs-of-inmates-phone-calls.html.

32. Alysia Santo, "When Freedom Isn't Free: The Bail Industry Wants to Be Your Jailer," Marshall Project, February 23, 2015, accessed July 6, 2016, https://www .themarshallproject.org/2015/02/23/buying-time#.hCP5YaRAR.

33. Max Ehrenfreund, "What's Wrong with Making People Post Bail After Trial," *Washington Post*, March 16, 2015, accessed July 6, 2016, https://www.washingtonpost.com /news/wonk/wp/2015/03/16/whats-wrong-with-making-people-post-bail-after-trial.

34. In fact, the private bail system may be one area where privatization shapes policy meaningfully. There's evidence showing that those out on bail have better outcomes— they are less likely to be convicted, and they are punished less severely when convicted— even once we account for the differences between those who are out on bail and those who are denied or unable to make bail. The idea of money bail has come under attack lately due to concerns that many people who can't make bail aren't risks for fleeing or

reoffending—they're just poor. Money bail remains in no small part due to lobbying by the bail-bond industry.

35. Perhaps privatization matters more to prison conditions than it does to sentencing laws. In pursuit of profits, Aramark may be more willing to cut corners than state entities. Yet almost every analysis of the prison industrial complex points to bad outcomes by private actors without any comparison with what public actors have done in similar situations. Plus, we've already seen competing anecdotes of privates providing better conditions than publics.

36. Paul Egan, "Michigan to End Prison Food Deal with Aramark," *Detroit Free Press*, July 13, 2015, accessed July 6, 2016, www.freep.com/story/news/local/michigan /2015/07/13/state-ends-prison-food-contract-aramark/30080211.

37. I don't want to oversell this point. Aramark does highlight corrections as an important part of its revenue stream. But the overall share is nonetheless likely fairly small. Michigan has the nation's tenth-largest prison population, so providing it with food is likely among the larger food-service contracts available, and yet it came to a small fraction of Aramark's revenues. "Aramark Reports Fourth Quarter and Full Year 2014 Results; Posts Strong Sales and Profitability Growth," Aramark Corporation, November 14, 2014, accessed July 6, 2016, www.aramark.com/about-us/News/aramark-general /fourth-quarter-full-year-2014-results.

38. Dan Abrams, "No, Florida's Stand Your Ground Law Did Not Determine Either Zimmerman or Dunn Cases," ABC News, February 17, 2014, accessed July 6, 2016, http:// abcnews.go.com/US/floridas-stand-ground-law-determine-zimmerman-dunn-cases /story?id=22543929.

39. John Nichols, "How ALEC Took Florida's 'License to Kill' Law National," *The Nation*, March 22, 2012, accessed July 6, 2016, https://www.thenation.com/article /how-alec-took-floridas-license-kill-law-national.

40. James O'Toole, "Companies Pressured over Ties to 'Stand Your Ground' Group," CNN, April 10, 2012, accessed July 6, 2016, http://money.cnn.com/2012/04/10/news /companies/stand-your-ground-companies.

41. Most accounts make it seem like the state is contractually obligated to physically detain someone in the private prison bed. This is not the case—the state is agreeing to pay as if those beds were filled even if they are not.

42. See, for example, Donald Cohen, "'Lockup Quotas,' 'Low-Crime Taxes,' and the For-Profit Prison Industry," *Huffington Post*, November 26, 2013, accessed July 6, 2016, www.huffingtonpost.com/donald-cohen/lockup-quotas-lowcrime-ta_b_3956336.html.

43. Here, I'm using the NYSCOPBA as a proxy for the guards themselves. I'm not arguing that the union's specific goal is maximizing its dues, but that it aims to protect the total amount of money flowing to its members.

44. I don't want to create a strawman here. There are plenty of people pointing out the miserable conditions in public prisons, and there are movements all over the country to improve, if not simply shut down, the worst of the public institutions (like the campaign in New York City to shut down the Rikers Island jail). It's telling,

however, that Senator Sanders's first act in the name of criminal justice reform was to propose banning private prisons, not, say, repealing the Prison Litigation Reform Act, a Clinton-era law that makes it harder for inmates to file lawsuits about bad conditions in (public) prisons.

45. "State and Local Expenditures on Corrections and Education," US Department of Education, Policy and Program Studies Service, July 2016, accessed July 6, 2016, http://www2.ed.gov/rschstat/eval/other/expenditures-corrections-education/brief.pdf.

46. When translated into per capita terms, real per capita spending rises, too—though it levels off in the 2000s—so this is real growth over this time. For 1970s data, see "Justice Expenditure and Employment in the US, 1971–79," US Department of Justice, Bureau of Justice Statistics, August 1984, accessed July 6, 2016, www.bjs.gov/content/pub/pdf/jeeus7179.pdf. For 2013 data, see "2013 State & Local Government," US Census Bureau, accessed July 6, 2016, https://www.census.gov//govs/local (adding up police, corrections, and judicial/legal).

47. Some spending by states is mandated by state and federal statutes (like much of elementary and secondary education, welfare, medical spending, and transportation spending), and these areas are often heavily subsidized by the federal government as well. Spending in these areas cannot be cut to free up spending for more discretionary line items like corrections. Even looking just at discretionary spending, however, corrections' share of the budget remains fairly small. See William Spelman, "Crime, Cash, and Limited Options: Explaining the Prison Boom," *Criminology & Public Policy* 8 (2009): 29–77, one of the few papers to carefully examine the connection between fiscal capacity and incarceration. See also Pfaff, "Federal Sentencing in the States."

48. See, for example, Spelman, "Crime, Cash."

49. See note 47 above for a discussion of what differentiates the total budget from the discretionary budget.

50. Christian Henrichson and Ruth Delaney, "The Price of Prisons: What Incarceration Costs Taxpayers," Vera Institute of Justice, July 20, 2012, accessed July 6, 2016, www.vera.org/sites/default/files/resources/downloads/price-of-prisons-updated-version-021914.pdf.

51. Marc Schabses, "Cost Benefit Analysis for Criminal Justice: Deployment and Initial Application of the *Results First* Cost Benefit Analysis," New York Division of Criminal Justice Services, Criminal Justice Technical Report, October 2013, accessed July 6, 2016, www.criminaljustice.ny.gov/crimnet/ojsa/resultsfirst/rf-technical_report_cba1_oct2013.pdf.

52. See my Tweets of March 21, 2016, https://twitter.com/JohnFPfaff/status/711907958368694272.

53. Heather MacDonald coined the term "Ferguson Effect" to refer to the notion that greater scrutiny of police in the wake of the protests sparked by the killing of Michael Brown in Ferguson, Missouri, had led to reduced policing and thus higher crime. Heather MacDonald, "The New Nationwide Crime Wave," *Wall Street Journal*,

May 29, 2015, accessed July 6, 2016, www.wsj.com/articles/the-new-nationwide-crime-wave-1432938425. This fear and others were echoed by FBI Director James Comey in several speeches, such as one he gave at the University of Chicago in October 2015 (available at https://www.fbi.gov/news/speeches/law-enforcement-and-the-communities-we-serve-bending-the-lines-toward-safety-and-justice). Even though most criminologists viewed concerns about a new "trend" as premature, these fears quickly became part of the national conversation about crime and punishment. The official 2015 statistics, released just as ths book went to press, showed a nationwide increase in violent crimes, murder in particular. This increase certainly added to fears of a trend, even it is implications should be viewed carefully. See, e.g., John Pfaff, "Donald Trump's Wild Portrayal of Crime Is Simply Not True," *The Nation*, September 27, 2016. Accessed October 11, 2016. www.thenation.com/article/donald-trumps-wild-portrayal-of-crime-is-simply-not-true/.

54. Lauren-Brooke Eisen and Inimai M. Chettiar, "The Reverse Mass Incarceration Act," Brennan Center for Justice, October 12, 2015, accessed July 6, 2016, https://www.brennancenter.org/publication/reverse-mass-incarceration-act.

55. The $38 billion is the amount given over those years in real 2012 dollars. These aren't the only groups that gave money to the states, but they are likely the major ones, at least within the US Department of Justice. Other departments may also give money and aid to state criminal justice programs, including the Department of Homeland Security and the Department of Defense. But the funds from the eight agencies considered here (the Bureau of Justice Administration, the Bureau of Justice Statistics, the Community Capacity Development Office, the Drug Courts Program Office, the National Institute of Justice, the Office for Victims of Crime, the Office of Juvenile Justice and Delinquency Prevention, and the Sex Offender Monitoring, Apprehension, Registering, and Tracking Office) probably made up a lion's share of grants, and this list includes the most high-profile federal criminal-justice grant program, the Edward Byrne Memorial Justice Assistance Grants program.

56. The Laura and John Arnold Foundation, for example, developed a successful risk assessment tool for determining who should be detained pretrial that is now being used statewide in Kentucky. It cost the foundation only $1.2 million to design it. Shaila Dewan, "Judges Replacing Conjecture with Formula for Bail," *The New York Times*, June 26, 2015, accessed July 6, 2016, www.nytimes.com/2015/06/27/us/turning-the-granting-of-bail-into-a-science.html. There's no reason that narrow federal grants couldn't be equally successful.

57. For recent US Department of Justice budget data, see "US Department of Justice Overview," US Department of Justice, November 21, 2013, www.justice.gov/sites/default/files/jmd/legacy/2013/11/21/fy15-bud-sum.pdf.

58. For an example of people insisting that the truth-in-sentencing grants worked, see Lauren-Brooke Eisen and Inimai Chettiar, "How Washington Can Help End Mass Incarceration," *The Hill*, March 22, 2016, accessed July 6, 2016, http://thehill.com/blogs/congress-blog/273772-how-washington-can-help-end-mass-incarceration. For my rebuttal, see John F. Pfaff, "Bill Clinton Is Wrong About His Crime Bill. So Are the Pro-

testers He Lectured," *New York Times Magazine*, April 12, 2016, accessed July 6, 2016, www.nytimes.com/2016/04/12/magazine/bill-clinton-is-wrong-about-his-crime-bill-so-are-the-protesters-he-lectured.html.

59. In some cases, these partial effects were very small. Kansas, for example, already had an 80 percent truth-in-sentencing law prior to the 1994 Crime Bill; to get the federal money, it made a minor tweak to raise its cutoff to 85 percent. See William J. Sabol, Katherine Rosich, Kamala Mallik Kane, David P. Kirk, and Glenn Dubin, "The Influences of Truth-in-Sentencing Reforms on Changes in States' Sentencing Practices and Prison Populations," Urban Institute, April 2002, accessed August 24, 2016, www.urban.org/sites/default/files/alfresco/publication-pdfs/410470-The-Influences-of-Truth-in-Sentencing-Reforms-on-Changes-in-States-Sentencing-Practices-and-Prison-Populations.PDF.

60. "Truth in Sentencing: Availability of Federal Grants Influenced Laws in Some States," General Accounting Office, February 1998, accessed July 6, 2016, https://www.gpo.gov/fdsys/pkg/GAOREPORTS-GGD-98-42/pdf/GAOREPORTS-GGD-98-42.pdf.

61. Donna Murch, "Clinton's War on Drugs: When Black Lives Didn't Matter," *The New Republic*, February 9, 2016, accessed July 6, 2016, https://newrepublic.com/article/129433/clintons-war-drugs-black-lives-didnt-matter; Michelle Alexander, "Why Hillary Clinton Doesn't Deserve the Black Vote," *The Nation*, February 10, 2016, accessed July 6, 2016, www.thenation.com/article/hillary-clinton-does-not-deserve-black-peoples-votes. The most obvious defect in the argument blaming the 1994 Crime Act with "causing" mass incarceration is that the national prison population had grown by 244 percent between 1978 and 1994. For criticisms of these arguments more generally, see Leon Neyfakh, "The Clintons Aren't to Blame for Mass Incarceration," *Slate*, February 11, 2016, accessed July 6, 2016, www.slate.com/articles/news_and_politics/crime/2016/02/michelle_alexander_blames_hillary_clinton_for_mass_incarceration_she_shouldn.html.

62. See my tweets of April 13, 2016, https://twitter.com/JohnFPfaff/status/720272553093148672.

63. To be fair, a study by the Brennan Center for Justice suggests that New York's incarceration rate would have dropped even faster had it not adopted its truth-in-sentencing law, which seems right. James Austin, Michael P. Jacobson, and Inimai M. Chettiar, "How New York City Reduced Mass Incarceration: A Model for Change?," Brennan Center for Justice, January 30, 2013, accessed July 6, 2016, www.brennancenter.org/publication/how-new-york-city-reduced-mass-incarceration-model-change. But the law still failed to result in a net increase in incarceration in New York.

64. Office of Sex Offender Sentencing, Monitoring, Apprehending, Registering, and Tracking, http://www.smart.gov/sorna.htm; "Some States Refuse to Implement SORNA, Lose Federal Grants," *Prison Legal News*, September 19, 2014, accessed July 6, 2016, https://www.prisonlegalnews.org/news/2014/sep/19/some-states-refuse-implement-sorna-lose-federal-grants.

CHAPTER FOUR: COSTS OF THE STANDARD STORY

1. Pfaff, "Bill Clinton Is Wrong."

2. Peter K. Enns, "The Public's Increasing Punitiveness and Its Influence on Mass Incarceration in the United States," *American Journal of Political Science* 58 (2014): 857–872; Peter K. Enns, *Incarceration Nation: How the United States Became the Most Punitive Democracy in the World* (New York: Cambridge University Press, 2016).

3. Throughout the 2016 presidential campaign, there was a steady stream of articles blaming Bill Clinton—who didn't enter office until 1993—and the 1994 Violent Crime Control and Law Enforcement Act that he signed, for causing or contributing significantly to prison growth. See, for example, Alexander, "Hillary Clinton Doesn't Deserve," and Murch, "Clinton's War on Drugs." As I have pointed out, these arguments significantly overstate the impact of the act, and of the Clintons more generally. See, for example, Pfaff, "Bill Clinton Is Wrong," and Neyfakh, "Clintons Aren't to Blame."

4. Gottschalk, *Caught.*

5. Katherine Beckett, Anna Reosti, and Emily Knaphus, "The End of an Era? Understanding the Contradictions of Criminal Justice Reform," *Annals of the American Academy of Political and Social Science* 664 (2016): 238–257. Not only did the types of laws passed change after 2007, but so did the volume. According to the study's data, there were about 440 new laws in 2000–2007, and approximately 600 new ones in 2007–2012 (which is shorter by two years). The study focused just on laws intended to directly increase or decrease prison populations: a change in parole release procedures counted, but a change in the sorts of licenses a sex offender could not obtain did not.

6. Again, private prisons are not the only place where private firms play a role in criminal justice. While little action has been taken against private prisons, there has been a much more concerted effort to eliminate or restrict the use of cash bail, which has faced stiff opposition from private bail-bondsmen. See, for example, Christopher Moraff, "US Cities Are Looking for Alternatives to Cash Bail," *NextCity*, March 24, 2016, accessed July 6, 2016, https://nextcity.org/daily/entry/cities-alternatives-cash-bail.

7. Nicole D. Porter, "The State of Sentencing 2010: Developments in Policy and Practice," The Sentencing Project, February 2011, accessed July 6, 2016, www .sentencingproject.org/wp-content/uploads/2016/01/State-of-Sentencing-2010.pdf; Nicole D. Porter, "The State of Sentencing 2011: Developments in Policy and Practice," The Sentencing Project, February 2012, accessed July 6, 2016, www.sentencingproject. org/wp-content/uploads/2016/01/State-of-Sentencing-2011.pdf; Nicole D. Porter, "The State of Sentencing 2012: Developments in Policy and Practice," The Sentencing Project, January 2013, accessed July 6, 2016, www.sentencingproject.org/wp-content /uploads/2016/01/State-of-Sentencing-2012.pdf; Nicole D. Porter, "The State of Sentencing 2013: Developments in Policy and Practice," The Sentencing Project, January 2014, accessed July 6, 2016, www.sentencingproject.org/wp-content/uploads/2015/11 /State-of-Sentencing-2013.pdf; Nicole D. Porter, "The State of Sentencing 2014: Developments in Policy and Practice," The Sentencing Project, February 2015, accessed July 6, 2016, http://sentencingproject.org/wp-content/uploads/2016/02/sen_State_of

_Sentencing_2014.pdf; Nicole D. Porter, "The State of Sentencing 2015: Developments in Policy and Practice," The Sentencing Project, February 2016, accessed July 6, 2016, http://sentencingproject.org/doc/publications/State-of-Sentencing-2015.pdf.

8. The packages of reforms in each year were roughly the same, so I chose 2013 more or less at random. If anything, 2013 is one of the years *least* favorable to my overall argument here, since it is one of the few years in which a state implemented a major reform aimed at reducing punishment for people sentenced for violent crimes.

9. "Mississippi's 2014 Corrections and Criminal Justice Reform," Pew Charitable Trusts, May 2014, accessed July 6, 2016, www.pewtrusts.org/~/media/assets/2014/09 /pspp_mississippi_2014_corrections_justice_reform.pdf.

10. "Mississippi Department of Corrections: Daily Inmate Population," Mississippi Department of Corrections, February 2016, accessed July 6, 2016, www.mdoc .ms.gov/Admin-Finance/DailyInmatePopulation/2016–02%20Daily%20Inmate%20 Population.pdf; "Mississippi Department of Corrections: Daily Inmate Population," Mississippi Department of Corrections, December 2015, accessed July 6, 2016, www .mdoc.ms.gov/Admin-Finance/DailyInmatePopulation/2015–12%20Daily%20 Inmate%20Population.pdf.

11. State prison populations also fell during 2001, but the decline was less than 2,000 prisoners, which was more than offset by an increase of nearly 12,000 in the federal system.

12. Joan Petersilia and Francis T. Cullen, "Liberal But Not Stupid: Meeting the Promise of Downsizing Prisons," *Stanford Journal of Criminal Law and Policy* 2 (2015): 1–43. In all fairness, as we saw in Chapter 1, that 56,000 drop is the net decline, not the gross decline. Since 2010, twenty-five states have seen their prison populations shrink, for a total decline of over 77,000 (offset by a total increase of just over 21,000 in the other half of the states). California is "only" 45 percent of this gross drop—still an outsized portion.

13. See, for example, Marc Mauer, "Can We Wait 88 Years to End Mass Incarceration," *Huffington Post*, February 19, 2014, accessed July 6, 2016, www.huffingtonpost .com/marc-mauer/88-years-mass-incarceration_b_4474132.html.

14. According to the official statistics, the violent crime rate today is still more than twice as high as it was in 1960, and the property crime rate is 50 percent higher. Even if, as is likely the case, the official crime rates from the 1960s systematically undercounted crime, both violent and property crime rates today are still likely higher than they were back then.

15. Gottschalk, *Caught*; Hadar Aviram, *Cheap on Crime: Recession-Era Politics and the Transformation of American Punishment* (Oakland: University of California Press, 2015); Don Stemen, "Reconsidering Incarceration: New Directions for Reducing Crime," Vera Institute of Justice, January 2007, accessed July 6, 2016, http://vera.org/sites/default /files/resources/downloads/veraincarc_vFW2.pdf.

16. Prison and crime are highly endogenous. There are ways to tame the endogeneity, at least somewhat, but they are infrequently used—surprisingly so. For the impact of prison on crime, see the studies discussed in Stemen, "Reconsidering Incarceration," and Rucker Johnson and Steven Raphael, "How Much Crime Reduction Does the Marginal

Prisoner Buy?" *Journal of Law and Economics* 55 (2012): 275–310. For the impact of crime on prison populations, see Yair Listokin, "Does More Crime Mean More Prisoners: An Instrumental Variables Approach," *Journal of Law and Economics* 46 (2003): 181–206.

17. Levitt, "Understanding Why Crime Fell."

18. Johnson and Raphael, "Marginal Prisoner."

19. We often read about the need to never jeopardize the "hard-won" gains of the past thirty years. See, for example, "The Dangerous Myths of Drug Sentencing 'Reform,'" National Association of Assistant United States Attorneys, July 2015, accessed July 6, 2016, https://www.naausa.org/2013/images/docs/Dangerous-Myths-of-Drug-Sentencing-Reform.pdf.

20. Crime tends to be a young person's game; as people get older, their criminal activity generally subsides. As for culture, one analyst assembled ethnographic evidence suggesting that kids who witnessed the crack-fueled spike in violence in the latter half of the 1980s were more likely to swear off violence as a way of solving problems and to avoid using crack. Vanessa Barker, "Explaining the Great American Crime Decline: A Review of Blumstein and Wallman, Goldberger and Rosenfeld, and Zimring," review of *The Crime Drop in America*, rev. ed., by Alfred Blumstein and Joel Wallman, eds.; *Understanding Crime Trends: Workshop Report*, by Arthur S. Goldberger and Richard Rosenfeld; and "The Great American Crime Decline," by Franklin Zimring, *Law & Social Inquiry* 35 (2010): 489–516. Cars are harder to steal now than in the past, due to new anti-theft technologies; no one carries around much cash anymore, which makes robberies less profitable; and videos games, web surfing, and the like now keep young men inside, so they are less likely to be on the street getting into trouble.

21. See, for example, Kevin Drum, "Lead: America's Real Criminal Element," *Mother Jones*, February 11, 2016, accessed August 24, 2016, www.motherjones.com/environment/2016/02/lead-exposure-gasoline-crime-increase-children-health. Note that widespread, ongoing exposure to lead—like that in Flint, Michigan, and elsewhere—may lead to elevated levels of offending in the future, although the lead-crime connection has come under some criticism lately. See, e.g., Janet L. Lauritsen, Maribeth L. Rezey, and Karen Heimer, "When Choice of Data Matters: Analysis of U.S. Crime Trends, 1973–2012," *Journal of Quantitative Criminology*, 36 (2015), 335–355.

22. Barker, "American Crime Decline."

23. The cohort data are available in Lindsey M. Howden and Julie A. Meyer, "Age and Sex Composition: 2010," US Census, May 2011, accessed July 6, 2016, www.census.gov/prod/cen2010/briefs/c2010br-03.pdf.

24. John Roman, "Deciphering the Crime Decline," Urban Institute, July 27, 2011, accessed July 6, 2016, www.urban.org/urban-wire/deciphering-crime-decline.

25. Cullen et al., "Prisons Do Not Reduce Recidivism."

26. Daniel S. Nagin, "Deterrence in the Twenty-First Century," *Crime & Justice: A Review of Research* 42 (2013): 1–65.

27. Michael Mueller-Smith, "The Criminal and Labor Market Impacts of Incarceration," unpublished working paper, August 18, 2015, accessed August 24, 2016, http://sites.lsa.umich.edu/mgms/wp-content/uploads/sites/283/2015/09/incar.pdf. The paper

uses data from Harris County, Texas (Houston), and it finds that the incapacitation effects of prison were more than offset by the resulting higher rates of offending by those who were released from prison, and that the rate of reoffending rose the longer an inmate was confined. Like all empirical papers, it has some limitations, but it certainly indicates that the short-term gains from incapacitation may have long-term costs.

28. Levitt, "Understanding Why Crime Fell."

29. *Blakely v. Washington*, 542 US 296 (2004).

30. Joanna M. Shepherd, "Blakely's Silver Lining: Sentencing Guidelines, Judicial Discretion, and Crime," *Hastings Law Journal* 58 (2006): 533–589.

31. See the description of the stultifying boredom of prison, with the lurking *threat* of violence dominating actual acts of violence, in Norval Morris, "The Contemporary Prison: 1965–Present," in *The Oxford History of the Prison*, ed. Norval Morris and David J. Rothman (Oxford: Oxford University Press, 1995), 202–234. Or see this interview with Danny Trejo, a federal inmate turned Hollywood actor, on how polite people were in maximum security federal prisons, more or less for mutually assured destruction reasons: Bilge Ebiri, "Danny Trejo on *Machete Kills*, Randomly Meeting Clint Eastwood, and His Problem With *Oz*," *Vulture*, October 11, 2013, accessed July 6, 2016, www.vulture.com/2013/10/danny-trejo-machete-kills-interview.html.

32. That said, the *murder* rate in prison appears to be lower than that nationwide, and thus likely lower still than the murder rates in the communities in which many prisoners previously lived.

33. For mental health issues, see Craig Haney, "From Prison to Home: The Effect of Incarceration and Reentry on Children, Families, and Communities," US Department of Health and Human Services, Office of the Assistant Secretary for Planning and Evaluation, December 1, 2001, accessed July 6, 2016, https://aspe.hhs.gov/basic-report/psychological-impact-incarceration-implications-post-prison-adjustment. For the life-span argument, see E. J. Patterson, "The Dose-Response of Time Served in Prison on Mortality: New York State, 1989–2003," *American Journal of Public Health* 103 (2013): 523–528, which shows that the elevated risk of death that a formerly incarcerated person faces declines the longer he or she remains free.

34. European prisons are substantially more humane than American ones, which reflects, in part, different normative values about how prisoners deserve to be treated. A court in Norway, for example, held that mass murderer Anders Breivik's human rights had been violated by being detained under conditions that would seem impossibly pleasant by American standards. Jon Henley, "Anders Breivik's Human Rights Violated in Prison, Norway Court Rules," *The Guardian*, April 20, 2016, accessed July 6, 2016, https://www.theguardian.com/world/2016/apr/20/anders-behring-breiviks-human-rights-violated-in-prison-norway-court-rules. And a visit by several American prison experts to Germany revealed a system that treated its inmates far better than prisoners are treated in the United States. "How Germany Does Prisons," Marshall Project, June 2015, accessed July 6, 2016, https://www.themarshallproject.org/tag/how-germany-does-prison#.z0u2MWq8K.

35. Pfaff, *Sentencing Law*.

36. Bernadette Rabuy and Daniel Kopf, "Separation by Bars and Miles: Visitation in State Prison," Prison Policy Initiative, October 20, 2015, accessed July 6, 2016, www .prisonpolicy.org/reports/prisonvisits.html.

37. Donald Braman, "Families and Incarceration," in *Invisible Punishment: The Collateral Consequences of Mass Incarceration*, ed. Meda Chesney-Lind and Marc Mauer (New York: New Press, 2003), 117.

38. Leonard M. Lopoo and Bruce Western, "Incarceration and the Formation and Stability of Marital Unions," *Journal of Marriage and Family* 67 (2005): 721–734.

39. Tracey L. Meares, "Social Organization and Drug Law Enforcement," *American Criminal Law Review* 35 (1998): 191–227; Jeffrey Fagan and Tracey L. Meares, "Punishment, Deterrence, and Social Control: The Paradox of Punishment in Minority Communities," *Ohio State Journal of Criminal Law* 6 (2008): 173–229.

40. Braman, "Families and Incarceration."

41. Perhaps the most high-profile and controversial assertion of this point was made by MacDonald, "Nationwide Crime Wave."

42. This claim is not at all inconsistent with the work of Michael Fortner and James Forman Jr., who have demonstrated that black political elites often pushed for tough-on-crime laws, including harsh sentences for drug trafficking, precisely because their communities incurred so much of the cost of crime. Michael J. Fortner, *Black Silent Majority: The Rockefeller Drug Laws and the Politics of Punishment* (Cambridge, MA: Harvard University Press, 2015); James Forman Jr., "Racial Critiques of Mass Incarceration: Beyond New Jim Crow," review of *The New Jim Crow* by Michelle Alexander, *NYU Law Review* 87 (2012): 21–69. Put aside the fact that the elites do not always speak for the general public, and that even among the elites there was disagreement, such as when the Congressional Black Caucus only grudgingly helped President Bill Clinton pass the 1994 Crime Act. Karen Hosler, "Black Caucus Yields on Crime Bill," *Baltimore Sun*, August 18, 1994, accessed July 6, 2016, http://articles.baltimoresun.com/1994–08–18/news/1994230118_1_black -caucus-crime-bill-clinton. When the elites came out in favor of tough laws, crime was high and prison populations were relatively low; there's no reason these elites and the general minority public wouldn't shift their views as crime fell and imprisonment rose.

43. Federal Bureau of Investigation, "Crime in the United States: 2015." Accessed October 11, 2016, http://ucr.fbi.gov/crime-in-the-U.S./2015/.

CHAPTER FIVE: THE MAN BEHIND THE CURTAIN

1. Travis et al., *Growth of Incarceration*.

2. National Academy of Sciences, www.nationalacademies.org/nrc.

3. Chapters 2–4 of the report focus on the causes of prison growth. Chapter 2, which provides a broad overview of trends, never discusses prosecutors after a cursory mention in the opening paragraph. Chapters 3 and 4, which explore the causes of growth in more depth, do refer to prosecutors a few times, but usually in passing (" . . . foster circumvention by prosecutors, juries, and judges . . ." or "All found that prosecutors and judges (and sometimes police) . . .").

4. See, for example, Robert M. Ireland, "Privately Funded Prosecution of Crime in the Nineteenth-Century United States," *American Journal of Legal History* 39 (1995): 43–58.

5. Roger A. Fairfax Jr., "Delegation of the Criminal Prosecution Function to Private Actors," *UC Davis Law Review* 43 (2009): 411–456; Joan E. Jacoby, *The American Prosecutor: A Search for Identity* (Lanham, MD: Lexington Books, 1980); Stuntz, *Collapse*; Jed H. Shugerman, *The People's Courts: Pursuing Judicial Independence in America* (Cambridge, MA: Harvard University Press, 2012).

6. Michael Edmund O'Neill, "Private Vengeance and the Public Good," *Journal of Constitutional Law* 12 (2010): 659–750.

7. Stephen Deere, "Ferguson Takes Steps to Remove Controversial Prosecutor," *St. Louis Post-Dispatch*, May 4, 2016, accessed July 6, 2016, www.stltoday.com/news/local/crime-and-courts/article_2a627bbd-0cc9–5b83–8b4b-8c642de204af.html.

8. In Alaska and Delaware, the state attorney general (appointed in Alaska, elected in Delaware) is the chief prosecutor and appoints all local prosecutors. In Connecticut and New Jersey, the county prosecutors are viewed as the chief prosecutors for their counties—so they have more independent authority than the prosecutors in Alaska and Delaware—but are still appointed by the attorney general (who is elected in Delaware, and appointed in New Jersey). In Maine, the state attorney general handles all murder cases, but all other crimes are dealt with by the locally elected prosecutor. Note that, except for New Jersey, all of these are small-population states where county-level elections may not make much sense. For information on the number of full-time prosecutors, see Steven W. Perry and Duren Banks, "Prosecutors in State Courts, 2007—Statistical Tables," US Department of Justice, Bureau of Justice Statistics, December 2011, accessed July 6, 2016, www.bjs.gov/content/pub/pdf/psc07st.pdf; John M. Dawson, "Prosecutors in State Courts, 1990," US Department of Justice, Bureau of Justice Statistics, March 1992, accessed July 6, 2016, www.bjs.gov/content/pub/pdf/psc90.pdf. The newer data here are from 2007, so they are almost a decade old. Unsurprisingly, that's the most recent data we have.

9. Perry and Banks, "Prosecutors in State Courts, 2007."

10. The median number of prosecutors in communities of 250,000 to 999,999 was 44; in communities with over 1 million people, 156. These offices are surely more professionally run and managed.

11. For drug arrests I use total drug arrests here, even though a significant majority of drug arrests in each year are for possession (on the order of 72 to 83 percent), and therefore unlikely to result in prison sentences. These cases still take up prosecutors' time, however.

12. *Wayte v. United States*, 470 US 598 (1985).

13. All of New York's Assault Laws are under Chap. 120 of the New York Penal Code. Second Degree Assault is NY Penal Law §120.05, Assault on a Judge is NY Penal Law §120.09.

14. Several states use sentencing guidelines that require judges to impose sentences in a narrow range based on the crime charged and the defendant's prior criminal history. Prosecutors have tremendous power in these states to limit the range of time a defendant faces.

15. Greg Newburn, Tweet, October 9, 2015, https://twitter.com/gnewburn/status/652489497742077952.

16. *Bordenkircher v. Hayes*, 434 US 357 (1978).

17. To be fair, there may be internal rules in a prosecutor's office about how to make these sorts of charging decisions, but if they exist they are often not public, they can change at any time without notice, and they are not legally binding (so public defenders cannot appeal excessive aggression).

18. Cohen and Kyckelhahn, "Felony Defendants, 2006." Note that out of every one hundred felony arrests, only sixty-five result in pleas. That's a plea-bargaining rate of 65 percent. But only sixty-nine arrests turn into prosecutions, and of those, sixty-five (or 94.2 percent) end in plea bargains. So the oft-cited "95 percent of all cases end in pleas" turns to some degree on where we start counting.

19. NAAUSA, "Dangerous Myths."

20. "Gun Mandatory Minimum Sentences," Families Against Mandatory Minimums, accessed July 6, 2016, http://famm.org/projects/federal/us-congress/gun-mandatory-minimum-sentences.

21. See, for example, Mona Lynch, "Reining in Federal Prosecutors," *The New York Times*, June 2, 2015, accessed August 24, 2016, www.nytimes.com/2015/06/02/opinion/reining-in-federal-prosecutors.html.

22. This is literally an example of the prisoners' dilemma. If all defendants refused deals, they would collectively be better off, since prosecutors would be forced to drop a lot of cases. Any one defendant, however, has a strong incentive to take the generous deal prosecutors would offer to get the system moving again.

23. Scott W. Howe, "The Value of Plea Bargaining," *Oklahoma Law Review* 58 (2005): 599–636, 611–612.

24. Although defendants have no constitutional right to discovery, some offices have adopted "open file" policies that give defendants more access to information even during the plea process.

25. At more local levels, efforts to cut back on jail populations have targeted prosecutorial practices, especially case-management ones. See, for example, "Costly Confinement and Sensible Solutions: Jail Overcrowding in Texas," Texas Criminal Justice Coalition, October 2010, accessed July 6, 2016, www.texascjc.org/sites/default/files/publications/Costly%20Confinement%20Sensible%20Solutions%20Report%20(Oct%202010).pdf. Such efforts appear to be restricted to the local level, in part because local officials are more sensitive than state ones to the costs imposed on them by prosecutors.

26. Mark Guarino, "Chicago Prosecutor Loses Reelection Battle in the Shadow of the Laquan McDonald Video," *Washington Post*, March 15, 2016, accessed July 6, 2016, https://www.washingtonpost.com/news/post-nation/wp/2016/03/15/chicagos-prosecutor-faces-a-reelection-battle-in-the-shadow-of-the-laquan-mcdonald-video/?tid=a_inl&utm_term=.71eb986343e2.

27. Leon Neyfakh, "How to Run Against a Tough-on-Crime DA—And Win," *Slate*, November 12, 2015, accessed July 6, 2016, www.slate.com/articles/news_and_politics/crime/2015/11/district_attorneys_scott_colom_proves_you_can_run_against_a_tough_on_crime.html.

28. "ABA-LDF Joint Statement on Eliminating Bias in the Criminal Justice System," NAACP, July 16, 2015, accessed July 6, 2016, www.naacpldf.org/press-release /joint-statement-eliminating-bias-criminal-justice-system.

29. Meagher, "13 Questions."

30. Josh Keller and Adam Pearce, "This Small Indiana County Sends More People to Prison Than San Francisco and Durham, N.C., Combined. Why?" *New York Times*, September 2, 2016, accessed September 2, 2016, www.nytimes.com/2016/09/02/upshot /new-geography-of-prisons.html.

31. Recall the argument by Stuntz raised in Chapter 3, that prosecutors may actually value longer sentences negatively. Stuntz, "Disappearing Shadow."

32. As with so many other vital criminal justice statistics, we have very little data on how many Americans have criminal records. An interstate FBI database reports over 100 million arrest records, but it notes that some people may have multiple arrest records in different states. "Survey of State Criminal History Information Systems, 2012," US Department of Justice, Bureau of Justice Statistics, January 2014, accessed July 6, 2016, https://www.ncjrs.gov/pdffiles1/bjs/grants/244563.pdf. A report by the BJS suggests that as many as 25 percent of people released from prison end up with at least one out-of-state arrest, so the double-counting in that 100 million could be extensive. Matthew R. Durose, Howard N. Snyder, and Alexia D. Cooper, "Multistate Criminal History Patterns of Prisoners Released in 30 States," US Department of Justice, Bureau of Justice Statistics, September 2015, accessed July 6, 2016, www.bjs.gov/content/pub /pdf/mschpprts05.pdf. Nonetheless, these numbers still imply that tens of millions of Americans have criminal records of some sort. A smaller set of studies of defendants in urban counties supports this idea, showing increases over the 1990s and 2000s in the share of defendants with prior arrests and prior convictions. Brian A. Reaves, "Felony Defendants in Large Urban Counties, 2009—Statistical Tables," US Department of Justice, Bureau of Justice Statistics, December 2013, accessed July 6, 2016, www.bjs.gov /content/pub/pdf/fdluc09.pdf.

33. *Gideon v. Wainwright*, 372 US 335 (1963); *Argersinger v. Hamlin*, 407 US 25 (1972).

34. It was about 80 percent in 1992, and still about 80 percent in 2007. See Steven K. Smith and Carol J. DeFrances, "Indigent Defense," US Department of Justice, Bureau of Justice Statistics, February 1996, accessed July 6, 2016, www.bjs.gov/content/pub/pdf /id.pdf; "OJP Fact Sheet: Indigent Defense," Office of Justice Programs, December 2011, accessed July 6, 2016, http://ojp.gov/newsroom/factsheets/ojpfs_indigentdefense.html.

35. In Tennessee, for example, appointed counsel are paid about $40 to $50 an hour and face caps on how much they can earn per year. Chris Seaton, "Tennessee's Indigent Defense Task Force Does Nothing," Mimesis Law, February 15, 2016, accessed July 6, 2016, http://mimesislaw.com/fault-lines/tennessees-indigent -defense-task-force-does-nothing/6827.

36. Holly R. Stevens, Colleen E. Sheppard, Robert Spangenberg, Aimee Wickman, and Jon B. Gould, "State, County and Local Expenditures for Indigent Defense Services

Fiscal Year 2008," American Bar Association, November 2010, accessed July 6, 2016, www.americanbar.org/content/dam/aba/administrative/legal_aid_indigent_defendants /ls_sclaid_def_expenditures_fy08.authcheckdam.pdf.

37. Perry and Banks, "Prosecutors in State Courts, 2007."

38. "North Carolina's Criminal Justice System: A Comparison of Prosecution and Indigent Defense Resources," North Carolina Office of Indigent Defense Services, April 2011, accessed July 6, 2016, www.ncids.org/Reports%20&%20Data/Latest %20Releases/ProsecutionOfIndigentDefense.pdf.

39. One assistant public defender from New Orleans said her caseload was twice the recommended limit of 150 per year. As a result, she felt she couldn't properly represent her clients. Tina Peng, "I'm a Public Defender: It's Impossible for Me to Do a Good Job Representing My Clients," *Washington Post*, September 3, 2015, accessed July 6, 2016, https:// www.washingtonpost.com/opinions/our-public-defender-system-isnt-just-broken —its-unconstitutional/2015/09/03/aadf2b6c-519b-11e5-9812-92d5948a40f8_story .html; Hannah Levintova, Jaeah Lee, and Brett Brownell, "Why You're in Deep Trouble If You Can't Afford a Lawyer," *Mother Jones*, May 6, 2013, accessed July 6, 2016, www .motherjones.com/politics/2013/05/public-defenders-gideon-supreme-court-charts.

40. Jessica Miller, "State of Utah, Washington County Sued over Their Public Defender System," *Salt Lake Tribune*, January 22, 2016, accessed July 6, 2016, www .sltrib.com/home/3449965-155/state-of-utah-washington-county-sued; Kristine Guerra, "Lawsuit: Indiana County's Public Defender System 'Set Up to Fail People,'" *Indystar*, January 5, 2016, accessed July 6, 2016, www.indystar.com/story/news/crime/2016/01 /05/lawsuit-indiana-countys-public-defender-system-set-up-fail-poor-people /78301714; Colby Hamilton, "NYCLU Report Details 'Inadequate' Public Defense," *Politico New York*, September 17, 2014, accessed July 6, 2016, www.capitalnewyork .com/article/albany/2014/09/8552732/nyclu-report-details-inadequate-public-defense; Bill Wellock, "County Ordered to Justify Public Defender Funding," *The Citizen's Voice*, November 9, 2015, accessed July 6, 2016, http://citizensvoice.com/news/county -ordered-to-justify-public-defender-funding-1.1969018; Matthew Teague, "Why New Orleans Public Defenders Will Not Take Criminal Cases of City's Poorest," *The Guardian*, January 22, 2016, accessed July 6, 2016, www.theguardian.com/us-news/2016/jan /22/new-orleans-public-defenders-refuse-criminal-cases-aclu.

41. This isn't the first time criminal justice officials have tried to get sued as part of a battle for more funding. In the 1960s, prison wardens sometimes assisted prisoners suing in federal court over appalling prison conditions because the wardens saw it as the only way to get more money out of the state. Malcolm M. Feeley and Edward L. Rubin, *Judicial Policy Making and the Modern State: How the Courts Reformed America's Prisons* (Cambridge: Cambridge University Press, 1998).

42. Prosecutors have a huge carrot to use with defendants who can't make bail: plead guilty now, and the sentence recommendation will be for time already served in jail. A defendant faced with such an offer has to decide if staying in prison and fighting for an acquittal is worth more than just walking home that afternoon. It's a very powerful card for the prosecutor to hold.

43. Stuntz, *Collapse*.

44. Jed Shugerman, "Earl Warren, the Japanese Internment, and the Rise of the Prosecutor Politician," unpublished manuscript, 2016.

45. Even forceful critics of prosecutorial power, such as Angela Davis, readily acknowledge that prosecutors do need to retain some discretion. Angela J. Davis, *Arbitrary Justice: The Power of the American Prosecutor* (Oxford: Oxford University Press, 2007).

46. Ronald F. Wright, "How Prosecutor Elections Fail Us," *Ohio State Journal of Criminal Law* 6 (2009): 581–610. The study looks at elections in ten states over the years 1996 to 2006.

47. Colleen Long, "Losing Incumbent Charles Hynes Still a Part of Brooklyn DA Race," NBC, September 20, 2013, accessed July 6, 2016, www.nbcnewyork.com/news /local/Brooklyn-District-Attorney-Race-Charles-Hynes-Kenneth-Thompson-Ballot -GOP-Conservative-224487451.html.

48. "Statement and Return Report for Certification: Primary Election 2013," Board of Elections in the City of New York, September 10, 2013, accessed July 6, 2016, http://vote.nyc.ny.us/downloads/pdf/results/2013/2013SeptemberPrimaryElection /01019000123Kings%20Democratic%20District%20Attorney%20Kings%20 Recap.pdf; "Board of Elections, The City of New York: Annual Report 2013," Board of Elections in the City of New York, accessed July 6, 2016, vote.nyc.ny.us/downloads /pdf/documents/boe/AnnualReports/BOEAnnualReport13.pdf.

49. Joy-Ann Reid, "Tamir Rice Prosecutor Indicted Innocent Men, But Not Killer Cops," *The Daily Beast*, January 29, 2015, accessed July 6, 2016, www.thedailybeast.com /articles/2015/12/29/rice-prosecutor-indicted-innocent-men-but-not-killer-cops .html.

50. Steven W. Perry, "Prosecutors in State Courts, 2005," US Department of Justice, Bureau of Justice Statistics, July 2006, accessed July 6, 2016, www.bjs.gov/content/pub /pdf/psc05.pdf.

51. The victory of Scott Colom in Mississippi, discussed above, could be one such case, in which Colom ran on a general smart-on-crime platform. Of course, it likely didn't hurt that the incumbent was still burdened with several high-profile reversals over the years, including in a few death penalty cases. See Radley Balko, "Election Results: One of America's Worst Prosecutors Lost Last Night, But One of Its Worst Attorneys General Won," *Washington Post*, November 4, 2015, accessed July 6, 2016, https://www .washingtonpost.com/news/the-watch/wp/2015/11/04/election-results-one-of-americas -worst-prosecutors-lost-last-night-but-one-of-its-worst-attorneys-general-won.

52. In 2005, the last year for which there is data, over half of all DA offices received at least 82 percent of their funds from the counties, and nearly one-third were entirely county-funded. Perry, "Prosecutors in State Courts, 2005." In five states—Alaska, Connecticut, Delaware, Rhode Island, and Vermont—the state government pays for jails, since the jail and prison systems are unified under state control. See Carson, "Prisoners in 2014," Table 2 (note f).

53. According to Stuntz, this moral-hazard problem was ignored in the legal literature until Robert Misner wrote an article on it in 1996. Stuntz, *Collapse*, Chap. 9, n.

16. Of course, legal academics are not necessarily aware of everything state legislators are discussing, but if this were an issue that came up a lot it seems reasonable that someone would have raised it before we were more than two decades into the prison boom.

54. Oregon District Attorneys Association to Joint Committee on Ways and Means, January 28, 2015, accessed July 6, 2016, https://olis.leg.state.or.us/liz/2015R1 /Downloads/CommitteeMeetingDocument/48747.

55. Richard C. Dieter, "Millions Misspent: What Politicians Don't Say About the High Costs of the Death Penalty," Death Penalty Information Center, Fall 1994, accessed July 6, 2016, www.deathpenaltyinfo.org/millions-misspent. Sierra County is on the outskirts of Sacramento.

56. See, for example, Paula T. Dow, "Report of the County Prosecutor Study Commission," February 4, 2011, accessed August 24, 2016, www.nj.gov/oag/dcj/pdfs /Report-of-the-County-Prosecutor-Study-Commission-2011.pdf.

57. Khalil Gibran Muhammad, *The Condemnation of Blackness: Race, Crime, and the Making of Modern Urban America* (Cambridge, MA: Harvard University Press, 2010).

58. Beckett et al., "Lessons from Seattle."

59. *State v. Vasquez*, 129 NJ 189 (1992); *State v. Brimage*, 153 NJ 1 (1998).

60. "Revised Attorney General Guidelines for Negotiating Cases Under N.J.S.A.— Effective for Offenses Committed On or After September 15, 2004," Office of the Attorney General, State of New Jersey, www.state.nj.us/lps/dcj/agguide/directives/ brimagerevision.htm.

61. The one major difference from sentencing guidelines is that the permissible plea deal changes over time. The most generous deals are available pre-indictment. The choices narrow a bit in the "initial post-indictment" phase (basically, within twenty days of the first plea offer after indictment), and offers become even less generous in the "final post-indictment" phase, which is the rest of the time.

62. The only paper to talk about them at any length appears to be Ronald F. Wright, "Prosecutorial Guidelines and the New Terrain in New Jersey," *Penn State Law Review* 109 (2005): 1087–1105.

63. "Attorney General Guidelines," Office of the Attorney General, State of New Jersey, www.state.nj.us/oag/dcj/agguide.htm.

64. See, for example, John F. Pfaff, "The Continued Vitality of Structured Sentencing Following *Blakely*: The Effectiveness of Voluntary Guidelines," *UCLA Law Review* 54 (2006): 235–307.

65. Ronald F. Wright, "Sentencing Commissions as Provocateurs of Prosecutorial Self-Regulation," *Columbia Law Review* 105 (2005): 1010–1047.

66. Judith Greene, Kevin Pranis, and Jason Ziedenberg, "Disparity by Design: How Drug-Free Zone Laws Impact Racial Disparity—and Fail to Protect Youth," Justice Policy Institute, March 2006, accessed July 6, 2016, www.drugpolicy.org/docUploads /SchoolZonesReport06.pdf.

67. Ibid.

68. Brandon Martin, "Corrections Infrastructure Spending in California," Public

Policy Institute of California, March 2015, accessed July 6, 2016, www.ppic.org/main/publication_show.asp?i=1142.

69. *Brown v. Plata*, 563 US 493 (2011).

70. California Penal Code §1170(h). Almost all "serious" crimes, a legal classification in California, are also "violent," but there are some drug and other nonviolent crimes that are classified as "serious." Realignment also excluded some serious white-collar crimes from the "triple-non" category that are not otherwise viewed as "serious." "Serious Felonies Under California Three Strikes Law," Shouse California Law Group, n.d., accessed July 6, 2016, www.shouselaw.com/serious-felonies.html.

71. Magnus Lofstrom and Steven Raphael, "Realignment, Incarceration, and Crime Trends in California," Public Policy Institute of California, May 2015, accessed July 6, 2016, www.ppic.org/main/publication_quick.asp?i=1151; J. Richard Couzens and Tricia A. Bigelow, "Awarding Custody Credits," California Courts, February 2013, accessed July 6, 2016, www.courts.ca.gov/partners/documents/Credits_Memo.pdf.

72. "Realignment Cheat Sheet," California Public Defenders Association, October 1, 2012, accessed July 6, 2016, www.claraweb.us/wp-content/uploads/2011/09/2012-MEMO-Realignment.pdf, Appendix A.

73. Anat Rubin, "California's Jail-Building Boom," Marshall Project, July 2, 2015, accessed July 6, 2016, https://www.themarshallproject.org/2015/07/02/california-s-jail-building-boom#.x1zcVkCaI. Some of the funds are supposed to be used on programming, not just capacity expansion, but the decision is ultimately left to the county.

74. "Funding of Realignment," California Department of Corrections and Rehabilitation, n.d., accessed July 6, 2016, www.cdcr.ca.gov/realignment/Funding-Realignment.html.

75. Lofstrom and Raphael, "Realignment, Incarceration."

76. Ibid. The follow-up article is Jody Sundt, Emily J. Salisbury, and Mark G. Harmon, "Is Downsizing Prisons Dangerous? The Effect of California's Realignment Act on Public Safety," *Criminology & Public Policy* 15 (2016): 1–27.

77. Maureen Hayden, "Prison Officials Say Lighter Sentences Aren't Saving Money," *Herald-Bulletin*, March 9, 2016, accessed July 6, 2016, www.heraldbulletin.com/news/prison-officials-say-lighter-sentences-aren-t-saving-money/article_65e15ab6-e652-11e5-9672-6bf2b892e2d5.html.

78. Jessica K. Feinstein, "Reforming Adult Felony Probation to Ease Prison Overcrowding: An Overview of California S.B. 678," *Chapman Law Review* 14 (2011): 375.

79. Feinstein points out that the program wasn't indexed to inflation, so the value of $4,000 declined over time, yet the state still came to view the program as too costly.

80. Belden Russonello & Stewart Research and Communications, "Developing a National Message for Indigent Defense: Analysis of National Survey," October 2001, accessed August 24, 2016, http://66.35.48.28:21980/LegalDev/NLADA/DMS/Documents/1211996411.65/Polling%20results%20report.pdf.

81. "State-by-State Court Fees," National Public Radio, May 19, 2014, accessed July 6, 2016, www.npr.org/2014/05/19/312455680/state-by-state-court-fees.

82. John Pfaff, "A Mockery of Justice for the Poor," *The New York Times*, April 29, 2016, accessed August 24, 2016, www.nytimes.com/2016/04/30/opinion/a-mockery -of-justice-for-the-poor.html.

83. Bibas, "Plea Bargaining."

84. William J. Stuntz, "*Bordenkircher v. Hayes*: Plea Bargaining and the Decline of the Rule of Law," in *Criminal Procedure Stories*, ed. Carol S. Steiker (New York: Foundation Press, 2006), 351–379.

85. Richard Couzens, "Frequently Asked Questions," California Courts, November 2015, accessed July 6, 2016, www.courts.ca.gov/documents/Prop47FAQs.pdf.

86. The choice of the iPhone in this example is intentional. There are many reasons for raising the theft cutoff, including the fact that it had not been adjusted for inflation in years. But one possibly apocryphal explanation for the new minimums that several states have adopted for felony theft is that they wanted to make sure the theft of one iPhone was not a felony, which could often be the case for a $600 or $700 phone. If true, Apple is not just a powerful corporation, but a major unintentional criminal justice reformer.

87. Pew Center on the States, "South Carolina's Public Safety Reform"; "Mississippi's 2014 Corrections and Criminal Justice Reform," Pew Charitable Trusts, May 2014, accessed July 6, 2016, www.pewtrusts.org/~/media/assets/2014/09/pspp_mississippi _2014_corrections_justice_reform.pdf; Ram Subramanian and Rebecka Moreno, "Drug War Détente? Review of State-Level Drug Law Reform, 2009–2013," Vera Institute of Justice, April 24, 2014, accessed July 6, 2016, www.vera.org/sites/default/files/resources /downloads/state-drug-law-reform-review-2009–2013-v6.pdf.

88. NYPL §120.05, 720 ILCS § 5/12.2.

89. For the lawyers among you, I do not see the *mens rea* debate as part of the overcriminalization issue. The *mens rea* debate focuses on whether we are okay with strict liability crimes, not on whether the conduct itself should be criminal at all.

90. Dog waste: 16 USC §668dd & 50 CFR §32.42; spaghetti: 21 USC §§343(g), 333 & 21 CFR §139.110(c); marble: 15 USC §1264 & 16 CFR §1500.19(b)(4)(i). Note that all these examples come from the federal code. This is not a coincidence: for various reasons the federal system is much more prone to impose criminal sanctions in these sorts of unexpected situations.

91. Daniel C. Richman and William J. Stuntz, "Al Capone's Revenge: An Essay on the Political Economy of Pretextual Prosecution," *Columbia Law Review* 105 (2005): 583–640.

92. For one interesting take on why this is, see David Alan Sklansky, "The Nature and Function of Prosecutorial Power," unpublished working paper, accessed August 24, 2016, http://papers.ssrn.com/sol3/papers.cfm?abstract_id=2770815.

93. Perry and Banks, "State Court Prosecutors, 2007."

94. As noted above, just under 2 percent of all prosecutor offices are in counties with at least 1 million people, but in 2007 these offices handled over 26 percent of the 2.9 million felony cases closed out nationwide. Counties with at least 250,000 people closed out over 58 percent of that year's felony cases, despite being home to under 11 percent of

all DA offices. Conversely, just under 60 percent of all prosecutor offices were in counties with 99,999 people or fewer, but they closed out only 19 percent of felony cases in 2007. Perry and Banks, "State Court Prosecutors, 2007."

95. See, for example, Jason Kreag, "Prosecutorial Analytics," unpublished manuscript, April 12, 2016, accessed August 24, 2016, http://papers.ssrn.com/sol3/papers.cfm?abstract_id=2764399.

CHAPTER SIX: THE BROKEN POLITICS OF PUNISHMENT

1. Whitman, *Harsh Justice.*

2. Josh Page, "Why Punishment Is Purple," The Society Pages, September 26, 2012, accessed July 6, 2016, https://thesocietypages.org/papers/purple-punishment.

3. Carlos Berdejó and Noam Yuchtman, "Crime, Punishment, and Politics: An Analysis of Political Cycles in Criminal Sentencing," Haas School of Business, University of California at Berkeley, April 2012, accessed July 6, 2016, http://faculty.haas.berkeley.edu/yuchtman/Noam_Yuchtman_files/Berdejo_Yuchtman_April2012.pdf; Sanford C. Gordon and Gregory A. Huber, "The Effect of Electoral Competitiveness on Incumbent Behavior," *Quarterly Journal of Political Science* 2 (2007): 107; Gregory A. Huber and Sanford C. Gordon, "Accountability and Coercion: Is Justice Blind When It Runs for Office?," *American Journal of Political Science* 48 (2004): 247; Jason J. Czarnezki, "Voting and Electoral Politics in the Wisconsin Supreme Court," *Marquette Law Review* 87 (2003): 323.

4. In one 2012 survey of Republican voters in Florida who were likely to vote in the next primary—a group of older, more conservative, politically active white voters—respondents opted for a hypothetical "smart on crime" prosecutor over a "tough on crime" one by a 2–1 margin. "Smart Justice Poll Results," Florida Tax Watch, January 19, 2012, accessed July 6, 2016, www.floridataxwatch.org/resources/pdf/SmartJusticePoll11912.pdf.

5. Gill, "Correcting Course."

6. See, for example, Bridget Bowman, "Ayotte Pushes Opioid Penalties on Defense Bill," *Roll Call*, June 3, 2016, accessed August 24, 2016, www.rollcall.com/news/policy/opioid-kelly-ayotte-pushes-penalties-defense-bill.

7. Brian Elderbroom, Samuel Bieler, Bryce Peterson, and Samantha Harvell, "Assessing the Impact of South Dakota's Sentencing Reforms: Justice Reinvestment Initiative," Urban Institute, May 5, 2016, accessed July 6, 2016, www.urban.org/research/publication/assessing-impact-south-dakotas-sentencing-reforms-justice-reinvestment-initiative.

8. See Levitt, "Understanding Why Crime Fell," for the claim that $1 spent on policing is likely at least 20 percent more effective than that same dollar spent on corrections. Prison appears to work mostly via incapacitation, not deterrence, while policing in fact does deter. If a crime is deterred, there are no victimization costs, and the offender does not suffer all the various collateral costs of incarceration. We currently spend more on policing than on prisons, although we spend about the same on prisons and jails combined, and as a share of spending, prison spending has grown more.

9. For New York City, policing's share of the budget comes to about 10 percent, but in Chicago and Houston the shares are much bigger. Dean Fuleihan, "Budget Summary," City of New York, 2015, accessed July 6, 2016, www.nyc.gov/html/records/pdf/govpub /OMB%202015%20Exec%20Budget%20Summary.pdf; "2016 Budget Overview," City of Chicago, accessed July 6, 2016, www.cityofchicago.org/content/dam/city /depts/obm/supp_info/2016Budget/2016BudgetOverviewCoC.pdf; Jeanne Chipper-field, Chief Financial Officer, "Memorandum," February 6, 2015, accessed August 24, 2016, http://dallascityhall.com/government/citymanager/Documents/FY14-15%20 Memos/Council%20Memo%20-%2015.02.06.pdf.

10. Nancy G. La Vigne, Samuel Bieler, Lindsey Cramer, Helen Ho, Cybele Koto-nias, Debbie Mayer, Dave McClure, Laura Pacifici, Erika Parks, Bryce Peterson, and Julie Samuels, "Justice Reinvestment Initiative State Assessment Report," Urban Institute, January 27, 2014, accessed July 6, 2016, www.urban.org/research/publication /justice-reinvestment-initiative-state-assessment-report/view/full_report.

11. The $165 million is about 0.08 percent of the over $200 billion spent on criminal justice in 2014. But the JRI is intended as a pilot program, so this isn't really a criticism, more an indication of how new this process is, and how far we still have to go.

12. Gottschalk, *Caught*. As one psychologist, Phillip Atiba Goff, puts it, "before any-body's had contact with law enforcement, they've had contact with schools, with jobs, either getting them or not, with the health care system and the housing systems, all of which suffer from many of the same and sometimes even worse forms of bias than does law enforcement." Improvements at any of these points would surely keep some people out of the criminal justice system altogether down the road. Colleen Walsh, "The Costs of Inequality: Goal Is Justice, but Reality Is Unfairness," *USA Today*, March 1, 2016, accessed July 6, 2016, www.usnews.com/news/the-report/articles/2016-03-01 /the-costs-of-inequality-goal-is-justice-but-reality-is-unfairness.

13. James C. McKinley Jr., "In Unusual Collaboration, Police and Prosecutors Team Up to Reduce Crime," *The New York Times*, June 4, 2014, accessed July 6, 2016, www .nytimes.com/2014/06/05/nyregion/in-unusually-close-partnership-police-dept-and -district-attorney-team-up-to-reduce-crime.html.

14. See, for example, David Garland, *Culture of Control: Crime and Social Order in Contemporary Society* (Chicago: University of Chicago Press, 2002); Jonathan Simon, *Governing Through Crime: How the War on Crime Transformed American Democracy and Created a Culture of Fear* (Oxford: Oxford University Press, 2009); Katherine Beck-ett, *Making Crime Pay: Law and Order in Contemporary American Politics* (Oxford: Oxford University Press, 1999); Thomas Baker, "Most Americans Support Reha-bilitation Compared to 'Tough on Crime' Policies," London School of Economics and Political Science, United States Centre, American Politics and Policy blog, August 25, 2015, accessed July 6, 2016, http://blogs.lse.ac.uk/usappblog/2015/08 /25/most-americans-support-rehabilitation-compared-to-tough-on-crime-policies.

15. Garland, *Culture of Control*; Simon, *Governing Through Crime*; Alexander, *New Jim Crow*.

16. The terminology here is taken from medicine: a negative result means one that says the person doesn't have the looked-for problem—here, the risk of recidivating. Those labeled low risk who in fact don't pose a risk are "true negatives," while those labeled low risk who are high risk are "false negatives."

17. Bartleby, number 953, "Benjamin Franklin," www.bartleby.com/73/953.html.

18. Amy Brittain, "How an Accused Rapist Kept Getting Second Chances from the D.C. Justice System," *Washington Post*, May 14, 2016, accessed July 6, 2016, https://www.washingtonpost.com/investigations/off-the-grid-how-a-violent-offender -slipped-through-the-dc-justice-system/2016/05/13/ba4ca96c-ebba-11e5-bc08 –3e03a5b41910_story.html.

19. A prosecutor once told me that someone asked him what he did, adding, "You defend criminals, right?" Other prosecutors at the table nodded their heads knowingly.

20. Justin McCarthy, "Most Americans Still See Crime Up over Last Year," Gallup, November 21, 2014, accessed July 6, 2016, www.gallup.com/poll/179546/americans -crime-last-year.aspx.

21. Steve Borgia, *Courtroom 302: A Year Behind the Scenes in an American Criminal Courthouse* (New York: Vintage, 2006).

22. Trial judges in Illinois are appointed and then must be retained every six years. Retention elections are not head-to-head competitions. Instead, voters are essentially being asked if they approve of how the judge is doing. Any judge who gets at least 60 percent of that vote keeps his seat; below 60 percent, he loses it.

23. See, for example, Wright, "Prosecutor Elections."

24. James Alan Fox, "The Facts on Furloughs," *Christian Science Monitor*, September 28, 1988, accessed July 6, 2016, www.csmonitor.com/1988/0928/efur.html.

25. John Sides, "It's Time to Stop the Endless Hype of the 'Willie Horton' Ad," *Washington Post, Monkey Cage Blog,* January 6, 2016, accessed July 6, 2016, https://www .washingtonpost.com/news/monkey-cage/wp/2016/01/06/its-time-to-stop-the -endless-hype-of-the-willie-horton-ad. There's an irony here, that people who invoke the "Willie Horton effect" to talk about the problems of low-information voters often are low-information discussants.

26. Stuntz, *Collapse.*

27. Beyond the obvious racism, Stuntz, for one, further suggests that blacks were unable to gain control of urban criminal justice systems like earlier white immigrant groups because of a combination of professionalization (which made it harder to treat police positions as patronage jobs) and the growing power of all-white suburbs. Stuntz, *Collapse.*

28. John F. Pfaff, "Why Do Prosecutors Go After Innocent People?" *Washington Post*, January 21, 2016, accessed July 6, 2016, https://www.washingtonpost.com/news /in-theory/wp/2016/01/21/why-do-prosecutors-go-after-innocent-people.

29. "New York Prison Population," *Democrat and Chronicle*, http://rochester.nydata-bases.com/database/new-york-prison-population; prison maps are at New York State, Department of Corrections and Community Supervision, www.doccs.ny.gov/mapselec .html.

30. In the 2012 presidential election, 87 percent of blacks and 61 percent of Hispanics were Democrats or leaned Democratic. "A Closer Look at the Two Parties in 2012," Pew Research Center, August 23, 2012, accessed July 6, 2016, www.people-press.org/2012/08/23/a-closer-look-at-the-parties-in-2012.

31. "New York," Prison Policy Initiative, Prison Gerrymandering Project, www.prisonersofthecensus.org/newyork.html; "New York State Legislature," Ballotpedia, accessed July 6, 2016, https://ballotpedia.org/New_York_State_Legislature; Sasha Chavkin and Michael Keller, "Proposed 63rd Senate Seat Would Negate Impact of Counting Prisoners at Home," *New York World*, January 10, 2012, accessed July 6, 2016, www.thenewyorkworld.com/2012/01/10/redistricting. That the Republicans regained control of the state senate since then says more about the bizarre politics of New York State—where the Democrats actually have a majority of one, but six of the Democratic senators caucus with the Republican Party, and where the Democratic governor appears to campaign for Republican senators—than anything about the importance of "prison gerrymandering." Thomas Kaplan, "Republican Candidates Embrace Cuomo's Appeal," *The New York Times*, October 14, 2012, accessed July 6, 2016, www.nytimes.com/2012/10/15/nyregion/new-york-republican-candidates-embrace-cuomos-crossover-appeal.html; Michael McKee, "How Andrew Cuomo Helped the Republicans Keep Control of the State Senate," Metropolitan Council on Housing, December 2012, accessed July 6, 2016, http://metcouncilonhousing.org/news_and_issues/tenant_newspaper/2012/December/how_andrew_cuomo_helped_the_republicans_keep_control_of_the_state.

32. Peter Wagner and Elena Lavarreda, "Importing Constituents: Prisoners and Political Clout in Pennsylvania," Prison Policy Initiative, Prison Gerrymandering Project, June 26, 2009, accessed July 6, 2016, www.prisonersofthecensus.org/pennsylvania/importing.html.

33. "The Problem," Prison Policy Initiative, Prison Gerrymandering Project, accessed July 6, 2016, www.prisonersofthecensus.org/impact.html.

34. "Frequently Asked Questions," New York State Legislative Task Force on Demographic Research and Reapportionment, www.latfor.state.ny.us/faqs.

35. Prison Policy Initiative, "The Problem."

36. Alexander, *New Jim Crow*.

37. Garland, *Culture of Control*; Simon, *Governing Through Crime*.

38. Obviously, the end of modernity and electoral manipulation theories are not the only ones. Theodore Caplow and Jonathan Simon, for example, argued that in an era of general economic well-being, political debates shift to more social issues, such as abortion and gay rights, where there is less room for compromise. Crime, they suggest, is one issue where politicians could skim voters off the other party. Theodore Caplow and Jonathan Simon, "Understanding Prison Policy and Population Trends," *Crime & Justice* 63 (1999): 63–120.

39. Amanda Taub, "The Rise of American Authoritarianism," *Vox*, March 1, 2016, accessed July 6, 2016, www.vox.com/2016/3/1/11127424/trump-authoritarianism.

40. See, for example, Muhammad, *Condemnation*.

41. Hilary Hanson, "Nixon Aide Reportedly Admitted Drug War Was Meant to Target Black People," *Huffington Post*, March 22, 2016, accessed July 6, 2016, www .huffingtonpost.com/entry/nixon-drug-war-racist_us_56f16a0ae4b03a640a6bbda1.

42. Beckett, *Making Crime Pay*.

43. Coates, "Black Family."

44. Beckett, *Making Crime Pay*.

45. Peter K. Enns, "The US Public's Support for Being Tough on Crime Has Been a Main Determinant of Changes to the Incarceration Rate," London School of Economics and Political Science, United States Centre, American Politics and Policy blog, May 21, 2014, accessed July 6, 2016, http://blogs.lse.ac.uk/usappblog/2014/05/21/the-u-s-publics-support-for-being-tough-on-crime-has-been-a-main-determinant-of-changes-to-the-incarceration-rate; Enns, "The Public's Increasing Punitiveness." The index Enns develops looks at several measures of the fear of crime: support for the death penalty, support for punishing criminals more, support for spending more on crime control, support for the claim that courts are not harsh enough on defendants, and a lack of faith in the police.

46. This fear was surely amplified by the fact that the decline in the early 1990s looked just like a similar lull between 1980 and 1984, which ended with a powerful upward spike thanks to crack-related violence. Although the superpredator theory, often invoked in racially charged ways, was ultimately proven incorrect, it is not surprising that the theory resonated with the public.

47. It's worth pointing out that both the Beckett and Enns studies rely on national-level data and federal crime responses. As we know, what we really should care about are state- and county-level attitudes and trends, which can diverge from national trends in important ways. These are much harder to study, however, owing to a lack of data.

48. Recall the point made by Muhammad in *The Condemnation of Blackness* that crime by blacks in the United States has persistently been viewed as a collective, group-level failure that demands aggressive group-level responses.

49. Finland is often held up as a country with a high incarceration rate that simply decided to adopt alternatives and push its incarceration rate down, despite facing similar crime trends as the United States. Such an approach would simply be impossible in the United States, given how fractured responsibility is.

50. Franklin E. Zimring and Gordon Hawkins, *Crime Is Not the Problem: Lethal Violence in America* (Oxford: Oxford University Press, 1999).

51. To be clear, only about 0.004 percent of burglaries result in death. The risk is minimal, but whenever such an event happens it gets a lot of media attention, making people fear it more than they should. Shannon Catalano, "Victimization During Household Burglary," US Department of Justice, Bureau of Justice Statistics, September 2010, accessed July 6, 2016, www.bjs.gov/content/pub/pdf/vdhb.pdf.

52. Stuntz, *Collapse*.

53. See, for example, Pew, "States Cut Imprisonment and Crime."

54. Brennan Center, "Reverse Mass Incarceration."

55. See, for example, Ethan Siegel, "Newt Gingrich Exemplifies Just How Unscientific America Is," Forbes, August 5, 2016, accessed August 24, 2016, www.forbes.com/sites/startswithabang/2016/08/05/newt-gingrich-exemplifies-just-how-unscientific-america-is/#e32c6fe28328.

56. See, for example, John F. Pfaff, "For True Penal Reform, Focus on the Violent Offenders," Washington Post, July 26, 2015, accessed July 6, 2016, https://www.washingtonpost.com/opinions/for-true-penal-reform-focus-on-the-violent-offenders/2015/07/26/1340ad4c-3208–11e5–97ae-30a30cca95d7_story.html; Andrea Roth, "Let's Consider Leniency for Many 'Violent' Offenders Too," Los Angeles Times, July 24, 2015, accessed July 6, 2016, www.latimes.com/opinion/op-ed/la-oe-roth-non-violent-prison-clemency-20150724-story.html; Naureen Kahn, "President Obama's Prison Visit Caps Big Week for Justice Reform," Al-Jazeera America, July 16, 2015, accessed July 6, 2016, http://america.aljazeera.com/articles/2015/7/16/obamas-prison-visit-caps-big-week-for-justice-reform.html; German Lopez, "Mass Incarceration Is About Way More Than the War on Drugs," Vox, July 16, 2015, accessed July 6, 2016, www.vox.com/2015/7/16/8978579/war-on-drugs-mass-incarceration; Charles Lane, "Ending the War on Drugs Would Not End Mass Incarceration," Washington Post, October 14, 2015, accessed July 6, 2016, https://www.washingtonpost.com/opinions/ending-the-war-on-drugs-would-not-end-mass-incarceration/2015/10/14/e08835a4-7295-11e5-8d93-0af317ed58c9_story.html.

57. Thomas D. Stucky, Karen Heimer, and Joseph B. Lang, "Partisan Politics, Electoral Competition and Imprisonment: An Analysis of States over Time," Criminology 43 (2005): 211–248.

58. Rachel E. Barkow and Kathleen M. O'Neill, "Delegating Punitive Power: The Political Economy of Sentencing Commission and Guideline Formation," Texas Law Review 84 (2006): 1973.

59. William Glaberson, "In Tiny Courts of N.Y., Abuses of Law and Power," The New York Times, September 25, 2006, accessed July 6, 2016, www.nytimes.com/2006/09/25/nyregion/25courts.html.

CHAPTER SEVEN: THE THIRD RAIL: VIOLENT OFFENSES

1. President Barack Obama echoed this idea in an interview conducted by the Marshall Project, walking back earlier comments he had made before the NAACP suggesting that prison populations were driven primarily by drug offenders serving long sentences. Obama acknowledged the limits of focusing on "low-hanging fruit" while pointing to the need to build alliances to push through more serious reforms in the future. Marshall Project, "Transcript."

2. "Armed" robbery does not necessarily mean armed with a gun, although I would be willing to bet that that is the mental image most people have when they see that phrase. This observation reinforces the point made by Frank Zimring and Gordon Hawkins that a major difference between the politics of crime in the United States and in

Europe is Americans' fear, reasonable or not, of lethal crime. Zimring and Hawkins, *Crime Is Not the Problem.*

3. The data come from the National Corrections Reporting Program. If two people spend one day each in prison, that counts as two person-days; if one person spends two days in prison, that counts as two person-days as well. While the NCRP data run from 2000 to 2013, I chose the 2003 wave because earlier waves lacked enough reliable data. Other admission years produced similar results, even though the states in the samples change each year.

4. Here's the math: 69.9 million days divided by approximately 60,000 people (or 20 percent of 300,000) comes to about 3.2 years per person.

5. Gary Strauss, "No Jail for 'Affluenza' Teen in Fatal Crash Draws Outrage," *USA Today*, February 6, 2014, accessed July 6, 2016, www.usatoday.com/story/news /nation/2014/02/05/no-jail-for-teen/5242173.

6. One example of this type of story that we saw earlier was the case of Sharanda Jones, who received a life sentence as the result of being the middleman in a low-level drug deal. Gillespie, "Life Without Parole." Tellingly, Jones's was a federal case, which is where such severe sentences often arise. Her sentence was ultimately commuted by President Obama. Sari Horwitz, "President Obama Commutes Sentences of 95 Federal Drug Offenders," *Washington Post*, December 18, 2015, accessed July 6, 2016, https://www.washingtonpost.com/world/national-security/president-obama -commutes-sentences-of-about-100-drug-offenders/2015/12/18/9b62c91c-a5a3 -11e5-9c4e-be37f66848bb_story.html.

7. That is, someone believes that the crime deserves either a longer sentence or a shorter one. There's no data or evidence, however, that can shape these sorts of philosophical and moral decisions. It's possible to get into deep philosophical debates about such issues—"If you really follow what Kant says, then you must think that . . ."—but however important those discussions are, they are beyond the scope of this book.

8. It might seem strange for me to trot out the " . . . and keeps us safer" line after attacking it so much just one chapter earlier. To be clear, I'm all for making us safer. Although I don't think it should be the sole metric, " . . . and keeps us safer" is certainly a benefit that must be included in any sort of cost-benefit comparison!

9. See, for example, Robert J. Sampson and John H. Laub, "A Life-Course View of the Development of Crime," *Annals of the Academy of Political and Social Science (AAPSS)* 602 (2005): 12–45; *AAPSS* 2005; and Elaine P. Eggleston, John H. Laub, and Robert J. Sampson, "Methodological Sensitivities to Latent Class Analysis of Long-Term Criminal Trajectories," *Journal of Quantitative Criminology* 20 (2004): 1–26.

10. Arjan A.J. Blokland, Daniel Nagin, and Paul Nieuwbeerta, "Life Span Offending Trajectories of a Dutch Conviction Cohort," *Criminology* 43 (2005): 919–954; Ashley K. Ward, David M. Day, Irene Bevc, Ye Sun, Jeffrey S. Rosenthal, and Thierry Duchesne, "Criminal Trajectories and Risk Factors in a Canadian Sample of Offenders," *Criminal Justice and Behavior* 37 (2010): 1278–1300.

11. This pattern applies even to people we think of as "never committed a crime."

Even someone who goes his whole life without an arrest was more aggressive at eighteen than at forty-five. That same person probably also can't honestly say he "never committed a crime," only that he was never *arrested* for one. Did he get in a fight in high school? That could technically be assault, maybe even aggravated assault, even if we often write it off as "boys being boys." (Of course, whether these sorts of youthful acts result in a formal arrest can depend critically on race. See Catherine Y. Kim, "Policing School Discipline," *Brooklyn Law Review* 77 (2012): 861–903, particularly 888 n. 130.)

12. See, for example, Raymond E. Collins, "Onset and Desistance in Criminal Careers: Neurobiology and the Age-Crime Relationship," *Journal of Offender Rehabilitation* 39 (2004): 1. These differences help explain not just trends over one person's lifetime, but differences across people as well: a man with higher natural testosterone levels, for example, will be more at risk of violent behavior.

13. This evidence is accepted enough that even the fairly conservative US Supreme Court has used it to declare the death penalty, life without parole for non-capital crimes, and mandatory life without parole for murder all unconstitutional when applied to juveniles. *Roper v. Simmons*, 543 US 551 (2005); *Graham v. Florida*, 560 US 48 (2010); and *Miller v. Alabama*, 567 US __ (2012).

14. Robert J. Sampson and John H. Laub, *Crime in the Making: Pathways and Turning Points Through Life* (Cambridge, MA: Harvard University Press, 1995). There's an obvious causal problem here: To what extent do marriage or employment lead to desistance, and to what extent does desisting from crime make someone a more attractive partner or employee?

15. See, for example, Clare Huntington, "Staging the Family," *NYU Law Review* 88 (2013): 589–651.

16. Gordon Dahl and Stefano DellaVigna, "Does Movie Violence Increase Violent Crime?" *Quarterly Journal of Economics* 124 (2009): 677–734.

17. Robert J. Sampson and John H. Laub, "Life Course Desisters? Trajectories of Crime Among Delinquent Boys Followed to Age 70," *Criminology* 41 (2003): 301–339.

18. Mike Males, "Striking Out: California's 'Three Strikes and You're Out' Law Has Not Reduced Violent Crime. A 2011 Update," Center on Juvenile and Criminal Justice, April 2011, accessed July 6, 2016, www.cjcj.org/uploads/cjcj/documents /Striking_Out_Californias_Three_Strikes_And_Youre_Out_Law_Has_Not _Reduced_Violent_Crime.pdf.

19. Erik Eckholm, "Out of Prison, and Staying Out, After 3rd Strike in California," *The New York Times*, February 26, 2015, accessed July 6, 2016, www.nytimes .com/2015/02/27/us/california-convicts-are-out-of-prison-after-third-strike-and -staying-out.html. The recidivism rate for the Proposition 36 releasees—whose releases also require court approval, which also means this group is carefully selected—is about 5 percent, compared to nearly 50 percent overall. Obviously, that's just part of the story. While it's true that these cases were selected by judges, it is also likely that age explains much of the low recidivism rates.

20. Bruce Western's *Punishment and Inequality in America* (New York: Russell Sage, 2007) is one of the best analyses of these issues.

21. Gary S. Becker, "Crime and Punishment: An Economic Approach," *Journal of Political Economy* 76 (1968): 169–217. The expected value of the first punishment is one year half the time, no years half the time, or six months on average. For the second sanction, five years is served one-tenth of the time, and no years nine-tenths of the time, for an average value of six months again.

22. Nagin, "Deterrence in the Twenty-First Century."

23. Daniel S. Nagin, "Deterrence: A Review of the Evidence by a Criminologist for Economists," *Annual Review of Economics* 5 (2013): 83–105.

24. See, for example, David P. Farrington and Brandon C. Welsh, *Saving Children from a Life Crime* (Oxford: Oxford University Press, 2006).

25. "National Clearance Data," in "2014: Crime in the United States," National Data, FBI, Criminal Justice Information Services Division, Uniform Crime Reporting, https://www.fbi.gov/about-us/cjis/ucr/crime-in-the-u.s/2014/crime-in-the-u.s.-2014/offenses-known-to-law-enforcement/clearances/browse-by/national-data.

26. Nick Gass, "Sen. Tom Cotton: US Has 'Under-incarceration Problem,'" *Politico*, May 19, 2016, accessed July 6, 2016, www.politico.com/story/2016/05/tom-cotton-under-incarceration-223371.

27. Angela Hawken and Mark Kleiman, "Managing Drug Involved Probationers with Swift and Certain Sanctions: Evaluating Hawaii's HOPE," US Department of Justice, National Criminal Justice Reference Service, December 2009, accessed July 6, 2016, https://www.ncjrs.gov/pdffiles1/nij/grants/229023.pdf.

28. For those in HOPE, the rate of use dropped from 54 percent to 9 percent. For the control group, use rose from 22 percent to 33 percent. Six months out, HOPE participants were down to 4 percent, versus 19 percent for the control group.

29. See Thomas B. Marvell, "Sentencing Guidelines and Prison Population Growth," *Journal of Criminal Law & Criminology* 85 (1995): 696–709.

30. John F. Pfaff, "The Continued Vitality of Structured Sentencing Following *Blakely*: The Effectiveness of Voluntary Guidelines," *UCLA Law Review* 54 (2006): 235–307.

31. Why the Court did this, and what exactly it did, is well beyond the scope of this book. Most textbooks on sentencing law dedicate about one hundred pages to the issue. A much shorter summary is available at Pfaff, "Continued Vitality," and Pfaff, "*Booker* in the States." The Court continues to make things complicated, though. A major part of Michigan's guidelines, which had survived the earlier round of Supreme Court cases, were declared unconstitutional by the state supreme court in 2015 in the wake of yet another US Supreme Court decision. *People v. Lockridge*, Docket No. 149073 (July 29, 2015), accessed July 6, 2016, http://courts.mi.gov/Courts/Michigan-SupremeCourt/Clerks/Recent%20Opinions/14-15-Term-Opinions/149073-Opinion.pdf?utm_source=hs_email&utm_medium=email&utm_content=20932961.

32. See, for example, Ronald F. Wright and Rodney L. Engen, "The Effects of Depth and Distance in a Criminal Code on Charging, Sentencing, and Prosecutor Power," *North Carolina Law Review* 84 (2006): 1935–1982.

33. A somewhat disappointing example comes from North Carolina, which adopted

guidelines that went into effect in 1994. In 1995, the legislature sought to amend the new guidelines because it feared they weren't sending enough people to prison. This case highlights the political vulnerability of guidelines, but it also shows that they can be designed to restrict prison growth, if so desired. Ronald F. Wright, "Managing Prison Growth in North Carolina Through Structured Sentencing," US Department of Justice, National Institute of Justice, February 1998, accessed July 6, 2016, https://www.ncjrs.gov/pdffiles/168944.pdf.

34. A large number of states now use risk-assessment tools in some way during the parole process: "Use of Risk Assessment Tools for Parole Boards," Association of State Correctional Administrators, October 31, 2014, www.asca.net/system/assets/attachments/7803/Risk%20Assessment%20tools%20for%20Parole%20Boards%20Sheet1.pdf?1419372316. The federal plan, called the Data-Driven Justice Initiative, is discussed in Issie Lapowsky, "The White House Is on a Mission to Shrink US Prisons with Data," *Wired*, June 30, 2016, accessed July 6, 2016, www.wired.com/2016/06/white-house-mission-shrink-us-prisons-data.

35. Eric S. Janus and Robert A. Prentky, "Forensic Use of Actuarial Risk Assessment with Sex Offenders: Accuracy, Admissibility and Accountability," *American Criminal Law Review* 40 (2003): 1443–1499.

36. See, for example, Julia Angwin, Jeff Larson, Surya Mattu, and Lauren Kirchner, "Machine Bias," *ProPublica*, May 23, 2016, accessed July 6, 2016, https://www.propublica.org/article/machine-bias-risk-assessments-in-criminal-sentencing.

37. Debating this issue would take a book in and of itself, and in fact entire books have been written on it. See, for example, Bernard E. Harcourt, *Against Prediction: Profiling, Policing, and Punishing in an Actuarial Age* (Chicago: University of Chicago Press, 2006). See also Nathan James, "Risk and Needs Assessment in the Criminal Justice System," *Congressional Research Service*, October 13, 2015, accessed July 6, 2016, https://www.fas.org/sgp/crs/misc/R44087.pdf; Sonja B. Starr, "Evidence-Based Sentencing and the Scientific Rationalization of Discrimination," *Stanford Law Review* 66 (2014): 803.

38. Bill Hughes, "Even Model NYS Inmates Face Steep Barriers to Parole," *CityLimits*, September 17, 2014, accessed July 6, 2016, http://citylimits.org/2014/09/17/even-model-nys-inmates-face-steep-barriers-to-parole.

39. New York Penal Law §140.25, MS Code §97–17–23. The thought here, obviously, is that any home break-in *could* result in violence. But the data argues otherwise. In a comprehensive review, several analysts found that the risk of violence during a burglary ranged from under 1 percent in rural counties to under 8 percent in the densest urban ones, with an average of under 3 percent, with most violence not being that serious. Richard F. Culp, Phillip M. Kopp, and Candace McCoy, "Is Burglary a Crime of Violence? An Analysis of National Data, 1998–2007," US Department of Justice, National Criminal Justice Reference Service, February 2015, accessed July 6, 2016, https://www.ncjrs.gov/pdffiles1/nij/grants/248651.pdf.

40. States remain free to choose different classifications, as New York and Mississippi do with burglary (which is classified as a property crime in FBI records).

41. Here, a person's "offense" is the one that received the longest sentence. This is how the NCRP prioritizes offenses when someone has multiple convictions, because there is no real intuitive way to rank offenses within categories. It is easy to say "violent outranks property," but how should we rank simple assault, nonforcible sexual assault, and blackmail?

CHAPTER EIGHT: QUO VADIS?

1. Sullivan's pioneering article is Andrew Sullivan, "Here Comes the Groom," *The New Republic*, August 28, 1989, accessed July 6, 2016, https://newrepublic.com/article /79054/here-comes-the-groom. See also David Cole, *Engines of Liberty: The Power of Citizen Activists to Make Constitutional Law* (New York: Basic Books, 2016).

2. In 1996, only 27 percent of Americans favored gay marriage. By 2015, 60 percent did. "In Depth: Topics A to Z. Marriage," Gallup, n.d., accessed August 24, 2016, www .gallup.com/poll/117328/marriage.aspx. Of course, the most obvious difference here is that the answer to the question, "But who is harmed?," is quite different for gay marriage than for prison reform.

3. Beckett et al, "End of an Era"; Gottschalk, *Caught*.

4. Aviram, *Cheap on Crime*; Gottschalk, *Caught*; Petersilia and Cullen, "Liberal But Not Stupid."

5. Sara Mayeux, "Federal Funding for State and Local Public Defenders—Some Historical Context," March 19, 2016, accessed July 6, 2016, www.saramayeux.org/2016/03 /federal-funding-for-state-and-local-public-defenders-some-historical-context.

6. Pfaff, "Innocent People."

7. "2016 Democratic Party Platform," Democratic National Party, July 21, 2016, accessed August 24, 2016, www.demconvention.com/wp-content/uploads/2016/07 /Democratic-Party-Platform-7.21.16-no-lines.pdf.

8. While it is true that within any state poorer people tend to be more Democratic than wealthier people, in many of the more conservative states a majority of the poor still vote Republican, making the class implications harder to map out. Andrew Gelman, *Red State, Blue State, Rich State, Poor State* (Princeton, NJ: Princeton University Press 2009).

9. Kay Levine, "The State's Role in Prosecutorial Politics," in *The Changing Role of the American Prosecutor*, ed. John L. Worrall and M. Elaine Nugent-Borakove (Albany: State University of New York Press, 2008).

10. David Simon, the former *Baltimore Sun* reporter and creator of *The Wire*, claimed in his blog that the state's attorney for Baltimore managed to cut the number of murders he prosecuted each year by almost half, not because the number of murders had fallen, but as a way of protecting his performance numbers. David Simon, "Dirt Under the Rug," June 18, 2012, accessed July 6, 2016, http://davidsimon.com/dirt-under -the-rug; David Simon, "You Did It, Mr. Bernstein. Now Own It," September 18, 2012, accessed July 6, 2016, http://davidsimon.com/you-did-it-mr-bernstein-now -own-it.

11. Adam Foss, "A Prosecutor's Vision for a Better Justice System," TED Talks, February 2016, https://www.ted.com/talks/adam_foss_a_prosecutor_s_vision_for_a_better_justice_system.

12. M. Elaine Nugent-Borakove, Lisa M. Budzilowicz, and Gerard Rainville, "Exploring the Feasibility and Efficacy of Performance Measures in Prosecution and Their Application to Community Prosecution," American Prosecutors Research Institute, July 2009.

13. See, for example, Foss, "Prosecutor's Vision."

14. As a much smaller-scale alternative, states could at least streamline their criminal codes. States often have many, sometimes dozens, of "overlapping" statutes that can be applied to the same criminal act. Culling the number of options available to prosecutors would leave them with fewer options when it comes to charging, curtailing their discretion to at least some degree. Mississippi, for one, took steps like this to clean up its criminal code.

15. Some states are using risk-assessment tools to help judges determine the optimal sentence at the time the sentence is imposed. Sonja Starr has pointed out that these tools—generally just repurposed back-end tools used by parole boards—frequently focus on the wrong factors. At release, for example, youthfulness is a risk factor for reoffending. At the front end, however, youthfulness should probably mitigate punishment, since evidence suggests that younger inmates are more scarred by prison than older ones. Starr, "Evidence Based."

16. Of course, this already exists at the state level, with poorer, higher-crime states forced to make choices that richer, lower-crime states do not; why one cost is viewed as problematic and the other as just the workings of federalism is unclear.

17. The Speaker of the Georgia House of Representatives admitted that the state's sex offender residency law aimed to drive all sex offenders into neighboring states. Jacqueline Canlas-Laflam, "Has Georgia Gone Too Far—or Will Sex Offenders Have To?" *Hastings Constitutional Law Quarterly* 35 (2008): 309–344.

18. John Eck, Cheryl Lero Jonson, and Francis T. Cullen, "The Small Prison," in *The American Prison: Imagining a Different Future*, eds. Francis T. Cullen, Cheryl Lero Jonson, and Mary K. Stohr (New York: Sage, 2013).

19. I suppose people may fear that criminal gangs could try to buy bed-years as well to make it harder to send their members to prison. This strikes me as unlikely; if it is a real concern, however, the state could agree to sell only to approved, registered groups.

20. Thomas J. Miles, "Does the 'Community Prosecution' Strategy Reduce Crime? A Test of Chicago's Experience," *American Law and Economics Review* 16 (2014): 117–143. As is often the case in the social sciences, the paper uses crime control as the primary metric of success. Academics and analysts should start measuring other impacts of law enforcement more consistently as well.

21. Studies in several cities have shown that half of all crime in any year takes place on something around 10 percent of all city blocks. Lawrence W. Sherman and David A. Weisburd, "General Deterrent Effects of Police Patrol in Crime 'Hot Spots': A

Randomized, Controlled Trial," *Justice Quarterly* 12 (1995): 625–648; David Weisburd, Shawn Bushway, Cynthia Lum, and Sue-Ming Yang, "Trajectories of Crime at Places: A Longitudinal Study of Street Segments in the City of Seattle," *Criminology* 42 (2004): 283–322.

22. Micah Uetricht and Derrick Clifton, "Kim Foxx Trounces Anita Alvarez, but Activists Say They Want More," *Chicago Reader*, March 16, 2016, accessed July 6, 2016, www.chicagoreader.com/Bleader/archives/2016/03/16/kim-foxx-trounces-anita -alvarez-but-activists-say-they-want-more.

23. Malia Reddick, "Judicial Selection," American Bar Association, June 2008, accessed July 6, 2016, https://www.americanbar.org/content/dam/aba/migrated /JusticeCenter/Justice/PublicDocuments/judicial_selection_roadmap.authcheckdam.pdf.

24. Kate Berry, "How Judicial Elections Impact Criminal Cases," Brennan Center for Justice, 2015, accessed July 6, 2016, www.brennancenter.org/sites/default/files /publications/How_Judicial_Elections_Impact_Criminal_Cases.pdf.

25. In fact, a lack of computerized records at the Santa Clara courthouse has made it hard to assess Persky's overall practice. See Paul Elias, "Judge in Stanford Rape Case Often Follows Sentencing Reports," AP: The Big Story, June 17, 2016, accessed August 24, 2016, http://bigstory.ap.org/article/a01788e9c0374cf19a942625fde93174/judge -stanford-rape-case-often-follows-sentencing-reports.

26. Andrew King, "Be Careful What You Wish For, McGinty & Alvarez Edition," Mimesis Law, March 22, 2016, accessed July 6, 2016, http://mimesislaw.com/fault-lines /be-careful-what-you-wish-for-mcginty-alvarez-edition/7949.

27. National Association of Sentencing Commissions, http://thenasc.org/aboutnasc .html; Robert Weisberg, "How Sentencing Commissions Turned Out to Be a Good Idea," *Berkeley Journal of Criminal Law* 12 (2007): 179–230; Rachel E. Barkow, "Administering Crime," *UCLA Law Review* 52 (2005): 715–814.

28. New York now has a commission, but it was established in 2010, long after prison populations began declining around 1999.

29. Barkow, "Administering Crime."

30. "Gubernatorial and Legislative Party Control of State Government," Ballotpedia, https://ballotpedia.org/Gubernatorial_and_legislative_party_control_of_state _government. In the remaining ten states, control is split between the parties, which should be enough to block reforms.

31. Ken Stier, "NYS Prison Budget Climbs, Despite Fewer Inmates," *City Limits*, November 10, 2015, accessed August 24, 2016, http://citylimits.org/2015/11/10 /nys-prison-budget-climbs-despite-fewer-inmates.

32. Kenneth R. Mayer, "The Base Realignment and Closure Process: Is It Possible to Make Rational Policy?" NYUWagner, December 2007, accessed July 6, 2016, http://users.polisci.wisc.edu/kmayer/Professional/Base%20Realignment%20and%20 Closure%20Process.pdf.

33. George Winner, "Legislature Rejects Prison Closure Commission Proposal," New York State Senate, April 3, 2007, accessed July 6, 2016, www.nysenate.gov/newsroom /in-the-news/george-winner/legislature-rejects-prison-closure-commission-proposal.

34. Stacie L. Pettyjohn, "Why the Pentagon Can't Bypass BRAC," RAND Corporation, March 24, 2014, accessed July 6, 2016, www.rand.org/blog/2014/04/why-the-pentagon-cant-bypass-brac.html.

35. Alexander Volokh, "Prison Accountability and Performance Measures," *Emory Law Journal* 63 (2013): 339–416.

36. "31 States Reform Criminal Justice Policies Through Justice Reinvestment," Pew Charitable Trusts, January 2016, accessed July 6, 2016, www.pewtrusts.org/~/media/assets/2016/01/pspp_jrireformmatrixoverview.pdf.

37. "The President's News Conference," Ronald Reagan Presidential Foundation and Institute, August 12, 1986, accessed July 6, 2016, https://ml.reaganfoundation.org/pdf/SQP081286.pdf.

38. Andy Cush, "The Randolph Holder Shooting Had Nothing to Do with Jail Diversion and Bill de Blasio Knows It," *Gawker*, October 22, 2015, accessed July 6, 2016, http://gawker.com/the-randolph-holder-shooting-had-nothing-to-do-with-jai-1738040218.

39. Seung Min Kim, "Cotton Leads Effort to Sink Sentencing Overhaul," *Politico*, January 25, 2016, accessed July 6, 2016, www.politico.com/story/2016/01/criminal-justice-tom-cotton-218121.

40. Howden and Meyer, "Age and Sex: 2010."

41. On how informed younger Americans are, see Lisa Johns, "What Factors Affect Americans' Perception of Whether Crime Is Increasing or Decreasing?," The Opportunity Agenda, June 2014, accessed July 6, 2016, https://opportunityagenda.org/pom_june_2014. According to Figure 4, a majority of Americans of all ages believe that crime is rising year over year, despite steady declines. For their attitudes on the proper response to crime, see "An Overview of Public Opinion and Discourse on Criminal Justice Issues," The Opportunity Agenda, August 2014, accessed July 6, 2016, http://opportunityagenda.org/files/field_file/2014.08.23-CriminalJustice Report-FINAL_0.pdf.

42. To be fair, many opponents of tighter gun regulations argue that broader access to guns improves public safety. But arguments built on the Second Amendment often emphasize that gun ownership is a right, independent of its net impact on safety.

43. Peter Weber, "How Ronald Reagan Learned to Love Gun Control," *The Week*, December 3, 2015, accessed July 6, 2016, http://theweek.com/articles/582926/how-ronald-reagan-learned-love-gun-control.

44. Some groups are already thinking along these lines. FreeAmerica, an organization assembled by the musician John Legend to push back against mass incarceration, describes itself as "a multi-year culture campaign . . . to change the national conversation about our country's misguided policies and transform America's criminal justice system." The impact of FreeAmerica remains unclear at this point. It could change the conversation, or it could fizzle and die out. What is worth noting is its focus on attitudes and perspectives down the road more than specific legal changes today.

45. Chettiar et al., "Reduced Mass Incarceration."

46. The Byrne JAG program is the largest criminal justice grant program the federal

government operates, but at about $400 million per year, it makes up about 0.2 percent of the over $200 billion that states and counties spend on criminal justice.

47. That bond failed, in that the program showed no signs of improved recidivism rates. The program was nonetheless viewed by many as a success, since it did what was intended, namely shifting risk from taxpayers to the private sector. Eduardo Porter, "Wall St. Money Meets Social Policy at Rikers Island," *The New York Times*, July 28, 2015, accessed July 6, 2016, www.nytimes.com/2015/07/29/business/economy/wall-st -money-meets-social-policy-at-rikers-island.html.

48. Eckholm, "Out of Prison."

INDEX

ACLU (American Civil Liberties Union), 138
Adam Walsh Child Protection and Safety Act of 2006, 103
admissions
    admissions and releases, 57–59, 58 fig. 2.1 (1980–2000s)
    arrests and, 73, 74 table 2.2 (1991–2011)
    changing of admission rate, 76
    collateral consequences of, 45, 69
    front-end admissions, 155–156, 234
    of older people, 75–76
    pretextual, 33–34
    prison growth and, 110
    prosecutor-driven, 70–71, 74–75, 98, 142–143
    restrictions of, 234
    to state prisons, 63 (2000–2014)
    for violent crimes, 6, 32–33
    See also drug-offense admissions
age
    aging out of crime, 193, 231
    lead exposure during youth, 115
    number of crime-aged young men, 115

older prisoners, 75–76
    patterns of violence, 190–191
alcohol, relationship to crime, 44
ALEC (American Legislative Exchange Council), 84, 92
Alexander, Michelle, 5, 21, 37, 50, 64, 187
Allgood, Forrest, 134
Alm, Steven, 195
Alvarez, Anita, 134, 216
American Bar Association, 54, 134
American Civil Liberties Union (ALCU), 138
American Federation of Teachers, 86
American Law Institute, 131
American Legislative Exchange Council (ALEC), 84, 92
American Prosecutors Research Institute, 210
Americans
    change in attitude toward responses to crime, 161
    historic attitude toward crime, 161
    as low-information, high-salience (LIHS) voters, 169, 170
Anamosa, Iowa, 173

Photo by Chris Taggart,
courtesy Fordham Law School

JOHN F. PFAFF is a professor of law at Fordham Law School. His work has been covered by the *Economist*, *New Yorker*, *New York Times*, *Washington Post*, *Los Angeles Times*, *National Review*, *Slate*, and *Vox*, among others. He has a JD and a PhD in economics from the University of Chicago. He lives in Brooklyn, New York.